P9-APC-104

The Spirit of Chinese Politics

To: Dick Newman
with Best Wishes
Lucian W. Pye

The Spirit of Chinese Politics

NEW EDITION

Lucian W. Pye

HARVARD UNIVERSITY PRESS
Cambridge, Massachusetts, and London, England

Copyright © 1968, 1992 by the President and
Fellows of Harvard College
All rights reserved
Printed in the United States of America
10 9 8 7 6 5 4 3 2

*Library of Congress Cataloging-in-Publication
Data*

Pye, Lucian W., 1921–
    The spirit of Chinese politics/Lucian W.
Pye.—New ed.
        p. cm.
    Includes index.
    ISBN 0-674-83240-X
    1. China—Politics and government—1912–
1949. 2. China—Politics and government—
1949– 3. Political culture—China.
4. Authority.
I. Title
JQ1508.P94 1992   91-34892
306.2′0951—dc20   CIP

CONTENTS

PREFACE TO THE
NEW EDITION

In the first half of 1964, when I was doing research in Hong Kong, China was relatively tranquil on the surface. It had emerged from the follies of the Great Leap Forward and had not yet plunged into the greater madness of the Cultural Revolution. Yet I became convinced that beneath the calm there were great tensions which might soon boil over. The Western consensus was, as usual, optimistic about China's prospects: China's leaders were rational, prudent people who learned from experience and were above all not given to rashness. So they could be counted upon to lead China in steady progress. In seeking to resolve what I saw as a set of profound and troublesome contradictions between surface appearances and masked realities, I arrived at an interpretation of Chinese political culture which became this book. During that time I also made public my dissent from the existing consensus, which I called the "prudence model" of Chinese Communism, in an article published in *Foreign Affairs* in April 1966, a few months before the Cultural Revolution exploded into public view. *The Spirit of Chinese Politics* was published when the world was just beginning to try to make sense of the massive disruptions of the Red Guards, and when there was still much skepticism about reports of widespread violence throughout China.

The Spirit of Chinese Politics was allowed to go out of print during the honeymoon phase of China's new opening to the West. But new interest in the book, especially among Chinese intellectuals, surfaced when Deng's "reforms" began to run into difficulties a year or so before the Beijing Spring of 1989 and the subsequent Tiananmen Massacre. As they wondered about the fate of China's modernization efforts and contemplated the character of their enduring culture, these intellectuals began talking about a "crisis of confidence." They saw *The Spirit of Chinese Politics* as less nihilistic than such Chinese interpretations as the six-part television series *River Elegy* or Bo Yang's *The Ugly Chinaman*. I have been told that there are several pirated translations circulating in both China and Taiwan.

In this new edition I have not altered or updated the first nine chapters. I have, however, replaced a chapter that is now considerably dated, a case study of the commune movement, with comparable but more up-to-date material from my *Dynamics of Chinese Politics* (1981). The basic tension between consensus and factions in the operation of Chinese politics illustrates the "spirit" in action. The final chapter, originally published in the Fall 1990 issue of *Foreign Affairs,* discusses the great gap that persists between the world of the political leadership and the activities of society in post-Tiananmen China. Reflecting prevailing usage both now and earlier, I have used *pinyin* in these last two chapters while leaving Wade-Giles spelling in the original text.

In the late 1960s many scholars became convinced that not just Chairman Mao but Fidel Castro and a variety of African leaders had changed the deep culture of their societies through sheer political will. The myth of Mao Zedong's revolutionary transformation of the character of the Chinese people contributed to a premature dismissal of political culture studies. With the opening of China in the post-Mao era, when it became clear that Chinese culture had indeed persisted despite decades of relentless attacks by the Communist Party, it also became clear that the study of political culture was still relevant.

In fact political culture continues for many reasons to be singularly important in shaping Chinese politics. There, more than in most countries, politics revolves around clashes of ideas and sentiments that have to be played out in the context of exaggerated notions of authority, on the one hand, and straitjacket controls on dissent, on the other. Conformity and rebellion have indeed been the lifeblood of modern Chinese politics. The centrality of hierarchy, the elaborate concerns involved in managing superior-subordinate relations, and a pervasive use of moralistic rhetoric have combined to produce in China a form of Confucianist Leninism that seems destined to outlive the model of Leninism in its homeland. But there is also the gap between formality and reality, which has produced the great Chinese political art form of feigned compliance. The center proclaims grand policies, the localities nod their assent but then test the limits by going their own ways— and the center, hesitating to expose its impotence, looks the other way. The tradition of rule by men instead of by law has also promoted an extraordinary mystique of leadership. Mao the Superman Chairman has been succeeded by Deng Xiaoping, the Paramount Leader who holds no office, is responsible to no institutions, but who dictates the fate of more than one billion Chinese. Consequently the future of Chinese politics, like its past, is destined to be one of continuous struggle over leadership succession.

The special importance of political culture for understanding China also lies in the ways in which China is unique at both the collective and the individual levels. As a collectivity, China is not just a normal nation-state; it is a civilization trying to squeeze itself into the format of a modern state. At the individual level, no society makes more of the importance of molding children into people who will honor correctness in both thinking and conduct.

Central to my interpretation of Chinese political culture are the problems arising from a deep crisis of authority in Chinese civilization, a crisis complicated by the frustrations created by the imperative of conformity; a combination that has produced a profound fear of disorder. Fueling these tendencies are Chinese socialization practices that severely repress expressions of aggression. The result is a pronounced idealization of harmony alongside a reality of diffuse, suppressed anger. (Some readers, apparently not comfortable with psychology, have said that *The Spirit of Chinese Politics* is tainted with Freudian insights, which I suppose can be taken as a compliment, however it was intended.) In recent years even before Tiananmen it has become more legitimate to point to the role of violence in Chinese culture—as for example in works such as *Violence in China* (1990), edited by Jonathan N. Lipman and Stevan Harrell, and *Sanctioned Violence in Early China* (1990), by Mark Edward Lewis. My interpretation dwells less on violence per se, although the horrors of the Cultural Revolution and the Tiananmen Massacre are a part of the story; instead my focus is more on orientations toward power and authority that have operated to impede China's modernization.

As China now moves into another succession crisis comparable to the end of the Mao era, and the problems of power relationships are likely to become critical once again, it seems appropriate to republish *The Spirit of Chinese Politics*. With the Deng era coming to a close China is caught in its Brezhnev phase: On the surface there is the order and tranquillity of political stagnation, while throughout society profound social and economic changes are taking place that will in time fundamentally alter the character of Chinese society. In the meantime the essential features of the political culture will operate to provide elbow room between the realms of conformity at the top and of spontaneity beneath the surface. Given the Chinese practice of feigned compliance, contradictions will be more readily contained than they would be in more rationalistic cultures, where logical inconsistency is less tolerated and becomes the grounds for adversarial tensions and conflicts. As at the close of the Mao era, the end of Deng's rule will intensify the inevitable factional struggles of succession. Elements of the public, especially the intellectuals and the emerging entrepreneurs, will become skilled in learning the limits of their respective freedoms, the boundaries of which will be drawn, first, by the pressures of conformity and, second, by the realities of state-sanctioned fear. In short, change is taking place, but certain continuities will endure.

Needless to say, we now have considerably more knowledge about the operations of Chinese politics than was available when I wrote either *The Spirit* or *The Dynamics*. Indeed, from the perspective of hindsight it seems incredible that on the eve of the Cultural Revolution, when China had barely recovered from the Great Leap Forward, which had produced the greatest famine in its history, the standard line of the China-watching community was that Chinese politics was operating according to the norms of prudent rationality, unencumbered by cultural predispositions or other marks of human frailty. (But then, on the eve of Tiananmen there was also near-universal belief that Deng Xiaoping and his legions of reform-minded cadres had found the formula for the intelligent solution of China's problems.) The context in which the succession struggles for leadership after Deng will be played out is of course different from that of the last days of Mao's rule. The haunting memories of both the Cultural Revolution and Tiananmen will no doubt inhibit violence but not passions of anger. Yet the very fact that the Chinese, after going through the trauma of Mao's succession, failed to establish any institutions and processes for orderly leadership succession suggests that the basic cultural predispositions remain remarkably the same. Awe of the magic of personal leadership rather than reverence for the majesty of law still governs Chinese feelings about power and authority. Deng's hapless selection of Hu Yaobang and Zhao Ziyang is a close enough parallel to Mao's equally ill-starred choices of Lin Biao and Hua Guofeng to suggest that *The Spirit of Chinese Politics* may still be relevant in efforts to understand the mysteries of Chinese political behavior. The very process of identifying where changes might be called for should prove enlightening.

I am grateful to *Foreign Affairs* and to the Rand Corporation for granting permission to reprint the material under their copyrights. I am indebted to Ann Hawthorne for exceptionally careful and thoughtful editing. I also thank Pamela Clements for her help in typing much of the manuscript.

Cambridge, Massachusetts
September 1991

The Spirit of Chinese Politics

THE AUTHORITY CRISIS
IN MODERNIZATION

China is not only Communist;it is a developing country. Strangely this second dimension of China has been more
appreciated in the popular press and in official policies than
in scholarly research. Academically there has been little inclination to apply to the analysis of Communist China the
concepts and theories that have given such vitality to the
study of political and economic development in the rest of
the Afro-Asian world. Among scholars the division has been
sharp between those working on Communist China and those
working on political and economic development. Each group
has gone its separate way, and there has been remarkably
little intellectual exchange. The China specialists have seemingly taken on some of the pride of their country of study
and have been anxious to stress its world-shaking importance,
often, possibly quite unintentionally, giving the impression
that the rest of the underdeveloped countries are insignificant
in comparison. This has helped to spread the impression that
China's problems and those of the other transitional societies
have little in common. The students of development, on the
other hand, have steadfastly ignored Communist China and
have generally displayed a strong distaste for any serious
analysis of communism. For these people Communist China
smacks too much of the Cold War, a reality they accept at

1

times when justifying the importance of development but which they prefer to live without. Although the search for theories of political, social, and economic development has sought to avoid excessive partisanship, the implicit bias of most scholars in the field has been toward democratic development; hence there has been a feeling that the blatantly Communist example of China can properly be ignored.

Possibly an even more significant element in this curious scholarly omission is the fact that China was a transitional society long before the world fully appreciated the inherent difficulties of modernization. If we were now to review the twentieth-century experiences of the Chinese in the light of what we currently know about the difficulties of achieving advancement in the Afro-Asian world we should have to revise many, if not most, of the conventional judgments and evaluations of Chinese performance. Throughout the 1920's and 1930's the Chinese received low marks and a bad press from scholars, diplomats, and journalists because everyone measured their efforts to modernize against the standards of the European world and not against those that are currently being applied to transitional societies in the former colonial areas. During these early decades of the century when China was seeking to break out of the traditional institutional molds there was little general understanding of the extraordinary complexity of economic and political development. At that time China stood largely alone in the world as an independently developing society; the rest of the still traditional and pre-nation-state societies were held together and given administrative order largely through colonial rule. Thus, in the decades when China was passing through the first phases of modernization, the world was not nearly as tolerant as it is now of the violence, confusion, and ineffectualness characteristic of developing societies.

During this period China was compared only with Japan, a country we now realize had unique potentialities for development. Certainly no other developing country in today's world has the likelihood of matching the Japanese record in modernization. The common Confucian-Buddhist tradition and the historic Japanese borrowing of Chinese culture, however, tended only to confuse the issue by suggesting that the Japanese experience should be relevant for judging Chinese potentialities.

The feeble afterglow of the 1911 Revolution, the period of the pathetic Phantom Republic in Peking, Sun Yat-sen's impotent efforts at economic planning, the sordid interplay of warlords, the students' explosive but ineffectual nationalism, the venal corruption of bureaucrats and office holders, the Nationalist government's shallow propagandist pretensions of progress — all seemed to suggest that something was wrong with the Chinese, that they lacked the ability to build a polity and to run a country. Since the forces of frustration and conflict inherent in the developmental process were being contained throughout the rest of Asia, Africa, and the Middle East by the intervention of European power, no one could envisage standards appropriate for measuring Chinese performance.

Now that the world has seen innumerable "phantom republics" in the ex-colonial world, the period of the early twenties in Peking seems less preposterous. The common phenomenon of military rule in postindependence societies makes the emergence of the Chinese military and the rule by warlords less disgraceful and more sociologically understandable.[1] Indeed, considering the intellectual vitality and the exciting traffic in ideas of the warlord period, military rule in China was seemingly less handicapping to development than it has been in most contemporary cases.

If we use the measures of progress currently applied in the Afro-Asian world, we see that significant advances in Chinese development occurred in the 1930's and 1940's. During this

[1] For a general discussion of the military and the problems of political development see John Johnson, ed., *The Role of the Military in the Underdeveloped Areas* (Princeton, N.J.: Princeton University Press, 1961).

period, increasing numbers of Chinese were trained in modern skills, and elite cadres were developed in a variety of fields and were eager and able to perform the functions necessary in a modern secular society. The war against Japan, which has generally been thought to show up Chinese weaknesses, was in fact a remarkable performance for a transitional society. It is questionable today whether any developing country could, with almost no outside assistance, mobilize so large a proportion of its human and material resources for so long a period of time. The Americans who knew wartime China were largely disappointed and frustrated because they expected too much of their ally. Today we are wiser and expect less of a transitional society.

The reason for attempting to analyze contemporary China in the light of our knowledge about political development in other countries is less to achieve justice in historical evaluations and more to discover what may be unique and what may be universal in China's experiences with modernization. Although we cannot as yet say how successful the Chinese will be in time, we can certainly begin to isolate the ordinary and the peculiar in their pattern of development. It is at this point that a comparative perspective is critical.

The Chinese themselves would insist that because of the historic greatness of their civilization their experiences with modernization must be significantly different from those of other traditional societies with less impressive histories. In their minds China represents the agonies of a great civilization in turmoil and not just a traditional culture adapting to modern ways.

The key problem that has plagued a hundred years of efforts to respond to the challenge of a dynamic outside world has been the inability of the Chinese to reconcile the manifest accomplishments of their traditional civilization with the requirement that their society would have to be radically made over. According to the straightforward logic that greatness should sire greatness the Chinese felt they had the right

4

to expect that their philosophically sophisticated traditional civilization, with its partially urbanized way of life, should give them unquestionable advantages in accommodating to the demands of the modern world. Yet these manifest advantages may also have been subtle and intractable liabilities for truly effective development. In clinging to both the legitimacy and the virtues of a past civilization the Chinese have necessarily inhibited their commitments to change and to modernization.

It is rarely appropriate to take seriously the historical pretensions of a people, but there are grounds for recognizing that the Chinese experience in modernization has differed in certain critical respects from the typical pattern of transitional societies. It is equally proper to discount the earlier Chinese protestations that they were unique in their suffering from the Western impact and the current Communist claim of having a unique "Chinese model" for all developing societies. Yet there are deeper analytical reasons for believing that the Chinese experience has been significantly different.

It will be the theme of this book that the critical difference between the Chinese and most of the other developing countries begins with the fact that the Chinese have been generally spared the crises of identity common to most other transitional systems. The basic problem in development for the Chinese has been that of achieving within their social and political life new forms of authority which can both satisfy their need to reassert a historic self-confidence and also provide the basis for reordering their society in modern terms.

We shall have to reserve for later discussion the complex implications for national development of the Chinese sense of historical greatness; at this point we need only note that in the modern era the Chinese have had little doubt about their identities as Chinese, and the more they have been exposed to the outside world the more self-consciously Chinese they have become. Indeed, their psychological sense of cultural and social identity has in many respects blurred the extent of regional, class, and linguistic divisions in Chinese society. Thus, the Chinese have not been psychologically confused over who they are, instead they have been distressed and frustrated over the fact that they have been weaker and poorer on the world scene than they have felt it right and proper for them to be. Modernization has created for them a long-persisting sense of dissatisfaction with their leaders and deep cravings for the decisive power of truly effective authority. It has given them a crisis of authority.

An authority crisis arises when the cultural and psychological bases for the legitimacy of political power are radically undermined by the developmental process. This can occur, in the first instance, when the traditional political forms of authority prove to be manifestly incapable of coping with the problems and demands of modernization. Legitimacy always needs competence; nothing so shatters the mystique of authority as helplessness. But beyond the question of the legitimacy of political institutions, the authority crisis gains depth and pervasiveness as the other structures of society lose their capacities to command easy compliance. Without the reinforcing powers of the social, religious, and cultural institutions that give form and order to the entire social structure a vacuum of authority appears.

In the last analysis, however, the acuteness of the authority crisis stems from disruptions in the prime socializing institution of the society, the family. The critical problem, ironically, is that the family does not necessarily lose any of its potency in socializing the offspring even when it is disrupted and weakened as a social and economic unit. The young will still be taught abiding sentiments and concepts about authority no matter what the fate of the family as an adult institution. Indeed, paradoxically, the very weakening of the family as a social institution tends frequently to increase the sense of dependency of the young. In short, in spite of all the disruptions of a society under the pressure of modernization the most intimate processes of learning can continue to operate, producing people who may still expect much from authority. The authority crisis thus involves far more than just the problem of establishing new sentiments and beliefs in legitimacy. Attitudes and sentiments about authority are shaped by both the earliest socialization experiences and the later cognitive political socialization process, and widespread frustration can occur when there is a serious breakdown in the continuity and reinforcing elements of these two socialization processes. The earlier process may produce people who cannot easily adjust to a political system with weakened forms of authority, because they have internalized various forms of dependency on an ordered social system. The failure of public authority can then release anxieties and produce frustration and aggression. Manifestations of such aggressive behavior may in turn produce not only increased anxieties but the release of sentiments that can only complicate the re-establishment of new forms of authority.

An authority crisis thus has several dimensions. At the most manifest level it calls for the creation of the myth of legitimacy for new governmental institutions. It becomes serious, however, only when this collective political process is complicated by an earlier socialization process in which sentiments about authority constitute a peculiarly important element of the individual's basic personality. Specifically, this is likely to occur when the ego-ideals that helped to shape the superego involve an inordinate awe of parental authority, as happens when a culture places unqualified stress upon filial piety. Thereafter the individual is likely to have a permanent ambivalence: On the one hand he feels a deep need for such an idealized authority, while on the other he can never find in reality an authority that can satisfy his ideals. The individual is left expecting more of authority than reality permits; he may also have problems about governing his own behavior, for in the process of molding his personality many of the mechanisms for controlling his emotions are inevitably tied to his ideals of authority and order.

In China the process of modernization was seen from the very beginning as a Western challenge to Chinese authority. At first the threat was to the authority of the Manchu dynasty, but quickly it became apparent that the requirements of performing in a world dominated by foreign concepts and practices would bring into question the authority of the Confucian traditions and of the whole Chinese imperial system.

Inevitably the system collapsed, and after 1911 the Chinese were thrown into a state of prolonged disarray as they desperately sought to find for themselves forms of authority that could meet the demands of modernization without violating too greatly their cultural concepts of the proprieties of government. From 1911 to 1916 the Chinese wavered between a return to some form of monarchy and an irrevocable commitment to republicanism. With the death of Yuan Shih-k'ai the option of monarchy disappeared, but the profound weaknesses of the republican governments that followed meant that authority increasingly gravitated to the provinces and to regional leaders.

The rebuilding of Chinese society now came to founder on the issue of provincial versus central authority. The subtle but profound processes of social and economic change tended to aggravate issues about the relative jurisdiction of different authorities. The introduction of the telegraph and the railroad, for example, raised this question directly, since central and provisional authorities were soon competing for the control and management of the revenues raised in different localities. The requirements of modern financing for such national systems conflicted with the age-old accommodation that imperial authorities had had with local authorities, and provincial governors naturally expected to have the first say about the disposition of any revenues collected in their territories.

Lacking authority, the Chinese system in the 1920's failed to mobilize the necessary resources for modernization and national development. Any essential effort by a provisional authority to press ahead with social development became a challenge to the concept of a national authority; and any attempt by a presumed national authority to encourage modernization tended to disrupt the legitimacy of the more localized authorities, who were in fact closer to the great masses of the people. During the years from 1916 to 1927 when the warlords dominated the political scene the crisis of authority became increasingly acute; more and more Chinese were frustrated by the lack of a coherent and decisive system of authority that could unambiguously resolve all the jurisdictional issues between central and local authorities, between public and private authorities, and between the authority of the family and clan and the authority of the school and government.

As long as the Chinese were plagued with this crisis of authority it was impossible for their governments to advance national political development, because they could not meet the essential requirements of penetrating more thoroughly into the society and mobilizing human and material resources more extensively than had been possible in the traditional system. Out of the frustrations the stage was set for widespread receptivity to one-party rule, first by the Kuomintang and then by the Communists. Yet the problem of authority was not to be solved quite so easily. Imposed national authority could only be a façade as long as the Chinese had deeper problems about the moral basis of legitimacy and authority. The attempts by Nationalist and Communist leaders to press the pace of national development tended in the decades of the 1930's and 1940's to provoke moral issues and hence raise questions about the intentions and moral proprieties of those with power. By its very nature a crisis of authority means that power is limited by the suspicion that it lacks a proper moral basis, and hence lacks legitimacy. The more the Nationalists tried to achieve substantive advances the more they seemed to raise suspicions about their ultimate intentions.

Throughout this whole period the central articulated theme of Chinese politics was revolution and nationalism. The emotional content of the Chinese sense of revolution was singular in that it dwelt upon the need for a strong and more complete authority. Instead of picturing revolution as an assault by the weak upon the strong so as to do away with a dominating and repressive authority, the Chinese have tended to conceive of revolution as the collective assertion by a people of their need for more, not less, authority.

What is distinctive about the Chinese sense of nationalism is that it has come in great waves, with massive outbursts of great emotions, which quickly subside as the people sink back into their normal state of accepting their Chineseness as the most obvious thing in the world. The ease with which national activities are quickly drained of any significant emotion suggests not a problem of national identity but rather one of handling affect in relations beyond the confines of the family and clan. For the Chinese there has been an element of artificiality in expressing strong emotions about such distant and abstract relationships as the bonds of the national community.

By relying so much upon the family to instill civic attitudes about authority, the Chinese political culture has had to pay a high price, for the individual has always been taught not to make emotional commitments outside of the institution of the family. Thus the great problem that the Chinese have had in modern times with the control of affect in nonkin relationships has been linked directly to the question of authority.

Today in the Great Proletarian Cultural Revolution and in the movements of the Red Guards we see the same themes bedeviling the Chinese. Revolution still means that those in authority have failed to live up to expected standards, and the demand of the revolutionaries is for a more complete disciplining of life. Similarly, we still see the problem of vacillation between overcharged emotionalism and routinized performance as the Chinese continue to work at developing new patterns for the commitment of their emotions in non-kinship relationships.

Before we turn to the more psychological aspects of the Chinese authority crisis we need to review some of the historical and social factors that set the stage for their problems with modernization. We shall first want to isolate some characteristics of the classical Chinese political system that have persisted into modern times and that have impeded modernization. The peculiar relationship between the political realm and the society in traditional China produced a system in which government continued to be remarkably insensitive to the consequences of change in the rest of the society. Thus the authority crisis in China was further intensified by the way in which men who had little exposure to the modern world could continue to be the nation's leaders. From this analysis of the character of the Chinese political elite we shall go on to a more detailed examination of the reasons why the Chinese have not been troubled by problems of national identity. We shall then return to a discussion of the psychological basis of the Chinese political culture.

CHAPTER TWO

THE COMFORTS OF
HIERARCHY AND IDEOLOGY

The search for an understanding of the roots of the authority crisis in Chinese modernization must begin with a study of some of the distinctive and peculiarly persistent qualities of the traditional Chinese social and political order. Although our concern will be with the dynamics of attitudes and sentiments we must start with the environment that shaped behavior. More particularly, it is essential to establish at the outset certain structural and institutional features of the traditional Chinese political system which have complicated the processes of modernization.

Traditional China was one of the most remarkable and certainly the most stable and enduring of political systems in human history. For nearly two thousand years the essential ingredients of Emperor and bureaucracy, of Confucian ideology and family authority, were held together with very little basic change. The system operated when Chinese culture was confined to the Yellow River basin, but it served equally well when China expanded to become a great empire. Here we can touch only briefly upon those conditions of Chinese politics which at the institutional, rather than the psychological, level set the stage for a peculiarly intense authority crisis.

The tenacity with which Chinese politics has been able to resist modernizing influences stems in no small part from certain key structural characteristics, its hierarchical nature, and its heavy dependence upon formal ideologies. As though immutably decreed, Chinese politics after chaos and revolution has always returned to being elitist and hierarchical in organization, closed and monopolistic in spirit; and while the content and the goals have now been irrevocably changed, the Chinese system still steadfastly depends for integration upon an overweening sense of righteousness. The entire structure of both imperial and Communist politics has rested upon self-cultivation as the ultimate rationale for legitimizing high office and the manipulations of political power. Mandarins and party cadres alike have believed that all those who know well and cherish the conventional ideology of the day should be rewarded with formal office and that once in positions of responsibility all officials should feel assured that their doctrines provide infallible answers to questions of justice. Confucianism and communism in their different ways have sustained this unique Chinese belief in authority's rights to arrogance. Each ideology has dwelt long on the rigorous self-discipline expected of officials, on the essence of virtue and wisdom, and on the ultimate importance of the common people; but both have been equally absolute in upholding the monopolies of officialdom.

Thus the first and most essential characteristic of the persisting structure of Chinese politics has been the degree to which it has been a self-contained system very little influenced by citizens or nongovernmental elites. Neither in old nor in new China have there been significant informal power structures, and those outside of recognized ranks and grades have been helplessly ineffectual. Chinese politics has also been unique in the degree to which official rank and formal office have accurately reflected the realities of relative power. Thus to a degree unknown in any other modern political system, and unusual even in most transitional systems, Chinese politics has been confined to a world of officials and apprentice officials. It has been so nearly coterminous with government that it has represented a direct contradiction to the basic beliefs of sophisticated, modern, political scientists, who are inclined to suppose that formal government is only a small part of politics in any society.

It has been this cardinal belief in the proper autonomy of government and in the need for officials to be responsive only to their ideals that has made Chinese politics so peculiarly insensitive to changes in the social and economic environment. The Chinese political class has focused its attention on intra-elite relations and has concerned itself with general developments in the society only to the extent that these threatened the security of the class or were the objects of governmental policies. Those without any obvious station on the political pyramid have felt that they had no right to make open demands upon the system; all they could do was hope and perhaps insist that the rulers adhere to their self-disciplining ideologies.

Much has been written about the two central features of traditional Chinese government, its bureaucracy based on a competitive examination system and its Confucian ideology. The Chinese bureaucracy was not only a model for the ancient world of East Asia it was also a prototype explicitly examined in establishing the modern British and American civil services. Of all non-Western ideologies Confucianism has probably received the greatest attention among educated people throughout the world.[1] Since so much has been written about

[1] So much has been written about Confucianism that it is almost invidious to single out any particular studies, but special recognition must be given to the volumes published under the auspices of the Association for Asian Studies: Arthur F. Wright, ed., *Studies in Chinese Thought* (Chicago, Ill.: The University of Chicago Press, 1953); John K. Fairbank, ed., *Chinese Thought and Institutions* (Chicago, Ill.: The University of Chicago Press, 1957); David S. Nivison and Arthur F. Wright, eds., *Confucianism in Action* (Stanford, Calif.: Stanford University Press, 1959); Arthur F. Wright, ed., *The Confucian Persuasion* (Stanford, Calif.: Stanford University Press, 1960); and Arthur F. Wright and Denis Twitchett, eds., *Confucian Personalities* (Stanford, Calif.: Stanford University Press, 1962).

these two features of traditional China, we need pause only to refresh our memories and to ask what aspects of Chinese politics produced a political culture so vulnerable to an authority crisis.

The traditional Chinese political order was remarkably monolithic, with all political action centered in a single bureaucracy headed by the Emperor. Although there was little sense of specialization, there was a strong appreciation that all officials shared a common ideological orientation based on the Confucian tradition and an informal understanding of the realities of life within officialdom. The entire thrust of traditional Chinese politics was upon the having and holding of office and the seeking of favors from an all-powerful bureaucracy.

The Confucian ideology stressed above all the importance of private morality and public rituals for officials. Individual behavior weighed more heavily than institutional mechanisms or specific public goals. Much in the Confucian philosophy dealt with the nature of the good life and the possibilities for peace and tranquillity that would automatically follow if each individual adhered to the highest ideals of his particular social role. The ultimate test in Confucian thinking was the sincerity of officials, which in theory meant that beliefs and motives were more important than actions. In practice, the test of the sincerity of officials generally became the evidence of their personal loyalty, which in any hierarchical system of politics is always an ultimate value. The central values of Chinese political behavior thus became sincerity, loyalty, reliability, and steadfastness — all values that ensured predictability in an ordered system of interpersonal relations.

The combination of bureaucratic hierarchy and ideological conformity governed nearly every dimension of the traditional Chinese political culture. As numerous observers have noted, the Communists have once again given the Chinese a political system that centers around a bureaucratic hierarchy,

15

this time in the form of the Communist Party, and is again integrated by an all-pervasive ideology, that of Marxism and Maoism.

The Chinese have always felt profoundly uncomfortable, dissatisfied, and threatened whenever their politics has not been characterized by a dominant hierarchy and a single ideology. It is this sense of all-pervasive malaise, which they exhibit whenever they are without a one-party, one-ideology system, that proclaims the extent to which the Chinese, both in their collective national history and in their personal views, have tended to treat politics as a matter essentially of authority.

It is significant that the imperial bureaucracy and the Communist Party in procedural practices, and both Confucianism and Maoism in ideological content, have explicitly stressed the problems of authority and order. In addition, however, from this traditional combination of hierarchy and ideology there followed certain other characteristics of the Chinese political system which, in turn, further reinforced the central importance of authority. In this study we can make only certain rather gross and unqualified statements about these distinctive characteristics of the traditional system that will set the stage for our subsequent analysis.

Sympathy in Place of Representation

First, we should note that the extreme stress on hierarchy and ideology meant that the Chinese political system lacked any explicitly acknowledged and legitimately accepted linkage between the realm of government and that of private interests. In traditional China there was no legitimized interplay among privately based power groups, and people had to be taught that it was improper and dangerous to assert self-interest in making any claims upon the political system. Subjects were supposed to be dependent on, not demanding of, the political system. That is to say, the functions of interest articulation and interest aggregation have always been monopolized by the governing class and subsumed under the accepted ideology.

Stated more positively, the Chinese recognized far more explicitly than most traditional peoples the central role of government in shaping a society and giving definition to a people. Politics and government supported the structure of the culture in a direct and intractable fashion. Elsewhere in the developing regions traditional societies were generally organized around more intimate and fragmented social institutions. In many of these societies it was only when the Western impact introduced much of the infrastructure of the modern nation-state by superimposing a higher level of organization where little had existed before that politics took on the role of giving identity to a people. Thus for the Chinese the autonomy of the political system and its immunity from social influences were in some respects essential; their own appreciation of authority was supported by their sense of cultural identity.

The importance of a pure and uncompromised concept of authority was further reinforced by a strong belief in the impropriety of government officials yielding to private interests. One of the most extraordinary facts about the traditional Chinese system is that it was the most stable and long-enduring political system known in history and yet it was based upon strangely confused and ambiguous concepts of the presumably fundamental relationship between polity and society. Specifically, the Chinese never achieved a clear definition of the proper basis for relations between citizen and official, between popular sentiments and imperial policies. In theory, the emperor ruled through a "Mandate of Heaven," which meant that his authority was in part divine and in part dependent upon the popular will, for Heaven was presumed to be in some degree sensitive to currents of popular contentment and of unrest.[2]

[2] Western scholars have always been fascinated with the Chinese concept of the "Mandate of Heaven," for it has always seemed to be

17

In practice the boundary between the world of officialdom and the shifting interests of private citizens was nearly absolute. This was particularly true in the sense that everyone — official and citizen alike — acknowledged that private interests had no legitimate claims on government. Any organized pressures or demands on the part of particular interests, if openly articulated, were treated as rude threats to public peace and order. There was no hint of the doctrine basic to Western thought that ideally government should be responsive to the spontaneous demands emanating from the larger society. In the language of structural/functional analysis it can be said that the functions of government did not explicitly include the processing of inputs from the society and their transformation into public policies. At no point did the Chinese idealize the notion that their society might be composed of legitimate interests which might be competitive and contradictory but which might all properly demand representation within the government and expect that the government should in some degree be responsive to them. Even in theory it was Heaven's wish that the officials do right by the people's needs and not that the people should make claims on the government.

In Chinese theory there was no need for either representation or the politics of interest groups, because if officials studiously adhered to the rules of conduct decreed in the formal ideology they could be confident that they were doing

---

a remarkably ingenious formula for combining the Western concept of the "Divine Right of Kings" with the recognition of a popular right to revolt. The formula was necessary to justify the replacement of one dynasty by another while ensuring that both in their time had divine sanction. In practice it would be difficult to determine whether the emperors saw the doctrine as providing a right to revolution. Historically, at least, they responded to any threat to their mandate not merely by trying to improve the righteousness of their conduct but by vigorously stamping out the rebels. In practice the doctrine may have increased coercion rather than civility, and it certainly reinforced the spirit of ideological conformity and the belief in the virtues of a monopoly of power.

18

everything possible to ensure justice and fair treatment for all elements of the society. The moral righteousness of government provided an absolute answer to the problems of representation and interest articulation. If officials behaved according to their highest ideals, everyone should be happy; and if any interest still felt it essential to make demands, it could be assumed that such an interest constituted an illegitimate and hence dangerous force.

Thus the boundary between public and private sectors was policed by the sympathy and generosity of officials. Officials were supposed to be sympathetic and understanding of the travails of individuals. A form of paternalism was the highest ideal of government, and everything was done to envelop transactions between government and the public in layers of diffuse human emotion. Citizens never demanded their rights; they sought instead the sympathy, and indeed the pity, of those more powerful than themselves. Officials, in turn, avoided as much as possible the confining discipline of any absolute and impersonal standards of treatment and demonstrated instead their capacity for human sentiment by giving free rein to discrimination in their treatment of each particular case. Above all else citizens were taught that they should never be aggressive or demanding in their relations with public authorities; and officials were expected to be considerate and understanding of those who were docile and properly dependent.

Needless to say, precisely because there was such uncertainty about the proper relationships between the public and private realms, the Chinese system was traditionally bedeviled by corruption. Because the formal ideology suggested the impropriety of government being responsive to private interests, relations between officials and citizens easily fell into a gray area, and almost all interaction initiated by nonofficials assumed immediately an illegitimate character. For officials, the problem of deciding whose difficulties should be given the most sympathetic treatment could be rationally settled

19

only by determining who was prepared to pay the most. We have no evidence to prove whether Chinese officials were more or less venal than officials of other countries, but it is clear that it was peculiarly difficult for them to uphold the proclaimed norms of their system.

The lack of recognized linkages between the polity and the society presented the most acute problem at the point where the formal reach of government came to an end at the outer limits of the bureaucracy. At this point local officials were supposed to go no further than to offer a sympathetic ear to private complaints, informally adjudicate or mediate disputes among citizens, and accept a tolerant live-and-let-live attitude toward private activities as long as they did not result in any demands upon the state. In practice, government officials had to adapt and respond to local interests, and the more powerful the private party the more likely it was to be influential. Officials were supposed to keep a sharp eye on any group that might become an organized interest group. Certain kinds of informal associations were historically tolerated, such as clans and provincial associations, trade guilds, and to a somewhat lesser degree the secret societies. Such groups were acceptable, however, only as long as they acted as protective associations assisting their individual members and made no generalized claims on government. Once a protective association sought to change its approach and act as a pressure group it was likely to be slapped down by the authorities. The basic notion about the illegitimacy of interest representation decreed that all informal associations would have to skirt the fringes of legality if they were to engage in any form of political activity.

Much the same pattern continues to this day, since under both the Kuomintang and the Communists it has been assumed that there is no need for the free interplay of private interests. Under the Communists the denial of legitimacy to autonomous interest groups is more absolute than at any time in Chinese history. Indeed, more than ever before it is assumed that officials know what is best for the people and that politics is a matter solely for those who are recognized by the regime as participants.

Today in Communist China the boundary between public and private sectors still remains somewhat ambiguous, and doctrine and practice are not entirely consistent with respect to the rules about traffic between the two. Officially the regime would like to suggest that the question of such a boundary has disappeared miraculously under their rule, for party, government, and society have presumably merged into one integrated system. Indeed, in practice the regime, seeking total control, has sought to push its influence into every nook and cranny of private life, so that the political sphere engulfs more of society than in any other country in history. In idealizing the new system the Communists like to pretend, however, that the exact opposite has taken place, that it is the people as a whole who have come forward spontaneously and given themselves and their problems to the care of the government. The end result in both theory and practice is that the Chinese still lack free and competitive interest articulation. Above all, the interests and well-being of the people are still assumed to be best guarded by the dutiful actions of ideologically inspired officials.

The model official in the Communist scheme has many of the same qualities as the idealized traditional official. He is expected, first, to be unqualifiedly loyal to a bureaucratic hierarchy and to the father figure at its pinnacle. In operating on the basis of a secure and well-defined position within the ranks of officialdom, the cadre belongs unquestionably to the side of authority. At the same time, however, those who stand at the outer boundaries of officialdom are supposed to mingle constantly with the people, in part so that they can convey to all the omnipotence of central authority, and in part so that they can know all that is going on in the minds of the people.

It is still assumed that the posture of friendship on the part of officials is adequate and, indeed, is the best method for handling relations between the public and government. As in traditional China, so in Communist China, it is believed without question that the needs of the public can be met by officials who pose as sympathetic and understanding. Hence there is neither need nor justification for informally organized interests. Power and authority are supposed to lie entirely within the single hierarchical structure of authority, and the fundamental belief remains that the masses of the people can be readily satisfied and, more important, kept docile and compliant merely by the appearance of a potentially sympathetic and not unreasonably hostile system of official authority.

The traditional denial of the legitimacy of claims on the political system by private interests also had the peculiar consequence of denying the legitimacy of diversity within the country. The universal rules of the political system were supposed to apply equally to all reaches of the empire. In practice, however, officials did have to make accommodations to local conditions. Here we come to a basic dilemma common to all Chinese political systems, imperial, Nationalist, and Communist alike. To overstate the issue slightly for the sake of clarity, we can say that because of the lack of effective institutionalized linkages between the polity and society, Chinese regimes have had to choose between preserving the integrity of the polity, and hence allowing for an ever-widening gap between it and the public — ideological sentiments to the contrary notwithstanding — or allowing officials to accommodate themselves to local realities, thus compromising the ideals of a fully integrated political system responsive only to the purity of the ideology.

Historically, all political systems that have ruled the diversity of China on the basis of bureaucracy and ideology have tended, gradually, to permit local accommodation. In doing so, however, the local as well as higher officials have realized that accommodation violated their mystique of absolute authority and introduced an element of pretense to their system

22

of rule. This has meant that the defenders of the imperial system have always had to pretend it was more centralized than it was, while their critics have always felt they were making telling charges against the essence of the traditional system when they pointed to the officially unrecognized powers of the gentry class which were the result of accommodation. It was the Marxists who derived the greatest satisfaction by focusing attention upon the realities that conflicted with official pretensions and suggested moral corruption.

Now, however, it is the Communists who feel the strains inherent in accommodation, and it will be the turn of the anti-Communists to believe that they are making telling points by drawing attention to patterns of local accommodation that are not consistent with Communist ideological pretensions. Such polemics aside, it is certain that the Communist system will eventually have to adjust to the realities of Chinese society, and it will have to do this in the knowledge that it is making a compromise with its own principles because those principles are inadequate to handle the boundary problem between the polity and the society.

In looking to the future, particular attention must be given to developments in local government where the gap between formal Chinese ideology and the necessities of accommodation between polity and society have always first appeared.[3] It

[3] It is indeed noteworthy that studies of Communist China have concentrated far more than Soviet studies on the local level of government. In part this may reflect only the personal intellectual interests of certain outstanding scholars whose work has properly influenced the development of the field. In part it may stem from the fact that the research perspective on Communist China is heavily influenced by the limitation of source material to Hong Kong, where peasants and former low-level officials from South China are readily available as interview respondents but exceedingly few from the higher echelons of the Chinese government. In any case, the quality of scholarship on local government in Communist China is high, and this is to be applauded in the light of our hypothesis that this is a critical point of contact in all Chinese political systems that have emphasized bureaucracy and ideology. Our knowledge about development in this area will be greatly increased with the publication of A. Doak Barnett's

is significant that while the drift toward accommodation with society has always been essential for the stability of Chinese political systems, this has had to occur without explicit ideological recognition and has therefore resulted in little uniform control over biases in the selection of those with whom accommodations will be sought. At present there is no indication that the Chinese Communist system is going to accommodate only to the interests of those who can do the most to advance modernization and development. Concessions have been made to private interests for the sake of incentives, such as in the grudging acceptance of private agricultural plots, but there are innumerable other examples where accommodation has not been used explicitly to advance development but to reduce the problems of individual officials. Indeed, it is this process of accommodation that has greatly compromised the centralized nature of the party hierarchy and opened the way to regional and local party interests. It is exceedingly significant that when factional struggles emerged in the Chinese Communist Party and the succession crises began they took the form of an attack on the Peking party organization by the Shanghai party organization. It would seem that by 1966 the trend toward local and regional accommodation was well advanced, and that local party leaders had to balance local accommodations against efforts to find security and accommodation with the central authorities. Yet as long as the system persists in denying the legitimacy of power outside of the formal domain of the hierarchy and the ideology, any act of accommodation with local interests can serve only to intensify the basic crisis of authority.

Greatness Lies in the Logic of the Political Order

A second distinctive feature of both traditional and Communist Chinese politics that follows from their structural char-

Cadres, Bureaucracy, and Political Power in Communist China (New York: Columbia University Press, 1967) and Ezra Vogel's detailed study of the government and life in the city of Canton.

24

acteristics is the sovereign importance that both have attached to the value of politics. In traditional China all avenues of social and economic advancement pointed to careers in government, and those within the ranks of officialdom dominated the society. More importantly, it was assumed that all the most important relationships for the society lay either within the activities of officials or in the complete privacy of the family and home.

The political system thus operated as the only society-wide system, and it could be assumed that all social requirements would be taken care of if the political order were properly maintained. The Chinese assumed that by preserving the logic of the political order they were doing everything possible or necessary concerning the economic, social, and legal orders. Authority therefore became a vital matter not just for power relationships but for all welfare and human concerns.

Historically the Chinese never developed the concept that governmental authority should be held in check in order to respect the integrity and the logical necessity of other large-scale systems of human interrelationships, such as, for instance, those that make up the economic system. In Europe, ever since the Middle Ages and the rise of institutionalized feudalism, there has been an appreciation of the possible co-existence in the same society of different systems of authority, both secular and spiritual, and of the specialization of separate role systems, each with its own dynamics and disciplines. Merchants, traders, moneylenders, and eventually bankers had to follow the logic of their callings, as did kings and soldiers. In a sense modern academic theorists were only elucidating the obvious when they talked about an economic order as a system with lawlike properties that had to be respected for the welfare of all.

Even in East Asia, in spite of the heavy influence of Chinese thought, the Japanese, long before any exposure to the West, developed out of their peculiar form of centralized feudalism an appreciation for the distinction between the economic and

25

the political spheres. Political authority in Japan acknowledged that it should respect the logic of economic considerations and accept the need to defer to "economic laws" and not merely to assert the forcefulness of political power. In China there was no such yielding to the concept of an autonomous economic system.

It is striking that in Communist China the need persists to assert the central importance of politics and to believe that the logic of the political ideology is adequate to handle all public problems. Communist officials, just as Nationalist officials before them, have found it painfully difficult to accept economic theory as a proper element in the determination of policies and priorities; for them the relentless mobilization of power alone governs the basic facts of public life.

Thus, when the Communists came to power and sought to define their goals, when they embarked upon their first five-year plan, when they initiated export drives in 1956–1957, and, above all, when they plunged into the Great Leap, they consistently underestimated the realities of economics and overestimated the potency of political control. The difficulty is that skilled economists have won little power or respect and the political leaders are nearly illiterate in economic theory. Yet the Chinese power holders seem undisturbed by their deficiencies in knowledge and feel no need to defer to the more technically skilled.

There are many other reasons why the Chinese place such an extreme value on political power (including a deep sense of insecurity over unstructured and ambiguous social relations —which leaves them with an insatiable need for total control or predictability in human relations), but one significant factor is the belief that the accumulation of redundant power is always prudent, because power can be used for so many things. Deficiencies in other matters can be compensated for by a determined use of political authority. The fact that political power can unquestionably deter and deflect economic and social forces, whether by hampering merchants and traders or by controlling intellectuals, seems to confuse the Chinese into believing that it can be used as readily for constructive developments. Since the will of government has kept people poor, the will of government should be sufficient to produce economic development.

Here again we find very powerful reasons why the Chinese attach so much importance to the concept of political authority and why they are inclined, when dissatisfied with the course of events, to believe that the source of their difficulties must be some inadequacies in their leadership.

This tendency to see the worst in their leaders whenever times are difficult has meant that in the process of modernization the Chinese have been devoid of genuinely popular heroes and of the advantages that come from this form of early constructive authority. In most transitional societies, in contrast, the lingering qualities of the traditional culture have normally tended to work in the opposite direction and to provide the basis for an easy acceptance of any proclaimed leader. The disruptive nature of the modernization process has usually meant that even rather small and petty men can become charismatic leaders. But not so in China, where the few men who have achieved popularity have quickly lost their appeal as soon as they were confronted with difficulties and setbacks.

In present-day China the problem of the relationship of political authority to the other spheres of life is reflected in a basic clash between ideological dogma and specialized skills. The "red and expert" issue is only a modern recasting of the old view that politics should govern all other considerations. At present Mao Tse-tung's intense orthodoxy in fighting any forms of "revisionism" is only another expression of the belief in the universality of politics. The Chinese are quite convinced that if scientists, economic technicians, or scholars are allowed to act according to their professional dictates they will compromise the political system, and this is exactly where they see the folly and sin of Khrushchev and the Russians. We shall return again for a more detailed look at this problem, but here

27

we need observe only that the Chinese political culture has never recognized that any autonomous bodies of knowledge can properly lie outside the reach of the formal political ideology.

Historically the Chinese escaped acute clashes over this matter because there was little or no sense of specialization in the elite society. It is the modern world that has brought increasing social differentiation and intellectual specialization to Chinese society. The trend toward modernization has universally compromised hierarchical forms of authority and favored divisions of authority in line with divisions of labor. Modern firms and enterprises that depend upon advanced forms of technology have tended to be more broadly structured, more decentralized, and more dependent upon cooperation among separate fields of competence than firms that have a much more elementary form of technology.

Thus, while hierarchical authority could easily be maintained in the past, the pressures toward specialization in contemporary China have created strains on the needs of the political system to maintain a single monolithic structure. Hence, the basic tendencies toward differentiation in the modernization process have contributed to the crisis of authority.

Moral Power and the Molding of Personality

A third persisting feature of Chinese politics that has contributed to the authority crisis has been its extraordinary concern for the efficacy of moral persuasion and the importance of self-cultivation.

Precisely because so much was expected of the political system, it became essential for individuals to be indoctrinated in the civic virtues and thereby establish their own internal restraints against antisocial behavior. The Chinese have always been peculiarly self-conscious about the process of political socialization and uninhibited in their faith in self-cultivation and political indoctrination.

28

In a sense so much was expected of government that it needed almost magical powers of persuasion; and in the Confucian ideology there was a naïve faith in the ability of rulers to shame their subjects into proper behavior merely by being exemplary models. At present the Communists have an equally unlimited faith in their capacity to persuade everyone of the correctness of their position and of the exemplary quality of their behavior. In practice this need for rulers to be persuasive has generally been understandably confused with the obligation of subjects to be accommodating to authority.

Historically the Chinese political system lacked the structural capability of imposing itself upon the entire society and of effectively monopolizing all social functions as it pretended to do. A citizenry was needed that was ready to accept the authority of the system and to share the values of the rulers. Thus from a very early time, because of the functional requirements of their hierarchical political system, the Chinese developed a keen awareness that power and authority were closely associated with morality and persuasion. They learned that there should be a peculiarly direct relationship between government and the socialization of the individual, and thus governmental and familial authorities tended to complement and reinforce each other. More than in any other traditional culture the Chinese insisted that the essence of government was to ensure that people were instructed in the proper civil virtues. The Chinese have long appreciated the fact that the younger the person the easier he can be molded, and that if children are properly socialized the task of ruling is greatly simplified. Thus the beginning of government lies in education and child training.

Since in subsequent chapters we shall have to examine the socialization process in considerable detail, it is necessary here only to dwell on the stress on morality as a contributing factor to the authority crisis in modern China. Historically the concern for the morality of officials ranked high as a problem of Chinese politics because few institutional or structural restraints were placed on the actions of those in power. Since the system lacked any form of open competition or public criticism, the prime restraint on officials had to be internal and subjective. The well-being of the political system seemed to require that it be managed by men of superior moral virtues. Nowhere in Chinese politics do we have a frank acceptance of the fact that men may be crass and self-centered and that it is only prudent in designing public institutions to insist upon checks and balances and to provide objective rather than subjective restraints on the use of power. The Confucian ideology stressed the belief that man was by nature good, and the Chinese generally acted in the hope that this was true. Operationally, rulers were supposed to appeal to everyone's better self, and all who aspired to be significant knew that they should apply themselves in self-cultivation according to the cultural ideal of an upright man. Of course, in the contemporary Communist political culture there is an even more intense moral fervor, and much of politics is directed toward influencing and inspiring the private conduct of individuals.

The Chinese problem has been further complicated by the fact that the ethical basis of the traditional public morality was relevant to only a highly stable and orderly situation. The expected morality of leadership could be realized only in an essentially peaceful and static environment. Leaders were supposed to demonstrate their moral fitness by handling predictable problems in a conventional manner. In contrast, in most of the societies of Africa and Asia the traditional concept of authority allowed for the epic hero, the bold leader, the imaginative warrior, the conqueror of the unknown. As we shall see later in this analysis, the Chinese have had little feeling for the potentialities of the virile, youthful, and dynamic leader.

All of this has meant that in the modernization process the Chinese have had to do more than most transitional societies to create an artificial image of their leaders. Whether it related to Sun Yat-sen, Chiang Kai-shek, or Mao Tse-tung, there had to be a planned effort to establish the cult of the leader.

Ideology to Make Reality Safe

Moralistic civic training and the creation of artificial images of leaders both suggest another characteristic of traditional Chinese politics that has contributed to the intensity of the authority crisis, and this is the long-established need to envelop political discussions in rather elaborate and moralistic ideologies. As realistic as the Chinese are in most matters, they have tended in political analysis, especially when seeking to be constructive, to shy away from realities and indulge in ideological discourse. This propensity appears to have been related to traditional anxieties about disorder and conflict. Thus, while in the West it is commonplace and far from shocking to assume that politics is in the last analysis concerned with the management of conflict, the Chinese have sought historically to deny the need for social conflict and to suggest that harmony should always prevail.

The importance of ideology to the operation of politics has been so great that both Chinese and Westerners have conventionally begun their studies of Chinese politics by detailed examinations of the content of the current ideology, whether Confucianism, San-Min-Chu-I, or Marxism-Leninism-Maoism. This approach has obscured the fact that the almost compulsive need for ideologies is far more significant than the content of any one of their ideologies. No other people in history have had as great a need to dress up their politics in formal ideological trappings.

All of this suggests that for the Chinese a basic function of ideologies has been to make it possible for them to avoid a direct confrontation with the realities of their politics. Political reality in any society must reflect disorder, potential or actual conflict, and the expression of open or latent aggression. These

31

are anxiety-provoking subjects for the Chinese. Thus the tradition developed that the elaboration of politics could be respectable only if it was enveloped in moral discourse, and any explicit discussion of the realities of politics without the wrappings of ideology was vulgar.

Furthermore, the extent to which the Chinese have had to rely upon ideology has been indicative of the degree to which they have tended to repress conflict; and more importantly they have related the need for authority to the need to control all manifestations of human aggression. From this exaggerated need for the comforts of ideology we can see a hint of the intensity of the concern about aggression.

Authority Crisis and Aggression

Having suggested a link between the repression of aggression and the tendency to verbalize moralistically about politics, we are in a position to move beyond our initial historical and institutional analysis and introduce the central hypothesis of this study. We argue that the Confucian tradition, both structurally and ideologically, created forms of authority that gained strength by denying the legitimacy of sentiments of aggression. Therefore, once this system of authority was disrupted, the problem of controlling aggression complicated the process of establishing new forms of authority. The release of repressed aggression through more popular forms has complicated the task of arriving at concepts of authority appropriate for more modern politics. On the other hand, the attempt merely to impose modern versions of traditional forms of authority involves the stifling of powerful emotions released by the overt expression of long-repressed aggression.

Theoretically, whenever there is a strong tendency for public authorities to support explicitly the socializing powers of the family and to mobilize familial authority to the task of making better citizens, it is likely to result in the suppression of all socially disruptive tendencies. This means that socialization processes strongly sanctioned by governments are likely to place great emphasis upon the repression of all signs of aggression. In a psychological sense one can indeed think of the prime function of government as this basic social need to control aggression; and therefore it is understandable that civic-oriented socialization processes would tend to focus on the control of aggression.

In fact the Chinese culture has given considerable empirical support to these theoretical speculations. In a sense it has represented historically a massive effort to repress all overt manifestations of aggression and to encourage the sublimation of this powerful force in human nature. What in other cultures has been the problem of controlling sexuality was replaced in some measure in the Confucian tradition by the problem of controlling all expressions of aggression. A host of Chinese behavior characteristics, ranging from their intense concern for form, ritual, and etiquette to their deep anxieties about social and situational ambiguity and uncertainty, their sensitivity to status issues, their acceptance of hierarchy, their dread of social confusion and political disorder, and their constant search for belonging, for identification with groups, and for the security of success and power—all fit together in a common pattern and in varying degrees are related to the control of aggression.

Our hypothesis helps to account for some of the extreme vacillations in Chinese politics between monolithic order and intense but not always bloody conflict. Once an element of competition enters the political scene it can result in a dramatic rise in tension. Thus Chinese politics can at one moment be more orderly than most and at the next violent and hostile. For example, communism in China could seem at one time to be more stable and free from internal leadership conflicts than other Communist movements and yet at another moment become severely torn with authority conflicts.

Aggression is present in all political cultures. In China, however, the problem is particularly acute because the impact of the modern world, which brought the imperatives of social change, disrupted the elaborate mechanisms by which the drives of aggression had been traditionally repressed and molded into the Chinese personality. At the same time, modern nationalistic politics opened up new channels for both the overt and the covert expression of aggression, and with the breakdown of the Confucian world order new antagonisms appeared that authorities could no longer easily contain.

Thus an emotional force has been let loose in modern Chinese politics which is far greater than that contained in the ideologies. It has given great strength and potential to Chinese politics but it is at the same time unreliable and frequently self-defeating. Our purpose in this study will be in considerable degree to measure and evaluate the potential and the limits of harnessing this force in the creation of a new Chinese social order, an order in which aggression will be handled differently than in either the traditional China or in the transitional culture of recent decades.

The need to control aggression once gave powerful meaning to the traditional Chinese stress upon accommodation and harmony. With communism there have come defiantly bold and awkwardly un-Chinese assertions about the merits of struggle and conflict. However, the Communists still retain some of the essential elements of the traditional spirit of accommodation, for to a degree unique among all Communist parties they have acted valiantly in the belief that all people can be converted to communism, that those who are enemies can be won over, and that the party should, in a sense, cooperate and harmonize with history in assisting others to become progressive. The Chinese Communists have tended to talk the language of class struggle but with the strange expectation that they are being only reasonable and that no one should take exception to them.

The real problem of Chinese political culture has not, however, been to deny conflict in the midst of the disruptions of social change but rather to work effectively with those with whom it has had clashes and disagreements. The control of aggression determines the capacity to respect the legitimacy of conflict and to accept the possibilities of disagreements without disrupting or rupturing social relationships. It is the lack of this capacity that has been so noteworthy in the history of contemporary Chinese politics. Once there has been serious disagreement, cooperation becomes impossible. The ability to give legitimacy to but still to manage conflict is precisely the quality essential for the creation of a modern open society. Their difficulty in coping with the realities and the emotional overtones of competition has denied the Chinese the possibilities of modernizing along competitive democratic lines. And now with the conflict over the succession to Mao Tse-tung and the clashes of the Great Cultural Revolution, this same problem is undermining the effort to modernize along Communist lines.

POLITICS WITHOUT
MODERN MEN

Now that we have observed how certain structural characteristics of the traditional Chinese political system helped to shape, and in turn became expressions of, certain dominant and persistent themes of Chinese political culture, we are ready to study the people who participated in this political culture. In modern times, who were the people most likely to be recruited into the ranks of the Chinese ruling classes? What were their predispositions about change and modernization? Why have the Chinese rulers of the twentieth century seemed so stubborn, so willfully hostile to imagination and creativity? Why have the modern Chinese intellectuals been so alienated from politics when elsewhere in the developing world the intellectuals have often dominated politics?

To understand the peculiar relationship of political recruitment to political development in China it is important to begin by observing that the Chinese pattern of modernization stands in sharp contrast to the general pattern of most transitional societies. In China the diffusion of Western practices and what we may now call the "world culture" came slowly and only indirectly to the political sphere. Elsewhere, and particularly in the former colonial countries, the Western impact was generally most intense within the political sphere. In China the modern world had its most direct influences in such private spheres as education, commerce, engineering, and journalism. The modern man was trained primarily in nonpolitical and essentially civilian skills and professions. Elsewhere in Asia and Africa people tended to expect that government and public affairs should be the natural preoccupation of the most modernized elements of their society. Subsequent to colonial rule the dominant pattern in the more typical transitional societies has been one of a relatively acculturated, and possibly alienated, political leadership striving to utilize the powers of government to change all the other segments of life that are lagging behind.

Not so in China. In striving to protect the nation from foreign domination, politics has succeeded mainly in defending its own limited world from modern currents, and thus the political sphere has consistently lagged behind the private, urban sector. To an extraordinary degree, recruitment into the political sphere has operated in a fashion to screen out the more Westernized and modernized Chinese. Consequently, those who have been successful in making careers of office holding and power manipulating have generally been less influenced by the outside world than their counterparts in most African and Asian countries. Chinese who have shown the skill and the ability to adapt themselves intellectually and emotionally to the modern world have had little opportunity to participate effectively in the day-to-day maneuverings of Chinese politics. Thus the relationship between political power and modernization in China is the exact opposite of what it is in most transitional societies.

At the time of the fall of the Manchu dynasty it appeared for a brief moment that modernized Chinese with experiences abroad might be able to rush in to take command of government and politics. But the very process of defeating the Manchus brought forward men who had been only faintly touched by modern ideas. Soon politics became the monopoly of warlords and locally based officials whose ties were with parochial traditions and who were largely insensitive to dynamic developments in the outside world. The

Nationalist revolution and the emergence of the Kuomintang tapped a more enlightened reservoir of talent, but even the Kuomintang, in both its leadership and its rank-and-file party members, consisted of men more at home in provincial than in cosmopolitan society. At present, although the Communists have been able to recruit some Westernized intellectuals, neither their leaders nor the great mass of their party cadres represent the most modernized segments of Chinese society. And when we look beyond the generation of Mao Tse-tung and note the character of the post-Long March cadres, the prospect is still one of supremacy for the less worldly, the less sophisticated, and the more parochially rooted.

Thus the first point to keep in mind is that while the gap of alienation in most transitional societies has been between a Westernized and modern inspired elite and a still traditionalist mass, in China the gap of alienation has been between the dispossessed Westernized intellectuals and a political elite that has remained closer to the masses. Chinese leaders, both Nationalist and Communist, have generally been men who have not been at home in any foreign language and who have not traveled extensively abroad.[1] In every other country of Asia the political class has had a larger proportion of men with a command of foreign languages and firsthand experiences of other parts of the world. The Nehrus and Ne Wins, the Souvanna Phoumas and the Sihanouks, the Magsaysays and the Tunkus — even the Sukarnos — are from a different stratum of Asian society than the Chiang

[1] Robert C. North's study of elites showed that at least until 1950 the Kuomintang and the Communist leaders were remarkably similar in class background, social status, education, age, and channels of advancement. In both groups those who came from better-off families tended to be downwardly mobile and worse off in personal circumstances. On the other hand, those of humble origins generally advanced through army channels. A third of the KMT Central Executive Committee and 54.8 per cent of the Communist CEC went to Chinese military schools. See Harold D. Lasswell and Daniel Lerner, eds., *World Revolutionary Elites* (Cambridge, Mass.: The M.I.T. Press, 1965), p. 382.

Kai-sheks and the Mao Tse-tungs, whose shrewdness in politics comes largely from an easy acquaintanceship with the oldest political traditions of their land.[2] The truth is that no other Asian society has so wholly left the management of its public affairs and its national interest to half-educated rulers and strong-armed bullies. This is all the more puzzling to foreigners and annoying to the Chinese in the light of their traditional notion that government should belong to the philosophers and the educated class.

Although modern Chinese politics has been the preserve of the less modernized, it has rarely reflected the higher ideals of the traditional political culture, for those who have controlled the movement of events have not been inspired by the higher traditions of a once sophisticated civilization. The linkage between contemporary Communist practices and historical politics is found less in the grand traditions or explicit philosophies of government than in the vulgar but popular traditions of day-to-day Chinese life. Thus when we speak of the persistence of elements of traditional culture in both Communist and Nationalist politics we are thinking not of the vestiges of Confucianism but of the spirit in which the Chinese have approached power and the necessities of government.

In any society the unfathomable nature of political prediction causes people at all levels to look for guidance from those who are presumed to have some specialized skills or some unique human capabilities or from those who may be situated close to the centers of decision and thus have relevant information. The common people generally believe that

[2] It is true that in many of the ex-colonial countries power has gravitated away from the more cosmopolitan to the more parochial elements, but these emerging elites are in their fashion concerned with modernization and reflect to some degree their societies' exposure to world culture. See Myron Weiner, "India: Two Political Cultures," in Lucian W. Pye and Sidney Verba, eds., *Political Culture and Political Development* (Princeton, N.J.: Princeton University Press, 1965). In China there has never been even a brief period during which cosmopolitan elements dominated politics.

their intellectual superiors, and especially those with skills that give them higher status, are better able to comprehend the rationally incomprehensible nature of much of politics. Thus a mark of political change and indeed a measurement of the nature of a political revolution can be found in the shifts that occur when one skill group replaces another as the most accepted interpreters and forecasters of political developments.

In traditional China it was universally assumed that the Confucian scholars were unquestionably the most knowledgeable about the affairs of state and the direction of history. What is striking about the modern Chinese political culture is not so much the declining influence of the traditional scholar but, rather, the failure of any other skill group to emerge as the new experts on the mysteries of politics. Those within politics have apparently felt no need for the private advice or the public pronouncements of journalists, business leaders, academic specialists, or any other kind of elite spokesmen common to most modern politics. The successive Chinese political classes have been self-sufficient, feeling little need for the intellectual or moral support of any group in society. The public has had a prolonged sense of futility about politics; and no detached elite has been recognized as an appropriate interpreter of public affairs.

Thus throughout the first half of this century China's politics has not been inspired, reinforced, or disciplined either by outside skill groups or by the more educated Chinese. Since the Communists assumed direction of the society the practice of rejecting native talent and specialized skills has continued, and the monopoly for interpreting public affairs has been firmly held by the current political insiders, the party cadres.

The Rock of Anti-Intellectualism

One must wonder whether any country, let alone one with China's massive problems, can hope to realize progress

40

without exploiting its most precious resource — its highest human talents. Since it is in the nature of revolutionary processes to cast aside much of the "capital" built up by the old order, many otherwise capable people find it impossible to adjust to the demands of a new order in any rapidly changing society and are pushed to the sidelines; but the situation in China has involved far more than this phenomenon. There has been conscious and ruthless action by the political class against those with constructive skills who would have been prepared to a large degree to contribute to the building of a more advanced nation.

The Kuomintang was never able to appreciate fully the importance of intellectuals. In alienating students, scholars, and the educated classes it tended to push them into the arms of the Communists. The general expectation when the Communists came to power was that the new regime would tenderly care for its more enlightened citizenry. But the Communist power holders and manipulators soon proved that their instincts on this score were little different from those of their predecessors.

In the first years after the Communists came to power, efforts were made to attract intellectuals and technically skilled personnel to the cause of national reconstruction. In the early 1950's a campaign was waged to bring back to the homeland Chinese with modern skills and knowledge. However, every year thereafter, in one campaign after another, the regime has cut away at this body of talented supporters. Gradually, through the lasting effects of such programs as the Three-Antis, the Five-Antis, the "Learn from Russia" drive, the Great Leap, the Anti-Rightists, the *Hsia-fang,* the thought remolding campaigns, the "Learn from the Thoughts of Mao Tse-Tung" drive, and the Cultural Revolution against "bourgeois" thinking in the universities, the Chinese political class has steadily alienated the intellectuals. Even within the party the process has occurred, because the efforts to resolve what the Chinese Communists call the "red and expert"

41

problem have tended to minimize the importance of intellectual talent as against other considerations.

Thus the sequence of commitment and disillusionment of the intellectuals is only the most recent chapter in the repeated story of the fundamental clash between Chinese power holders on the one side and intellectuals and technical specialists on the other. The intensity of this persisting conflict has usually become apparent only when the power holders have so alienated the specialists that the latter have given up all hope of influencing public affairs. At the beginning of each cycle, when new rulers have just come to power, the clash has been muted and less manifest because of the readiness of the intellectuals and specialists to support the new power holders in the anxious but inevitably forlorn hope of gaining some access to the direction of power.

It is possible to picture the dynamics of modern Chinese politics as one in which the hard core of political power has passed from one anti-intellectual political class to another, and to observe that in this movement through time the successive political classes have been surrounded by the ineffectual clamors of the enlightened, whether intellectuals or specialists, who have been persistently denied access to the realm of real decision making. From time to time individuals from the educated class have gained access to the hard-core political realm; but since the terms of admission have always involved the sacrifice of their moral principles and their rationalistic outlook, the anti-intellectualism of the politicians has not been diluted.

Students and intellectuals have occasionally injected themselves, sometimes violently, into Chinese public affairs and caused great embarrassment to the political class. The May Fourth movement in 1919 in response to the Versailles decision to transfer the former German concessions in Shantung to Japan — enraged students set fire to the home of a cabinet minister and chased another minister over his back fence — was the most dramatic instance of student involvement in

Chinese politics. The May Fourth movement pales, however, in comparison with later student demonstrations elsewhere in Asia and in the Middle East or Africa; and it is clear that students in Indonesia, Burma, Egypt, Turkey, and several Latin American countries have had more influence at particular junctures over the course of their nations' developments than did that early generation of Chinese youth. Comparisons aside, there is no question that students and intellectuals have at no time been regular participants in Chinese politics. They have been able to articulate the emotions of nationalism but never to shape the decisions of the nation. They have accelerated the decomposition of one group's power, but they have been irrelevant to the formation of new power. Now, of course, in the phenomenon of the Red Guards we see the extreme example of students in a transitional society being used and manipulated by public authorities who have little appreciation for intellectual values.

The frustration of the Chinese intellectuals has had unhappy — even tragic — results. Their natural articulateness has helped to accentuate the impression of the brutality of Chinese politics, for, with the door closed to them, the intellectuals have pictured politics as an unthinking process surrounded by disillusionment and alienation. This was how they expressed their feelings after the May Fourth movement proclaimed the republican politicians deficient in patriotism, after the professors and students in Kunming and Peking declared the Nationalists to be corrupt and venal, and after Mao decided that there would be no more Hundred Flowers campaigns. Thus the potency of Chinese intellectuals has been limited almost entirely to the harping, negativistic role of the purveyor of scandal. Unable to carry forward their own plans, and denied any possibility for vigorous constructive approaches, they have tended to concentrate on the moral and personal imperfections of those who have had the responsibilities for ruling China.

Although, admittedly, policies have changed during the

43

tenure of each successive political class, and although there are objective grounds for the rise and fall of popular hopes for progress, the intensity of the fluctuations of illusion and disillusionment that characterize Chinese politics stems in no small measure from the fact that the educated classes are constantly trying to mobilize themselves to gain access to the inner core of Chinese politics. The intellectuals have been steadily driven on by their unquenchable belief that politics rightfully belongs to the most educated class. This is the one element that even the most modernized intellectual still carries over from the great classical tradition of Chinese government.

The frustration of the intellectuals contributes to the spirit of hostility and hate that we shall identify as a basic ingredient of the Chinese political culture. The shame of the intellectuals for their failure to regain the place within the society that they feel is rightfully theirs is readily merged with their greater sense of shame over the weaknesses of China. Those weaknesses have hurt them, because manifestly their self-interest would have been advanced by modernization. On the other hand, the security and power of the political leaders, whether warlord, Nationalist, or Communist, has generally not depended upon the pace of modernization. On the contrary, they have often benefited precisely from what the intellectuals consider to be the shame of China.

Individual specialists and technicians have personally come to terms with Chinese politics, accepted innocuous employment within the various governments, and even served as members of the personal entourages of warlords and politicians. It has also been a common practice of warlord and commissar to utilize people from the modernized sector of society for high-prestige positions. But these have almost universally been positions of little power in domestic politics.[3]

[3] It is noteworthy that in a field that was seen as highly technical and nonpolitical, that of diplomacy, the Chinese in the 1920's and

Such involvement has been in essence nonpolitical, because the intellectual or technician has acknowledged his competence only to further the decisions of others and not to be a principal in the making of policies. In a sense the intellectuals and modernized specialists in modern China, whether among the hangers-on of a warlord or in a controlled office of the Communists, have at best only taken over the role that in traditional politics was filled by eunuchs.

In modern times the successive political classes have each in their turn displayed an awareness of the clash with the intellectuals, and in their separate ways they have shown uneasiness over the illegitimacy, in traditional terms, of denying government and influence to members of the educated classes. Since those who have held power have neither seen the intellectuals as a power threat nor appreciated their potential value, the aggressive treatment of intellectuals probably stems from a feeling for the impropriety of excluding the educated from the centers of politics. Power holders have often deferred to the intellectual but usually by trying to keep him happy *outside of politics.*

Although the anti-intellectualism of the Communists has differed in many respects from that of earlier political classes, the consequences for Chinese development have been much the same. The much more explicit and sophisticated ideological basis of the Communist political culture might have been expected to provide a peculiar appeal to intellectuals, but the central thrust of Maoism, with its exaggerated emphasis on the importance of men over machines, of the spirit over

---

1930's were represented by a remarkably skilled group of modernized men who had extraordinary success in international politics, especially considering how little power China had at the time. The field of foreign affairs could, however, be left to these talented men precisely because it was seen by the political class as lying outside the domain of politics. The Communists have treated foreign affairs more seriously, and hence the quality of Chinese diplomatic representation has declined to the general level of the current political class.

the mind, of ideological loyalties over pragmatic realism, has provided the basis for a more vicious attack on intellectuals than that of any earlier political class.

At present in China a struggle is clearly going on between those who would seek a more technocratic approach to problems and those who would stress the anti-intellectualism of ideological purity. One dimension of the conflict that led to the removal of P'eng Teh-huai and the rise of Lin Piao in the army and in party circles was the former's concern for the rational development of the People's Liberation Army and the latter's support for the principle of learning from the thoughts of Mao Tse-tung and for the belief that doctrinal enthusiasm can more than make up for material deficiencies. The party's position on the "red and expert" issue has been in the same spirit. Some young Chinese scientists tried to suggest that the correct formula should be that the more "expert" a man was the less he should have to be "red," that is, a deeply trained ideologue, and the less a man's intellectual skills the more he should have to prove ideological commitment, but the party leadership hit back by saying that the more "expert" a man was the more he would be expected to be "red." [4]

This controversy in a broader form has been at the heart of Mao Tse-tung's attack on "revisionism" and his deep anxiety lest the next generation of Chinese lose their sense of revolutionary fervor. The Cultural Revolution that began with the fall of P'eng Chen in the spring of 1966 has taken

[4] Tsien Hsüeh-sun, the leading Chinese rocket expert trained at the Massachusetts Institute of Technology and the California Institute of Technology, wrote an interesting criticism of the attitudes of young Chinese scientists and aspiring technicians, saying that the prevailing mood was one of "expert first and red second," and that too many scientists had the "three get-by-withs" attitude — get by with the least possible political involvement, get by with a secure and interesting technical job, and get by with a good private life. The article, entitled "One Must Be Both Red and Expert to Climb to the Mountain Top for the Benefits of the Revolution," appeared in the June 3, 1965, issue of *China Youth* and was reprinted on the next day in *People's Daily.*

the form of a peculiarly vicious attack upon the institutions of higher learning.[5] The Chinese leaders, in coupling the universities with "revisionist" tendencies, have been quite explicit in declaring that the great mistake the Soviets made was to permit their scientists to meet with American scientists and to allow technically oriented specialists to have excessive influence in economic planning. With determination to avoid the same mistake, Mao appears to be counting in a very particular way upon the anti-intellectualism of the political culture to protect his revolution from the dangers of a thaw in relations with the United States — through meetings of scientists or a return to capitalism through rational planning.

The Rooted and Unalienated Politicians

The corollary to the exclusion of the educated elements from central power is that the political classes of modern China have been more firmly rooted in social realities than have the political classes of most other transitional societies. Indeed, to understand the evolution of the political culture it is particularly important to recognize that the political classes have been close to the center of gravity of Chinese society while the educated classes have been more alienated in their search for modernization. This has had profound

[5] At the time of writing all major Chinese universities have been closed for one year while the whole system of student selection and admission is being revised so as to eliminate dependence upon examinations and objective measurements of academic capabilities — measurements that are supposed to be "bourgeois" in nature. Presumably the new system will favor ideological commitment and be sensitive to the class background and the political feelings of candidates.

This attack upon the universities reflects to some degree an idiosyncratic bias of Mao, who has always had a contempt for the academic world and whose hostility toward universities has increased over the years. He has informed both a Japanese and an Italian delegation that they were wasting their time in visiting Peking University, which he then characterized scatologically. Mao's anti-intellectualism is in tune with the modern Chinese traditions of political leaders; he is only less inhibited in expressing his prejudices.

psychological significance for the development of the political culture. Above all it has meant that the power holders have not been as haunted by fears of inferiority to the outside world, nor have they had a concern for the judgments of foreigners as have so many of the leaders of other transitional societies.

Within the province of their day-to-day activities, and as long as they kept the intellectual in the wings, the Chinese political classes have been able to find justification for their position; they have generally stood out as appropriate leaders with superior talent when compared with the great masses of the people. The warlords who shaped the first generation of the modern political classes were certainly no match in human talents and imagination for the modernized and cosmopolitan coastal Chinese, but within their provincial domains they were generally striking figures who stood out among the peasants. The same has been true of each succeeding generation, including the present Communist leaders — who are certainly provincial men if measured against the educated classes but in the peasant setting of the Long March and Yenan are manifestly natural leaders. Each generation of Chinese politicians has in this strange fashion been able to think of itself as upholding the tradition of government by educated and superior men.

The various Chinese political classes have been surrounded on one side by far more modernized and educated people and on the other by more deeply traditional masses. In this fashion they have been able to conduct their daily affairs shielded from a constant concern with the outside world. Their isolation has made them impervious to the psychic threats that might come from a constant awareness of the standards of government and public affairs in other countries. They have thus been remarkably secure both in their sense of identity as Chinese and in their unconcern with the need to justify the purposes for which they have employed the power at their disposal.

In examining more closely the emotional dimensions of the clash between the political and the educated classes, we find that the politicians have been securely rooted in their culture while the educated classes, as the articulate spokesmen of nationalism, have had ambivalent and alienated feelings about their heritage. During the 1920's and early 1930's it was clearly those who were outside of the arena of day-to-day politics who sought to infuse into public life a sense of nationalism and hatred toward the threatening foreigners. During this period the members of the political class, feeling secure in their parochial identity as Chinese, could not appreciate the passions of the anxious and psychically threatened modernized class.

One dynamic theme in the evolution of the modern political culture has been the gradual decline in self-assurance and a concomitant rise in assertiveness toward outsiders of each succeeding generation of power holders as they have been exposed to the taunts of the Westernized, and hence most nationalistic, elements of Chinese society. The old warlord, for example, was completely at home within his own world; he could recognize the existence of foreigners without permitting them to shake his own sense of cultural identity. In contrast, the Nationalist politician derived less security from his cultural roots and was more anxious about foreign judgments. And the present generation of Chinese Communists is far more preoccupied with meeting foreign standards than with living up to Chinese cultural traditions. Nevertheless, even though the trend has been in the direction of greater insecurity of identity, the political classes have remained remarkably rooted in their culture; and, in spite of the far-reaching effects of social and political change, the spirit of the modern Chinese political culture has remained close to that of the traditional political culture.

THE MILLSTONE
OF GREATNESS

As we begin to note the clash between modern and traditional in China we come to the realm of conflicting values, which have plagued the life of most transitional societies. For most of the countries of the Afro-Asian world, and particularly those that have experienced colonialism, this conflict has been played out in the personal lives of individuals, creating what has commonly been called "crises of identity." Although the Chinese have known these conflicts they seem to have been spared many of the psychological problems common to severe identity crises. Fundamentally, and largely because of their strong sense of history, they have had little confusion over the reality of their Chinese identity.

The most pervasive underlying Chinese emotion is a profound, unquestioned, generally unshakable identification with historical greatness. Merely to be Chinese is to be a part of the greatest phenomenon of history. The twists and turns of contemporary circumstance seem never to ruffle this diffuse and all-pervasive sense of personal association with a glorious and self-contained history that encompasses all of merit and greatness in the human experience. This is all so self-evident to the Chinese that they are hardly aware when they are being superior to others.

Manifestations of this bedrock sentiment have been noted

by most observers of Chinese behavior, whether Communist or Nationalist, traditional or modern. It has been labeled the "Middle Kingdom complex" and identified as an exaggerated sense of "national pride" or simply "racial arrogance." Yet the sentiment that allows the Chinese to believe they are the center of the world runs far deeper than what is customarily associated with the term "complex" and certainly involves more than what is usually thought of as pride.

As a historical theme the Chinese identification with greatness first appeared when the first Western visitors to the Celestial Kingdom were dismissed as mere "barbarians," and it rose to a crescendo in the mid-nineteenth century in the numerous memorials and imperial edicts that sought to bring the various European envoys to their knees in the proper postures of humility before the Chinese throne. The disintegration of the imperial system and the sorry confusion of the republican regime in no way eliminated the phenomenon. Western students of Chinese communism are repeatedly rediscovering it; and when such an experienced reporter of the Communist scene as Robert S. Elegant sought to sum up nearly a decade at the Hong Kong listening post he concluded that the theme that best supported his summation was the Chinese identification with historical greatness.[1]

Every confrontation between traditional societies and the modern world gives rise to an assertion of the integrity and greatness of each parochial history. Hence it might seem that the Chinese were making only a more elegant and more sophisticated assertion of the legitimacy of their own historical sense of identity than has been possible for most other peoples. In many respects the nineteenth-century confrontation between imperial China and Western technological society was merely the playing out on a much grander scale of the same drama that has been enacted on countless stages throughout the world. The clash between the universalism of

[1] Robert S. Elegant, *The Center of the World: Communism and the Mind of China* (London: Methuen & Co., 1963).

51

the modern world culture and the parochialisms of each society's roots in history has been felt by all peoples, non-Europeans and Europeans alike. In this view of history no peoples have been able to avoid the distorting effects of their own parochial cultural identities, and all have at times appeared to act in self-centered ignorance as they have striven to deny the ultimate potency of the modernizing world. Thus the stubborn resistance of the Chinese to the Western impact was only one well-documented chapter in the "passing of traditional society."

Yet once it is granted that the Chinese experience is part of a world-wide drama, it must still be conceded that the Chinese sense of historical greatness has an added and distinctive dimension: It is of a different order of magnitude from that of all other cultural traditions and it is documented by more than just the feeling of the Chinese about themselves; all peoples in some degree acknowledge the uniqueness of China and its historic civilization.

Without undue exaggeration it can be said that an awareness of the greatness of Chinese civilization, together with an appreciation of the distinctiveness of "Chineseness," is possibly one of the few cognitions shared by nearly the entire human race. Certainly during the last two hundred years, anyone at all enlightened about history has been at least vaguely aware of China, of Cathay. Even when the details of that civilization are unknown, the mere word "China" seems to excite the imagination. For early in the experience of each generation comes some feeling for the uniqueness and imponderability of Chinese civilization that subsequent experiences never seem to eradicate completely.

For others, as for the Chinese, the awareness of its greatness is little affected by the fortunes of present-day Chinese society. This sentiment is so closely associated with a sense of mystery about the endurance and development of human history that events of the contemporary world hardly touch it. The extraordinary and historically unique phenomenon of modern Japanese development and rapid progress is still seen as somehow more trivial than the historical phenomenon of China. Asians, particularly, appreciate only intellectually what Japan has done; their unconscious, spontaneous appreciation is for the supreme greatness of China.

Even when people acknowledge the failings of modern China, a feeling for its greatness is still sustained by awe at its mere size and its numberless people. Imagination falters at the thought of nearly 750 million people sharing a common national identity. The prospect that within our lifetime a third of the human race may be Chinese overshadows our feelings about the political and social failure of modern China. It is significant that China's huge population can conjure up a vision of immense power that might become a threat to others, while India's similarly huge population suggests in contrast a nearly hopeless situation.

Many who know the Chinese well lose the feeling for their historic greatness in exasperation with their arrogance and self-satisfaction. But even the Southeast Asians, who have little capacity for reverence toward anyone and who have long had to practice the art of keeping the Chinese in their place, have some feelings for the latter's distinctiveness. They recognize that precisely because of the depth of the roots of Chinese culture they can most effectively prove their own powers by stripping the Chinese of their national identity.

Within East Asia itself the Japanese have long been an appreciative audience for the mystique of Chinese greatness. The current protestation of the Japanese intellectuals that they somehow have a deeper understanding of and affinity for the Chinese than any other people is only a contemporary form of that age-old Japanese wish that somehow a bit of Chinese greatness could be rubbed off onto themselves. Although the Japanese long ago took a different fork in the road of national development, they persist in pretending that their earlier tie to Chinese civilization is still relevant to their own sense of self-dignity.

The spirit underlying this attitude was revealed by an American-educated, vibrantly energetic Japanese executive, who in a moment of candid introspection confided to an American friend that the one thing he envied the most in the world was the unsurpassable good fortune of the Chinese at simply being Chinese. As much as he accepted the advantages of modern knowledge and the scientific world culture, he could not escape from a deeper feeling that somehow all else was trivial and merely man-made in comparison with the immeasurable heritage that lay at the roots of Chineseness.

Standing in Awe of Biological History

Since others have not allowed the sorry history of modern China to blur their appreciation for her historical distinctiveness, it is understandable that the Chinese themselves have preserved their unquestioning faith in the greatness that was once theirs and that they feel *should remain* theirs forever. This unshakable tie to culture and race makes it peculiarly difficult for them to appraise their civilization in a critical manner except to note when they are not realizing their inherent capability. Even when they are prepared to admit that much must be changed and that revolution is the only solution for the moment, such admissions do not compromise their fundamental awe of their own history. Their effort at change is only a tactic to regain their place in history, not a denial or rejection of their past.

When pressed, however, to state what precisely they revere of their culture, even the most articulate Chinese tend to have difficulties. In large measure this is because they have so assumed the greatness of their ancient civilization that it has never seemed necessary to consider the details. Yet, it is remarkable how few specific features of their civilization the Chinese self-consciously value or feel that they must fight to maintain. Whenever Chinese communities feel they must make a self-conscious effort to preserve their traditions the results

have always been depressing. For example, when the Nationalists retreated to Taiwan and gave up their earlier quest for
modernization in their anxiety over the need to preserve the
heritage of Chinese civilization, their move resulted in a stulti-
fication of life that has been common to all other overseas
Chinese communities that have sought to do the same thing.
This is only to say that since it is peculiarly unnatural for the
Chinese to have to work at being Chinese there are no spontaneously acknowledged features of their civilization that they
see the need to preserve.

There is thus a strange paradox about Chinese culture. It
has had a remarkable endurance in history; yet it is a culture
that easily becomes artificially traditionalistic whenever a self-
conscious effort is made to preserve it. Although powerful and
persistent, Chinese culture seems to lose its essential spirit
when consciously defended. Other cultures, for example, the
Jewish, have long had to practice the art of enduring and
flourishing while on the defensive; but historically the Chinese
have not. This paradox also helps to explain why they have
been so awkward and artless in winning sympathy for themselves whenever they have felt compelled to be defensive.

The lack of strong attachments to specific institutions or
articulated values has given the Chinese the capacity to accept
a remarkable degree of change without compromising their
identity and their feeling of association with greatness. This
has been possible because in spite of all references to civilization and culture their sense of greatness has been rooted primarily in a profound, mystical, and self-conscious awareness
of the biological ties to their ancestors. The sense of identity
is thus derived less from the content of culture, which is always
somewhat vague and ambiguous, and more from the fact of
race, which is biologically unambiguous. The central place of
ancestor worship and the compulsive desire for sons are both
only surface manifestations of the deeper Chinese belief in the
significance of their own beings as a part of immemorial history. The individual is subconsciously aware of a unique link

with the past, and thus his very existence becomes the basis for an essentially mystical view of his unshakable roots in history. For other peoples the self-conscious awareness of the existence of the self can provoke questions about "Who am I?" "Why am I here?" and "What is the purpose of my existence?" For the Chinese it is precisely the awareness of physical existence as Chinese that resolves all such questions.

Somehow other people — who as "foreign devils" and "barbarians" have different origins — are not the products of the same process of family building with ancestral links; their existence is no more mystical than the process of breeding that produces generations of animals. The Chinese see such an absolute difference between themselves and others that even when living in lonely isolation in distant countries they unconsciously find it natural and appropriate to refer to those in whose homeland they are living as "foreigners."

The importance of biological considerations in establishing the Chinese sense of identity also helps to explain the peculiar difficulties that the Chinese have with emotions and feelings of association in relationships that go beyond the ties of kinship. The problem is not just that the Chinese value the family so highly that they have had difficulty in developing loyalty to the nation. More basic is the fact that they have not associated the ultimate test of identity with mere cultural similarity; for them like-mindedness has not been an easy substitute for the realities of the biological family. Only gradually, as they have been exposed to other cultures, have the Chinese been driven to realize that out of the fact of their biological identities as individual Chinese they must be associated also with all others who share the Chinese race and culture.

Awareness of their distinctive Chineseness has been a powerful factor inhibiting the rate of assimilation of overseas Chinese into foreign cultures. In Southeast Asia, moreover, the Chinese generally have had a higher economic position than the masses of the Southeast Asians and have adhered to distinct professions and occupations, factors which have tended to reinforce the boundaries of cultural differences. The Chinese thus readily confuse culture and biology and assume that it is in their nature to excel in some pursuits and to be more industrious, more sober-minded, more at home with urban life, and generally more successful than others.

In spite of these barriers and psychological resistances, assimilation does occur, and the Chinese are aware that their children may lose their sense of Chinese identity; hence the universal thrust in all overseas communities to establish "Chinese schools." In the recent past the problem has taken on different dimensions because the overseas Chinese, particularly in Malaysia, have had to ask themselves how they can become accepted members of the new national community. Changing circumstances have altered the dimensions of the problem, but the basic underlying sentiment has continued to be that it would be grotesquely abnormal for any Chinese to lose his identification with the roots of Chinese greatness.

Historically it is possible to explain the strong biological basis for the Chinese sense of identity in terms of the traditional place of the family in the culture and society. In modern times this institution has been compelled to undergo extensive changes. But, significant as these changes have been, most of the key features of the family socialization process that might affect the child's sense of identification with Chineseness have been little touched. As the smaller nuclear family has come to replace the traditional extended family, the pressures have been maintained, and in some respects increased, to ensure that the offspring will be constantly aware of their identity as Chinese. Whatever the setting may be, whether in China itself or in foreign lands, the biological family, the Chinese community, the outside social agencies, and peers have all combined to impress this upon the young.

Social Change with a Stable Identity

This capacity to appreciate their own existence has meant that as a people the Chinese have not been afflicted with the problem of identity so prevalent in most transitional societies. In the former colonial world Indian intellectuals worry about their state of rootlessness. African writers struggle to refine their racial identities, but for the Chinese the question is quite different. As a young Chinese anxious to become a good citizen of Malaya put it: No matter how he tries, how can a Chinese ever stop being a Chinese?

Since a Chinese cannot possibly conceive of not being Chinese, he cannot personally escape feeling threatened and humiliated by his nation's difficulties with modernization. When the Chinese have become self-conscious upon exposure to the modern world, their reaction has not been one of confusion about their individual or collective identities, rather they have been perplexed and vexed that China as a nation should be having difficulties and appear in any way inferior to other nations.

In looking for the sources of their difficulties the Chinese are quick to trace them to the political arena. This has been easy for the more modernized Chinese, for as we have noted they have been consistently excluded from positions of influence. But in a more general sense it has been logical for the Chinese to believe that their problems were in the political realm because of the central importance of government in traditional China. In so identifying their collective problem the Chinese have translated their difficulties with modernization into a problem of authority. It has therefore been easy and quite natural to believe that they have been let down and that they needed stronger leadership.

Thus their approach to modernization has not suggested the need to change fundamentally and irrevocably their basic nature or identity. Instead the Chinese have tended to believe that it should be necessary only to eliminate some surface defects and to allow the basic virtues of the people to reassert themselves. Even the most enlightened and sensitive have been easily convinced that national salvation would follow automatically if only the unfortunate influences of supersti-

58

tion and ignorance could be pushed aside. No Chinese would think of raising publicly the possibility that the problem might be deeper and that maybe there would have to be a change in Chinese identity. Serious searches for the heart of successful modernization have generally led to the belief that the precise qualities required were, in fact, once a part of the Chinese heritage.

The Natural Greatness,
and Hence Goodness, of the Self

Modernization has thus appeared as a somewhat less earth-shaking process to the Chinese than to people less certain of the durability of their traditional values in a modern world. They have been quite ready to talk about the need for revolution, but their sense of revolution has been limited psychologically to shaking off the layer of inappropriate custom so as to allow the true Chinese qualities to govern society once again. Indeed, this approach has given a profoundly different psychological basis to Chinese communism than is to be found in Russian Bolshevism. Since the Russian reaction to modernization was more in line with the feelings of transitional peoples experiencing a crisis of identity, it would be helpful at this point to note briefly the difference in attitude toward national character in the two Communist countries.

An essential feature in the shaping of Russian communism was a very conscious but deeply felt need to counter and repress many characteristics of the Russian national character that were accepted as the source of weakness and ineffectualness. Nineteenth-century Russian intellectuals loved Mother Russia and the Slavic tradition but they generally recognized the need to replace or repress certain elements of the native temperament and behavior if they were to create a modern and efficient national society. With the Bolsheviks this need became quite explicit, for the good Communist must be constantly on the alert to control his natural tenden-

59

cies. The dominant spirit of life as a dedicated party member became the demand that the individual constantly steel himself against his inclinations and always struggle against his own inner weaknesses.

In sharp contrast the Chinese Communists have never seriously entertained the notion that their national identity could be an obstacle to their communism. On the contrary, they seem to believe that by achieving the ideal of the good party member they are doing no more than giving expression to the inherent goodness of their national character. There may have been bad aspects to Chinese "feudalism," "bourgeoisie," and the corruptions that "imperialism" brought to the "Chineseness" of their character and their society. Above all, nothing in their struggle to become good revolutionaries suggests that the spirit of Chinese culture is not pure virtue. Mao himself lives at ease with his extensive knowledge of Chinese history, and he constantly relates the earlier greatness of China to the task of building communism today.

It is true that the Chinese Communists have had considerable difficulty in deciding precisely how they should treat their great historical heroes, particularly Confucius. Clearly they have been embarrassed by their desire not to discount the greatness of their own national civilization; but it is impossible to make the sage of the mandarin class into a forerunner of Marx. Thus, intellectually, their rationalizations display many ambiguities; but basically they are not ambivalent about the potential for greatness inherent in their culture.

In some ways the Russians have been more willing than the Chinese to face up to their own reasons for backwardness. This may be attributed to Russia's Christian heritage and to a fundamental belief in the doctrine of original sin. In order to achieve the ideal of the perfect man, the true revolutionary, the Russians recognize explicitly the need to grapple with the inner weakness of the soul, particularly the Russian soul, and to be constantly on guard against the triumph of evil.

In the Chinese view, as well articulated in the Confucian

60

as in the Communist traditions, man — that is, the Chinese man — is inherently good, and all he needs is education, training, or discipline to bring out his basic goodness. For the Russian the task of becoming a good Communist begins with an acknowledgment of the need to overcome the natural tendencies toward laziness, slovenliness, flights of fantasy, and undisciplined emotionalism and ends with a psychically exhausting struggle at the very roots of the personality. For the Chinese the task may be difficult and demanding and may be even cruelly painful but it does not involve a challenge to the basis of personality and it can be carried out in a pragmatic and utilitarian spirit.

Similarly, although the masses of the Chinese may have to be aroused constantly, this is not because of any flaws in their character but because they have been unjustly exploited for so long. The Russians, admitting that their peasants may, in their apathy and suspicion, lie on the borders of hopelessness, have been prepared to acknowledge that some people may never accept communism or become good party members; the Chinese have adhered to the fundamental position that all can be won over to their revolution. This essentially optimistic view of the attractive powers of communism touches on other features of the Chinese political culture which we shall come to shortly but it also reflects a conviction about the basic goodness and merit of the Chinese national character.

Impotence and Frustration Flow
from the Two Key Values of Chinese Culture

The optimism of the Chinese about their own potentialities has at every turn been challenged by the realities of China's record in modernization. The expectation of superior potentialities has produced only frustration and an exaggerated sense of humiliation. Since nothing can be wrong with the Chinese spirit and their inward identity, all problems must lie outside and therefore be the work of "foreigners."

Against this background, the rise of nationalism can be readily seen to revolve around the shame of the Chinese over the performance of their society and polity. We cannot document here the extent to which the Chinese have been embarrassed and humiliated by the performance of the Manchu dynasty and the period of warlord politics. What is important is that they have so exaggerated their sense of impotence that they have been blind to their own positive achievements during those periods. As we have already noted, the Chinese, even during the darkest periods of recent history, did have many significant successes.

What is striking, therefore, given their strong inclination to see only goodness in themselves and to believe that they are associated with greatness, is how little satisfaction they have been able to derive from these successes. It is true that in spite of its emphasis upon achievement, the Chinese culture has preferred to celebrate luck rather than attainment, for achievement is much too serious a matter to be in any sense confused with the passing sensations of joy. The restraint and modesty that are basic to good Chinese manners can always be expected to inhibit the joyful celebration of victory. Success should call only for more industry and hard work. Thus the Chinese have always preferred to dwell publicly upon humiliation than to acknowledge the exhilaration of success.

Although these puritan feelings about self-congratulation and the need to control one's feelings in victory no doubt explain the form of reaction to national successes, they provide only a partial reason for the dissatisfaction of the Chinese with their modern history. The tragedy is that modernization rather than tempting them with a new and different value pattern has brutally confronted the Chinese with failure in precisely those values most central to their traditional culture. What was most disturbing about the Western impact was not that it suggested a different set of values but that it made clear to the Chinese their lack of success in realizing what they thought were their own values. The Western impact chal-

62

lenged the Chinese squarely in terms of the two values that have always been central to their cultural identity: skill in the art of governance and the ability to maintain a superior material civilization.

Historically the Chinese felt that they were superior to all "barbarians" because of their ability to create and operate impressive governments and their capacity to live on a higher material plane than their neighbors. The essence of Confucianism was the recognition of the supreme importance of government in human affairs, while the daily conduct of the molders of Chinese civilization was a testament to the significance of material well-being in that culture. The Western impact on Asia directly and unambiguously challenged Chinese self-confidence in precisely these two areas of social life. Over time the administration of the treaty ports, contrasted with the confusion of the rest of China, provided concrete evidence that Chinese skill in managing public affairs was not outstanding. Similarly, European economic performance and the standards of Western living seemed to be as far above the Chinese level as the Chinese had been above those they had once scorned as "barbarians." Indeed, once the Chinese sensed that they no longer had a world order in which they could readily "manage barbarian affairs" — that it might be others who were manipulating Chinese affairs — then they were confronted with the question of who the "barbarians" might be.

Other societies have been able to some degree to protect their self-respect in the face of the Western impact by asserting the unique importance of traditional values that were manifestly different from Western values; and usually these values had the added merit that their significance could not readily be exposed to empirical testing. Thus, for example, the Indians have been able to claim a tradition of superiority to the West in the area of religion and other-worldly matters, and they have not had to be exposed to conspicuous evidence that they were wrong. It is true that the Chinese have on

63

occasion tried to rationalize their superiority by referring to "cultural and spiritual values," but this has never carried great conviction because the Chinese are not seen to be particularly sensitive to spiritual matters. In everyone's stereotype the Chinese are pragmatic, worldly, secular, and devoid of religious subtlety. Inescapably, the dominant features of the Chinese tradition have been the art of government, the effective management of public affairs, and the maintenance of an enviable standard of living through skill in the market place.

It follows that even modest threats to the Chinese sense of competence in government and economic matters have assumed great significance; and the demonstration of impotence in these matters has been truly shattering. Thus the Chinese have been harder on themselves for failures in the performance of their governments and their economy than others might consider justified.

Frustrations with the art of modern governance have been especially disturbing for the Chinese because they have found it so difficult to acquire a sense of what modern government might be for their country. Elsewhere in Asia, European rule provided a concrete and operational model of what modern government and administration might mean. For Indians, Burmese, Indonesians, Filipinos, and other former colonials it was possible to visualize independence and the standards of government in the modern world. For such peoples the task of nation building was in part blueprinted by developments during the colonial period, and the subject people could at least believe that they knew what had to be done to strengthen their nations: They had to take over and run the administrations that the Europeans had introduced, and they could aspire to modify and improve upon that reality. They could sense in concrete terms their own possibilities for progress, and they had visible guidelines for action.

We do not intend to minimize the objective and psychological problems of other peoples by suggesting that the Chinese were frustrated simply because they were never presented with a concrete model of a modern government. The Chinese could point out that foreign powers were administering urban governments in a few of their major cities and could therefore feel that they were sharing with most of Asia and Africa the humiliations and tribulations of colonialism. But they never experienced foreign domination in the way the colonial peoples did. Foreigners were just active enough to humiliate the Chinese with respect to their two key values, but they were not sufficiently involved in the control of China to establish the essential basis for subsequent economic and political development. The operations of the foreign concessions and the economic activities that rose within them were just enough to serve, in a sense, as pilot projects giving visible proof to all that foreigners could manage governments more effectively and maintain higher standards of living than the Chinese could but they were not enough to solve the question of an appropriate government for all of China.

The contrast between the islands of civil order that were the foreign concessions in the treaty ports and the confusion in the rest of China served only to show up the inability of the Chinese to manage their national affairs. These enclaves of isolated Westerners became in time the stable centers of administrative rule benefiting the millions of Chinese who sought them out. Elsewhere in Asia and Africa there was no escape from colonial rule, for the entire society was controlled, but in China it was individuals alone who sought out the foreign rule of the concessions: In their daily behavior thousands of Chinese demonstrated that foreign rule was preferable to their own government.

More disturbing, possibly, to the Chinese was the fact that since their experiences with Westernized governments were limited to urban concessions and not to full colonial rule they could not find a convincing solution to their problems of national development simply with the termination of the treaty port arrangements. They could desire intensely to remove these blots on their national honor but they could not really believe that the result would be a radical change in the condition of government throughout the rest of their land.

The result might be only a further demonstration of their ineptness in government, the realm in which they desperately believed themselves superior. Other colonial peoples could argue that they preferred to be free even if it meant the mismanagement of their public affairs, but not the Chinese, who could feel free only if completely "freed of" their awareness of the very existence of the West.

Yet just as it was patently impossible to believe that Chinese control of the treaty ports might in itself dramatically transform the realities of government for the entire country, so was it difficult to believe that foreign concessions were enough to produce foreign control of the entire country. The Chinese resented the role of the foreigner in their society but they could not put their fingers on the visible source of this frustration as could the subjects of explicit colonialism. What they had to point to as the cause of their difficulties could serve only to remind them of their own failings.

All of this was peculiarly galling for Chinese revolutionaries and modernizers because so many of them personally had had to rely upon the security and order of the foreign concessions while they dreamed of improvements in their society. On all sides the Chinese modernizers were exposed to evidence of their own impotence, which in turn was fed in no small measure by their inability to arrive at a positive and constructive course of national development. This situation helps to explain why the modern Chinese have generally been much more aware of what they dislike and of what disturbs them than of what they really want. Whenever the Chinese have been able to assert what they feel they desire this has served only to highlight the extent to which others appear to be superior. Above all, the Chinese seem to have been frustrated by their inability to find operational meaning in a modern context for those values that they have always felt were uniquely theirs. And from these frustrations have come profound feelings of hostility and the need to hate all who act as constant reminders of China's inadequacies.

THE DISCOVERY OF HATE

Since the Chinese political culture is rooted in a psychic sense of identification with greatness, one might assume that it would be based on a mood of serene self-confidence. Yet the dominant emotion of modern Chinese politics has been a preoccupation with hatred coupled with an enthusiasm for singling out enemies. Historically the assumption of greatness conformed enough to reality so that the Chinese could safely ignore others and express arrogance toward all enemies. Reality was once close to pretension. But when reality changed, the Chinese refused to acknowledge it and adhered to the dignity of their traditional political style; and then, when this was no longer possible, they released such a flood of emotion as to make all reality irrelevant.

No other political culture places as much stress upon the emotion of hate as does the Chinese. Both in extolling hate as a positive virtue and in seeking to tap hostile feelings, the Chinese Communists have carried to new extremes a trend that was well established in modern Chinese politics. What makes this development significant and of interest for the behavioral sciences is that hate is concentrated so intensely in the political culture. It was not a conspicuous part of traditional Chinese life, nor has it been a particularly outstanding feature of personal relations in modern Chinese life. It is true that socially there has been far more bickering, arguing, and the expression of sullen emotions than the ideals of Chinese etiquette would suggest; but the norms of the culture have always been that personal feelings of hatred should be repressed and passions hidden. In politics, however, hate and hostility have now taken on dramatically unqualified forms. In discussing politics in modern China one talks about who hates whom, and a man's position can be defined by identifying his enemies.

The contemporary legitimacy of hate is related largely to the historical evolution of the modern political process. The capacity of Chinese political activists to manifest and sustain the emotion of hate is the product of the peculiar pattern of political socialization that has shaped the last two generations. In traditional politics there was a great deal of plotting and scheming, and the search for revenge was often a powerful motivating force. Violence and torture were always far more widespread than Confucian ideals would apparently allow. In modern times, however, hate and hostility are not only more openly acknowledged but they are extolled as positive virtues of the political activist. Clearly the theme of hate is related to the sense of humiliation and shame that has been so much a part of the Chinese modernization process.

In seeking the roots of this new quality it is noteworthy that there is a diffuse, free-floating, and unfocused aspect to the modern Chinese feeling of hostility and aggression. Although there are certain notable exceptions, there has generally been little tendency to couple the need for hostility with an exaltation of violence. For all their recent cries for passionate action and hatred the Chinese have not tried to make a moral virtue, but only a political necessity, of physical violence.

This characteristic is significant because it distinguishes Chinese feelings of hostility and resentment from those found in ex-colonial countries that are experiencing identity crises. In such societies the appeal for political passions, aggressive actions, and the assertion of power and hostility toward the more powerful states seems to be closely associated with the belief that such displays of hostility are a necessary part of achieving self-respect and acceptance. In these cultures fear-lessness and hostility are extolled as if necessary to the proof of a people's collective manliness, and in this sense they are a part of the rites of passage from acknowledged dependency to respected independence and an "adult" identity in the international community.

For the Chinese the expression of hostility is less associated with a demand for the recognition of manhood and more with the desire to show that they were once mistreated and that it is the mature powers who lack morality. The appeals to hostility are closely related to moralistic statements. It is this strange juxtaposition of intense feelings and childlike morality which suggests that the expression of hostility is indeed closely associated with attitudes about authority. The Chinese, apparently, can still become emotionally agitated over the discovery that the great powers of the world do not always live up to their ideals — that the older generation is not as virtuous as it pretends to be. They are also frustrated by what they see as the failure of the leaders of former generations to deal effectively with an amoral world — their fathers have shamed them by being so innocent.

The anger of the Chinese is that of a people frustrated not just about their power but about both power and morality, that is, authority. This is the anger of moral indignation and of impotence. In seeking the cause of their frustrations with modernization the Chinese are still concerned with finding fault. And they would like to believe that the fault of their impotence lies with the immorality of others. The readiness with which they have tended to associate their own weak-nesses with the immorality of others stems in part from their cultural image of authority: Moral rectitude can be so com-plete a substitute for physical power in establishing authority that it is natural to imagine that complete impotence can be identified with high morality — while any threatening force is readily associated with immorality.

Political Awakening as a Fit of Anger

Before the advent of Chinese communism it was common-place for Westerners and Chinese alike to characterize the first stirrings of nationalism as the "political awakening" of the Chinese people. In public life those who could display passion, anger, and a sense of national humiliation were quickly identified as the politically awakened, while those who might be rationally concerned with solving China's problems were seen as less nationalistic.

The acceptance of the virtues of passion and hostility represents a complete reversal for the traditional Chinese ideals of the masterful political activist. Historically the ideal stressed such qualities as wisdom, cleverness, shrewdness, and the capacity to deceive others by hiding one's emotions and appearing to be guided solely by reason and morality. The modern ideal of the political activist, however, is one who can forget everything except the object of his anger.

This strange coupling of rationality with traditional politics and emotionalism with modernity emphasizes the way in which rationality developed in China as a defense of the established order and not, as in the West, as a force to oppose the status quo. In modern times, when the Chinese began anxiously to seek ways of changing the conditions of their society, it was natural for them to look for something more than rationality.

Thus in modern China the emotional basis of all movements that have been relatively popular has been the explicit appeal to anger and humiliation. Nationalism in China has steadfastly involved hostility toward one or more foreign nations, whether it was to hate the British, denounce the "unequal treaties," proclaim the May Fourth movement, or resist Japanese aggression. In contrast, the more sober expressions of nationalism — the early reform movement of 1898 or the Chinese Renaissance movement of the 1920's — have tended to founder. Within Chinese intellectual circles in the early twentieth century there was probably greater explicit association of science, mathematical reason, and objective, dispassionate analysis with the essential characteristic of modernization than has been common in most transitional societies. But this intellectual acknowledgment of the importance of rationality hardly touched on politics. The very fact that these modernizers stressed rationality and a programmatic approach toward solving the problems of their country was taken by all to mean that they were nonpolitical individuals. Thus, while it was recognized that national development demanded men with modern skills and knowledge, in practice it was assumed that political advance was being effectively carried out only by displays of passion and mass excitement.

Strength from Humiliation

It is noteworthy that in seeking to incite passion Chinese political leaders have not turned spontaneously to charismatic appeals and the themes of heroic glory that characterize the nationalism of most transitional societies. Instead, to a large degree they have sought to detail the real and imagined ways in which China has been humiliated by others. There seems to be a two-edged quality about this emphasis upon humiliation: It should provoke the Chinese people to anger, and it should also embarrass, and therefore hurt, those who caused the humiliation. The manipulators of popular passions have acted on the assumption that by stressing humiliation they could produce in the Chinese people the sentiments of anger that they identified with politics and political awakening. They have also tended to see the connection between humiliation and anger largely in terms of the role of shame in their culture. The propagandists of political awakening have anticipated that if the Chinese can in any way be "shamed" their spontaneous reaction will be immediate hostility toward those who caused their shame. And the propagandists seem to feel that in proclaiming China's anguish they are directly attacking those who caused it: The shame of the self can be overcome by shaming the cause of one's distress. This behavior conforms to a Chinese cultural pattern in which the weak, as a last resort, can publicly seek to embarrass the strong by stripping aside their respectability. (In the Chinese village a wife could always strike back against her husband by going out into the street and making a public spectacle of herself, vividly describing at the top of her lungs her husband's faults, particularly his lack of manliness — which was clearly evidenced by his inability to keep her in place.)

One effect of this development has been to give a strange respectability to public discussions about the way in which the self has been taken advantage of by others. Thus, in trying to stimulate patriotism, the Chinese Nationalists never found it odd to establish "National Humiliation Days," a concept for a national holiday that is unknown elsewhere. In giving expression to what is assumed to be patriotism, publicists and political leaders have been tireless in recounting the innumerable ways in which others have taken advantage of China. It is noteworthy that the Chinese public communications in the Sino-Soviet polemics have been guided by the same assumptions. Similarly, the Communists seem to feel that it is to their advantage to publicize the 350-odd times they say their air space has been violated by U.S. planes; from a different point of view such announcements might seem only to underline the impotence of their government.

A consequence of this tendency has been the practice of proclaiming the self blameless and of asserting that there is no justice in international politics. According to the political mythology that they have sought to build up, the Chinese have invariably suffered unjustly at the hands of all nations. Communist propaganda has strengthened the imagery of a China that could be mistreated by even the smallest foreign powers:

> In a hundred years or so prior to the victory of the Chinese revolution the imperialist and colonialist powers — the United

States, Britain, France, Tsarist Russia, Germany, Japan, Italy, Austria, Belgium, the Netherlands, Spain, and Portugal — carried out unbridled aggression against China.[1]

In deriving satisfaction from the injustices that their nation has suffered in modern times, the Chinese seem to be completely insensitive to what others might consider the "crybaby" character of their protests. In matters of national sentiment, objective facts are of minor importance in comparison with psychological considerations, but it would be hard to make a convincing case that, objectively measured, the Chinese have been treated worse than most peoples by history and the interplay of international forces. Most European nations have had to endure a far more competitive existence, and most of them have experienced more frequent conquests and more severe destruction of their material resources than have the Chinese. And most Asian and African peoples have had far more intimate experience with colonial rule.

What is important is that the Chinese political class has been unable to see the history of its Western relations as a process of give and take, of benefit and liability. In opposing colonialism, even the most ardent nationalists in Asia and Africa have been able to accept the possibility that while there were overwhelming injustices in Western rule there were also benefits to be gained from contact with Western civilization. Such an admission seems to have been completely impossible for the politically articulate Chinese.

No doubt the historical reason for the strong need to appear blameless but wronged is that the record for China's relations with the West was so ambiguous. Western behavior in some fields could be seen as self-sacrificing and genuinely charitable, but arrangements that had once been beneficial to the Chinese eventually had to be identified as damaging to the self and extremely unjust. This was true, for example,

[1] Hsinhua News Agency, March 8, 1963, quoted in Guy Searls, "Communist China's Border Policy," *Current Scene, II,* No. 12 (April 15, 1963), 4.

73

of the complex pattern of relations involving the treaty ports, the foreign concessions, and the explicit treaty provisions covering the legal status of Western nationals. In the nineteenth century these arrangements provided a *modus vivendi* for regulating relations between two quite different civilizations, and the Chinese clearly realized that they gave some protection and that they bottled up the "foreign devils" in their enclaves and isolated them from the main body of Chinese society.[2] In time, however, these arrangements, quite understandably, became less and less satisfactory to the Chinese, and their reaction took the form of a fantasy about the blameless and pure self being violently and grossly mistreated by all outsiders.

In this connection it is appropriate to note the intense concern about injustice in Chinese social relations. Adult Chinese who feel they have been mistreated seek out any sympathetic ear for their passionate protestations of innocence and unjust treatment at the hands of someone more powerful. The wailing, aggrieved individual, proclaiming to the skies his bad fortune was as common a sight in the social landscape as that of the tearful child, in the complex world of parents, siblings, aunts, uncles, and grandparents, seeking out the one person who might be prepared to give him unqualified solace for his damaged feelings.

At a deeper psychological level the moral masochism of the Chinese is apparently related to their rather strong narcissistic needs. As we shall observe, the oppressive demands of filial piety frequently compel the Chinese child to seek satisfaction in yielding submissively to the cruelties of his authoritarian father; as a result he learns when he grows up that he can gain self-esteem by finding enjoyment in being

[2] There is a rich documentation of the changing Chinese position toward foreigners in two monumental collections: W. T. de Bary, W. T. Chan, and B. Watson, *Sources of Chinese Tradition* (New York: Columbia University Press, 1960); and Ssu-yu Teng and John K. Fairbank, *China's Response to the West: A Documentary Survey, 1839–1923* (Cambridge, Mass.: Harvard University Press, 1961).

"beaten" by "fate" or "circumstances" as he once was by his father. At the earliest phase of infancy the child gains a sense of omnipotence; he is unable to differentiate between the self and the environment, and he feels that he is controlling everything when he cries and the stimuli of his displeasures are removed. This omnipotence later becomes closely associated with self-esteem when the child learns to make others extend love and affection toward him. If this cannot readily be achieved, as in the demanding and undemonstrative Chinese family, there is a tendency for the child to seek omnipotence again by refusing to differentiate between his self and the overpowering realities of "circumstances." He then finds strength and self-esteem from narcissistic satisfactions gained through suffering and humiliation.[3]

Wallowing in self-righteous humiliation in politics is an improvement in adulthood upon the condition of childhood. The child can never express himself clearly, but in politics it becomes possible to shout aloud that the "great powers"

[3] More specifically, the dominant Chinese pattern of socialization seems to be characterized by considerable adult responsiveness in the early years, so that children learn early that they are liked and that they can take the initiative to gain self-esteem. It is at about the Oedipal period that change begins, and life steadily becomes more demanding as ideals of behavior and suffering are introduced. It is at this point that the secondary narcissistic pattern emerges; the craving for self-esteem, the awareness of moralistic ideals, and the experience of suffering at the hands of authority converge to produce the basic ambivalence about autonomy and submissiveness.

We are here touching upon the dynamic basis of certain distinctive, and to the Western mind contradictory, Chinese characteristics: the characteristics of being equally sensitive to moral idealism and to fatalistic accommodation to circumstances, of seeking dignity by indulging in pretense while remaining easily vulnerable to the opinions of others, of indulging enthusiastically in make-believe while remaining hypersensitive to the dangers of losing face. The quality of narcissism allows the Chinese to link moral idealism and self-esteem with social conformity and timidity toward fate and circumstances. It helps to explain both the difficulties that they have had in learning to hold their moral liquor, and not become drunk with aggrieved self-righteousness, and the ease with which they can unemotionally adapt to reality.

have been bad. The socialization process distinguishes rather sharply the difference between thought, word, and action. The Chinese child is expected at first to see no faults in his parents; even if with age he learns of their shortcomings, he can never speak about them and certainly he can never act against them. Traditionally the child was taught to separate emotion from action, and his capacity for feeling, shouting, and, above all, acting against adult power was eliminated. To be able to live with strict and inhibiting norms was in the Confucian view the path to omnipotence.

"Coming of age" involved the "discovery" that parents did not have to live by norms as strict as they pretended, and thus to some degree one could do what one wanted. The traditional child learned this but kept his wisdom to himself. In modern China the first break has come with children asserting the right to speak out in their own self-defense; politically this step in the direction of modernization has brought the possibility of public expressions of hostility, but without engaging in action. At this stage, the earlier Confucian belief that power came from the complete adherence to norms has been replaced by the view that power, and indeed omnipotence, can come merely from having suffered at the hands of the older generation or the great powers. The pure and blameless self is invariably weak and helpless, and the initiator of injustice is always strong — and should be, but is not, controlled by moral principles. There is a certain innocence, and even moral virtue, in being impotent, whereas manly strength always runs the risk of being the cause of injustice and unhappiness. This view of the relationship between power and impotence seems to be closely associated with the idea that ultimate power should not place any demands upon the self, particularly the need ever to prove one's powers. If one cannot have such an undemanding and unthreatening form of pure omnipotence, the next best thing is to seek the purity of impotence. For complete impotence is associated with absolute adherence to norms, an incapacity to see or even think evil — and this, as we have just suggested, is the Confucian ideal of omnipotence.

Internationally the Chinese by articulating the purity of innocence and the degree to which they have been unjustly treated have in fact been acknowledging the superiority of the West. To give up the theme of humiliation, however, would mean giving up the main device for awakening the Chinese people. This has been the dilemma of both the Nationalists and the Communists in seeking to reassert the power and authority of China.

In Politics There Are No Equals, Only Superiors and Inferiors

The hierarchical nature of Chinese politics has, as we have noted, provided a structural basis for the view that the only well-defined roles in politics are those of the superior and the subordinate. In other political cultures, such as the American, actors will begin by seeking to expand as much as possible the scope for equals and only gradually and subtly move toward a superior-inferior relationship.

The lack of scope for equals in the Chinese culture is a constant source of tension and bickering. The result is an unusually strong tendency toward hurt feelings and imagined insults. This problem is particularly acute in more modern situations that require complex and functionally specific role relationships. The superior-inferior dichotomized view of human relations calls for an all-or-nothing pattern of functionally diffuse relationships; the superior is superior in all respects, and the inferior is totally subordinate. Modernization demands greater functional differentation and recognition of the place of specialization and the need for experts. In short, in the areas of his specialization the subordinate must be recognized as having greater competence and appropriately greater influence than his hierarchical superior.

The process of modernization has thus created a conflict

between the lingering belief that superiors have a universal claim to dominance and the modern requirement that various specialized skills need to be given their proper, albeit limited, areas of dominance. Since, for the Chinese, the inability to fit everyone into an appropriate superior-inferior pattern of relationships can only result in anarchy and confusion, this inherent conflict helps to explain the peculiar belief that modernization has threatened their country with disintegration and chaos. The only way to overcome the anarchy of relationships among equals is for all participants either explicitly or tacitly to recognize some sense of hierarchy of relations. National pride, if not merely the logic of power relations, demands that every effort be made to demonstrate one's own superiority and to humble others.

It is not strange, then, that the Chinese in modern times have never been able to maintain stable and amiable relations with any foreign power. Whether it has been with Britain or Japan in the nineteenth or early twentieth centuries, with America in more recent decades, or with the Soviet Union, India, and Indonesia in the last few years, the invariable turn has been toward hatred and away from what had once been acceptable and even warm relationships.

The intensity of Peking's present bitterness toward Moscow stems in part from the fact that during the 1950's the Chinese Communists subordinated China so completely to the Soviet Union. Never before had China openly acknowledged that it was subordinate to anyone; even the puppet regimes established by the Japanese did not characterize China as the "younger brother" who must rely entirely upon another power. The present Chinese leaders seem determined to make Moscow "pay" for this loss of self-discipline and the non-Chinese behavior of the 1950's.

The Sharp Divide Between Friend and Foe

The several characteristics of the Chinese political culture that we have discussed culminate in a vivid distinction between friend and foe — which for the Chinese are absolute categories. Affectively neutral attitudes are possible only toward those who lie outside the system of role relationships. When some political actor is not a clear friend, that is, he does not fit comfortably into the system of role relationships explicitly recognized, then the Chinese tend to suspect that he is a potential enemy. This suspicion reinforces the expectation that the world is populated more by enemies than by friends, since the latter are limited mainly to those with whom one has intimate and clearly structured relations. Particularistic associations are a prerequisite for true friendships.

This vivid distinction between friend and foe seems to be closely associated with the tendency of the Chinese to picture themselves in a pure and innocent light. Their overwhelming need to see only goodness in themselves makes it necessary to attribute to others all the badness they know. Friendship, therefore, is not easy in politics because others always have aggressive intentions.

The tendency to project aggression and identify it in the intentions of others is greatly reinforced by the assumption that all participants are likely to arrive at the same conclusions about the reality of any situation. The Chinese have tended to believe that all people are as anxious as they to establish who is superior and who is inferior. Thus, whenever they sense that they are weak, they are strongly inclined to believe that their feelings are being matched by the other party's sense of superiority. Historically, the more the Chinese have become a part of the modern world, and the more they have been accepted by others as equals, the more sensitive they have become to the belief that others might be treating them with scorn.

Living in a world that is filled with the extremes of friend and foe, they fall back upon their typical defense, which is to ignore the existence of others if they cause unpleasantness. Such behavior is related to their anxieties about social confusion and the need to have everyone fit into well-structured

79

patterns of relationships. That which will not fit into the Chinese scheme of things must be ignored; and thus there is something fundamentally threatening about those they would ignore. The Chinese child in being permitted no explicit means of expressing aggression, particularly against parents, can only employ silence, turn inward, and ignore them. Ignoring becomes an ultimate act; it is a form of "killing." In reverse, of course, Chinese parents have always had the right to "ignore" the child.

We are once again being drawn into a discussion of the psychological dimensions that stem from the Chinese socialization process, and the time has come to turn to an analysis of the cultural basis for many of the attitudes and sentiments we have been observing in the Chinese political culture. But before doing so let us pause briefly to summarize our analysis to this point.

We began by observing that this political culture rests upon a powerful sense of identification with greatness. The Chinese, in facing the challenge of modernization, in coping with foreign innovations, have not been as vulnerable to the crisis of identity as have most other transitional societies. They have been mystified that others could be their superiors, and they have been aware that something must have gone wrong in their recent history. They have not, however, been inundated with self-doubts, and they have not experienced the moods of elation and depression, the fantasies of omnipotence and the realizations of incompetence that have characterized societies in the throes of major identity crises. It is not solely for historical reasons that the Chinese have had no doubts about their identity. Certainty on this matter has been irrevocably established by the socialization process, which has tended to build within the personality a peculiarly strong sense of the ego and has not produced the ambivalence of personality that has made the Burmese, the Indians, the Javanese, and other transitional peoples predisposed to problems of collective identity.

The second characteristic we have observed in the Chinese political culture is the emotion of hate, which has increased in strength over the decades of modernization. We have noted that this key emotion is characterized by the belief that political self-consciousness involves a fit of anger, that strength and comfort can be derived from humiliation, that in politics there can be no justice, that the self is always blameless, that there can be no equality, only superiors and inferiors, and that there is a sharp divide between friend and foe. It is noteworthy that there is an extraordinarily sharp contrast between the extent to which hostility can be expressed freely in political life and the extent to which it must be suppressed in the nonpolitical realms of the culture. It seems as though the Chinese, confronted with all the frustrations of social change and modernization, have found it increasingly difficult to maintain their traditional repression of aggression and have discovered in politics a legitimate outlet for it. In this view, the very degree to which they have had to repress aggression helps to explain the intensity of their feelings when it has become legitimized.

Passion and Action

In communism the Chinese have, of course, a basis for giving legitimacy to hate; all Communist movements emphasize conflict and the evils of the enemy. The Chinese Communists, however, are unique in the extent to which they have sought explicitly to associate strong emotionalism and effectiveness in revolutionary actions. In describing the "good Communist," the Chinese, far more than the Russians, have emphasized a capacity for passion, mainly but not exclusively that of protracted and unfaltering hatred for enemies both domestic and foreign. But the difference between the Soviet and Chinese Communists goes further. In Soviet communism passion by itself has always been suspect; the Bolshevik leaders early recognized that a weakness in the Russian character

81

was the pervasive tendency to dissipate emotions without political effect, and hence their stress on the control of feelings.[4] In Chinese communism, by contrast, it is assumed that nothing can be accomplished unless people are stirred to passion. In the Chinese imagery of revolution, ineffectualness is related to indifference and to the dull unemotional acceptance of life as routine. For the Russians ineffectualness stems from vacillation between passionate, verbose outbursts of unharnessed exuberance and lapses into lazy unfeeling stupor. In a sense both Communist parties are reacting against strong characteristics of their different cultural heritages. The Russians need to counter the violent and self-destructive moods of the Slavic temperament; the Chinese need to counter the historic stoicism of the masses in fatalistically accepting their lot. The Chinese Communists' assumption that passion can intensify action is a relatively new development, for in the traditional socialization process every effort was made to separate emotion from action. Now, however, they seem to be saying that it is permissible to act in response to passion if the passion is directed toward the correct enemy.

In the Chinese Communist portrayals of revolutionary heroes a key ingredient of personality is a deep and essentially blind capacity for prolonged hatred. The conventional hero invariably discovers, with the arrival of communism — always labeled by the psychologically significant term "the Liberation" — that he has long possessed a deep hatred for the landlord and other class enemies and that in the post-Liberation era he can prove his abiding revolutionary qualities through his ability to find joy and satisfaction in that hatred. In emotional terms, "the Liberation" in no small measure provided a dividing point after which suppressed hatreds could be exposed and given glorious legitimacy.

It is significant that the targets of hostility have mainly been particular individuals or classes of people and not so

[4] Nathan Leites, *A Study of Bolshevism* (New York: The Free Press of Glencoe, 1953).

much the evils of abstract systems. Personal morality and personal corruption are far more important than the iniquities of a particular social order; the evils of the landlords as individuals called for hatred and not the system of landlordism itself. Here again we see the tendency to stress personal morality in public affairs, the propensity to dwell on the performance of individual roles rather than to think in terms of the general structure of society, and conversely, the lack of interest in abstract descriptions of the perfectly evil society.

At present one of the fears of the aging rulers in Peking is that the revolution may become routinized and the younger generation lose its capacity for hatred. The leaders act as though they believed that the very legitimacy of their rule would be compromised if their followers became less hostile. Instead of welcoming the prospect that the charismatic dimensions of their revolution might become institutionalized through increasing bureaucratization, the Chinese persist in calling for more passion even when it compromises the effectiveness of bureaucratic rule. The example of what happened in the Soviet Union, particularly with the transition from Stalin to Khrushchev, has only made the Chinese more determined to raise the level of passion within their own political culture. This again is evidence of the peculiar belief that the routinization of behavior can lead to ineffectualness and that emotionalism is the key to great achievements. It is particularly interesting in view of the historical distrust of emotions and the classic belief that the essence of willpower is purposeful, determined, but unemotional action.

Here we see a clue to Mao's deep concern about the ritualization of his revolution; the separation of emotion and action was the basis to so many of the strengths of the traditional China that he wished to overthrow. To settle for routinization, even of the revolutionary ardor, would be to fall back into the ways of old China. For Mao, passion has become more important than action because, psychologically, it represents a revolutionary advance. His dogmatic demand that emotionalism should be a constant that informs all behavior calls for a fundamental change in the Chinese personality.

Before we begin to speculate on the significance for the future if the Chinese personality should lose its qualities of self-control, it is necessary to examine more closely the details of the socialization process. In particular we shall want to understand the Chinese attitude toward authority and power, for it is clear that much of the frustration with modernization has been wrapped up in disappointment with the leadership, confusion about the legitimacy of power and the appropriate morality in intercultural relations, and anxieties over the weaknesses of China and its failure to be as great as it once was.

CHAPTER SIX

AUTHORITY,
SELF-DISCIPLINE,
AND ORDER

We are now ready to turn from our broad analysis of the historical experience to an examination of the psychological roots of the Chinese authority crisis. In doing so we shall be concerned with the gross outlines of the political socialization process, and this will require that we speak in very general terms about the Chinese family and, more particularly, about Chinese images of authority. Our objective will not be to give a detailed description of how the Chinese in fact have been socialized but rather to utilize whatever specific knowledge is available to capture the spirit of their sentiments and attitudes.

Therefore, rather than trying to mobilize all that is known about the Chinese family and childhood training — subjects that could fill several books — we shall set forth various hypotheses about Chinese feelings toward authority and explore their origins and functions in the personality. We shall have to move back and forth between adult attitudes and behavior and the family setting. In doing this we are fully aware that the development of political attitudes in the life of any particular individual is infinitely complicated. Our concern must be limited to the general patterns that can shed light on the character and intensity of the authority crisis. We shall therefore seek to keep a firm footing at the general historical and political level and venture into the realm of personality formation only when this seems profitable.

In the Chinese civilization the basic themes of social, political, and philosophical life all tended to converge in accentuating the importance of the collectivity. The individual found his identity only as a functioning member of the social order and the family order. More particularly, the definition of the self in terms of status in the collectivity was governed by relations to the appropriate form of authority. The central concern of both individual and collective life was thus propriety with respect to authority.

Since it bulked large in life and was critical to so many human relationships, the concept of authority was inevitably broad, diffuse, and lacking in precision. Although the Chinese were endlessly active in trying to define the appropriate attributes of authority, they attached so much importance to the concept that they were unprepared to strip it down to essentials. Hence there was even much that was contradictory in their image.

Authority was supposed to be absolute, harsh, and even ruthless; yet it was also seen as being subtle, wise, and the source of morality. It was to be feared and distrusted, yet also to be revered and relied upon. The demands of authority added up to tremendous social pressures and sanctions on the individual. Although he had an appreciation of the absoluteness of external social authority, the Chinese individual was left with the belief that social control should come from within the self. The ideal of social order rested upon self-discipline; but that meant that the absolute quality of authority did not carry with it complete responsibility. There was thus considerable vagueness about what should be expected of any authority and what were the boundaries between different authorities.

The imperial system was unique in that the Emperor was

an absolute, omnipotent, and unquestioned authority under whom there could be other absolute, omnipotent, and unquestioned authorities, ranging from mandarins, viceroys, and magistrates down to the heads of clans and the fathers of families. Although the structure was monolithic and hierarchic, there was considerable vagueness as to where the authority of one figure ended and that of another began. Also, since all authorities were cut from much the same model, Emperor and father had many characteristics in common. Conflict was reduced by tolerance and lethargy and by the fact that there was enough room in the system for all the claimants to authority to find status.

Whenever a dynasty fell, the Chinese suffered great anxiety over the lack of a single, central authority and feared that their society was on the verge of being torn apart by power struggles. Yet when one considers what was at stake and the rewards of expanding power, what is striking about Chinese history is how little competition there was and how easily new authorities became enduring imperial dynasties. In short, not everyone wanted to be the head of the family, but everyone was anxious to have a head of the family.

The Balance Between Family and Government

Articulated sentiments about authority in the Chinese political culture have been shaped largely by historical developments and the basic structural characteristics of government; but for the individual the critical experiences in learning about the nature of authority have been largely within the context of the family. Expectations about how authority is likely to behave, how it can be controlled, and the limits and requirements of legitimacy for authority are generally well established on the basis of experience with family authority.[1]

[1] Lee Shu-ching, "China's Traditional Family; Its Characteristics and Disintegration," *American Sociological Review, 18* (1953), 272–280; Yen Ching-yueh. "Crime in Relation to Social Change in China,"

The Chinese family system has been one of the great and distinctive institutions in all human history, and it has understandably fascinated Westerners because of its intrinsic characteristics. But the family was also distinctive in China because of the degree to which it reinforced the entire traditional political structure. In most societies there is some degree of tension and clash between the private domain of the family and the role of public institutions. Historically in China the family was not only explicitly recognized as the most efficient institution for socializing individuals, it was also given a broad range of responsibilities that reduced the strain on public institutions. The family system produced attitudes remarkably consistent with those essential to the maintenance of the political culture and also so reduced the problems of ruling that it could make the government appear to be highly effective. Indeed, in many spheres formal government did not have to govern at all because the family assumed all responsibilities. For example, in the maintenance of order and the apprehension of criminals, an area that customarily taxes the capacities of governments, the Chinese greatly reduced the problem by the simple expedient of holding the entire family or clan, or even village, responsible for the wayward behavior of any particular member. Formal authority, in short, did not have to bother about bringing the actual lawbreaker to book; it was enough merely to identify his family and then bring the appropriate pressure to bear on the head of the family or group of families.

This balance between primary social groupings and formal government is common to most traditional systems, and the universal pattern of modernization has been a decline in the role of the first set of institutions and an increase in the "load" of responsibilities to be assumed by the formal government. Colonial governments could easily be established and run by

American Journal of Sociology, 40 (1934–1935), 298–308; Liu Hu-chen, *The Traditional Chinese Clan Rules* (Locust Valley, N.Y.: Monograph of the Association for Asian Studies, 1959).

a few people because as long as the country was largely traditional the people governed and controlled social relations through the power of the family, village, caste, tribe, or other traditional institution. Similarly, with the breakdown of these primary institutions under the process of modernization, the "costs" of formal government went up and eventually became prohibitive for the colonial powers. This is why the newly independent governments find their task much greater than that of their colonial predecessors. Even in Europe and America we can observe the same trend, with the family and church losing control and government gaining greater responsibility over the lives of the people.

In China the difference has been one of degree; originally there was a much more subtle but explicitly acknowledged interdependence between the family system and formal government. Confucianism formally recognized that government would be impossible without the support of the family system, and thus family authority was peculiarly closely associated with attitudes and images about authority in the political culture. It is also true that in China, as in other transitional societies, the breaking down of the family and other primary institutions has created greater demands upon formal government. Even before the Communist regime, governments in modern China had already been disturbed and frustrated by this shifting of "tasks" to the public authorities. The Kuomintang practice of extolling the Confucian virtues of family was only in part a reflection of a basically conservative and traditionalist ideology. Nationalist officials were also aware that the basic costs of government were rising steeply because of the declining responsibilities of the family to bear the exceedingly high "costs" of socialization and social control. To some degree therefore the Nationalists were disturbed, like the governments of most traditional societies, by the increasing difficulty of governing people who were not being trained to social responsibility in their homes.

The Communists, in contrast, seemed, at least initially,

to welcome the weakening of any possible competitive source of authority and enthusiastically sought to assume full responsibilities for nearly all phases of socialization and the maintenance of order. More recently they have been pushing more of this responsibility back upon the family as they have come to realize that it is extremely costly for formal government to try to do everything. They have learned that families can be much more efficient than a formal bureaucracy so long as what they teach is compatible with the requirements of the higher authorities. In the next few years we may very well see the Communists giving greater and greater responsibilities to the family; and there may even be a strengthening of the family's role in Chinese society. This is likely to happen, however, only to the degree that the legitimacy of family authority acts in full support of the ideals of social conduct that the regime is seeking to establish. It is interesting that prior to the Red Guards the Communists were beginning to preach the doctrine of reverence and respect for age. Earlier, in the 1950's, they seemed to be unqualifiedly on the side of youth, demanding that children should report any deviant political thoughts or actions of their parents; but now, when China is ruled by a gerontocracy and Mao is an old man, youth is being told that experience is priceless and that the older generation has much to teach.[2]

Whatever the future may hold, it seems that the revolution has already taken place and that a new balance between family and government is being worked out.[3] Traditionally government had a low degree of penetration into Chinese

[2] See Ai-li Chin, "Modern Chinese Fiction and Family Relations," Cambridge, Mass.: Center for International Studies, Massachusetts Institute of Technology, 1966.

[3] See Olga Lang, *Chinese Family and Society* (New Haven, Conn.: Yale University Press, 1946); Marion J. Levy, Jr., *The Family Revolution in Modern China* (Cambridge, Mass.: Harvard University Press, 1949); Lin Yueh-hwa, *The Golden Wing* (New York: Oxford University Press, 1947); C. K. Yang, *The Chinese Family in the Communist Revolution* (Cambridge, Mass.: The M.I.T. Press, 1959).

society because its authority was strongly complemented by the role of a powerful family system. During the Nationalist period the system of order was greatly weakened because the decline in the family was not matched by an increase in the capacities of formal government. During that period all authority seemed threatened and relatively impotent. The Communist system represented a great strengthening of governmental authority and at first seemed completely to overshadow any role for the family, but now it has produced a new balance. Family authority is strengthened but only as it operates to support the greatly expanded role of governmental authority. To some degree the trend is the same as that in all industrialized societies in which formal government and public institutions, such as welfare agencies and schools, have assumed greater roles in the socialization process. The great difference, however, is that in China the scope for family initiative is greatly limited, and there is no recognition, as there is in all Western industrialized societies, of the legitimacy of the family to be autonomous in the raising of children so long as it does not produce socially undesirable consequences.

The Sanctity of Authority, Suppression of Aggression, and the Comforts of Order

Historically the three most striking characteristics of the Chinese family were the paramount value of filial piety, the absolute denial of the legitimacy of all forms of aggression, and the vision of a rigidly defined order of role relationships. These three characteristics were closely interrelated and of critical importance in shaping the personality.

No other culture in history has placed such a stress upon filial piety as has the Chinese.[4] Traditional Chinese literature

[4] Of all the literature on filial piety in Chinese culture the most psychologically insightful is probably Robert J. Lifton, *Thought Reform and the Psychology of Totalism* (New York: W. W. Norton, 1961).

91

and philosophy constantly held up as the ultimate virtue the spirit of dutiful respect for parents. In recording their history the Chinese developed as cultural heroes the individuals who excelled in this particular virtue. Thus the dynastic histories recorded the lives not only of great officials, conquering soldiers, and distinguished scholars but also those of exemplary filial sons and daughters. While it may be debated how much social mobility existed in traditional China, there is no question that a form of status mobility, involving the opportunity to gain immortality, was open to children from even the most humble families. No family was too mean or lowly to have a child who could bring it the highest social respect and regard.

Observance of the dictates of filial piety provided a concrete behavioral expression of the belief in ancestor worship, which we have already observed was of such importance in giving the individual his strong sense of identification with greatness. The mystique of filial piety thus surrounded both the individual's sense of identity and his feelings about authority; and from an early age the child learned that his feelings toward authority could not be separated from his feelings about himself. The self became meaningless without authority, and the outward response toward authority could never be divorced from subjective attitudes.

The child's first experience with authority was thus in the acceptance of the omnipotence of his father; he realized that the worth of the self depended completely upon the display of respect for his father's authority. The child learned that authority was an absolute monopoly of the father or the eldest male and that no diffusion of it was acknowledged. At the same time he was made to feel that if he should in any way think ill of parental authority he would have committed a most serious crime. Other members of the family might have their special functions, and the mother in particular might have considerable power and influence, but it was the father

92

who had absolute authority. The relationship with the father usually involved considerable fear and anxiety.

One of the most important dynamic aspects of Chinese personality development was that passion and action were rarely harmonized. This was explicitly acknowledged in the way the child was taught that he had to display respect, awe, and honor for his parents no matter how badly they might treat him. A striking characteristic of *The Classic of Filial Piety,* the text that has provided twenty-four models of the ultimate ideals of filial behavior for countless generations of Chinese youth, is the depiction of the parents of model children as far from model people. Father after father is described as ruthless, brutal, completely without love or compassion, and even stupid and willfully "childlike" in giving vent to emotions. Probably in no other culture could parents be as evil and yet be deserving of respect. They surpass even the evil "stepparents" in the fairy tales of other cultures — stories that may make a child happy with the real parents he has. The prime point of the *Classic of Filial Piety* is that filial obligation is an absolute requirement and exists without regard to the quality of parental behavior.

The relationship with authority was thus not a reciprocal one in which the obligations of obedience and respect were contingent upon the model behavior of those with power. On the contrary, the Chinese child learned early that he could not express either his emotions or his thoughts about authority, that he must be dutiful regardless of parental behavior, and that those with power were likely to be unfeeling toward those who were weak. The very stories that were supposed to teach the young Chinese his proper morals also taught him that authority itself could be unbelievably cruel. Certainly it would always be fearsome, and one had to be on one's best behavior before it.[5]

[5] See such anthropological studies as R. Bunzel and J. H. Weakland, "An Anthropological Approach to Chinese Communism," New York,

More important, the great chasm that has separated father and son and the lack of strong and overt affective feelings has meant that there has been a striking absence of empathy in the political culture between those with authority and those without. Subjects have not felt a natural and compelling need to sympathize with the problem and difficulties of those in power, and power holders have had little inclination to be liked or to appear as likable. This contrasts sharply with American culture in which affection is such a powerful and complicating element in the father-son relationship. The need to demonstrate love does seem to contribute to the American willingness to sympathize in some degree with those who have the responsibilities of authority; and of course American power holders are well recognized for their unquenchable desire to be liked and to be popular. Those with power in China have seemed to be peculiarly insensitive to any such desires. The political leaders have had no more need for warm affection than have Chinese fathers: leaders must be leaders, just as fathers must be fathers.

In the Chinese culture the acceptance of unambiguous authority is coupled with a process of strict disciplining in proper role relations in general. The child is taught conformity to specific and rigid patterns of conduct in all of his relationships and made to realize that these constitute a well-defined hierarchy within which he has a definite and more or less permanent place. The younger brother, for example, will always be the younger brother and will always have to defer in some respects to his elder brother, who can never lose his superior position.

This training in role relations, which becomes intensified

Columbia University, Research in Contemporary Cultures, mimeographed, no date; and Francis L. K. Hsu, *Under the Ancestors' Shadow* (New York: Columbia University Press, 1948). See also the following autobiographical accounts: Chiang Yee, *A Chinese Childhood* (New York: John Day, 1952); Chang Tchang, *A Son of China* (New York: W. W. Norton, 1950); Jede Snow Wong, *Fifth Chinese Daughter* (London and New York: Hurst & Blackett, 1952).

after the age of six and the beginning of school, makes the child believe that social relations can be and should be strictly ordered and that there need be little uncertainty or unpredictability in life. In the traditional family the child was taught that there was a correct way to deal with all the specific sets of relationships that mattered for his existence. The burden of the socialization process was directed toward making the child internalize an orderly universe of human relations and toward assuring him that if he conducted himself properly he could expect security and well-being.[6]

From a very early stage the Chinese child is taught that there is a great gap between the right and the wrong way of doing things. It is most important to be right at all times, for only then can he expect any warmth and affection from his family. Whenever he makes mistakes he will be disciplined by authority; and the essence of Chinese discipline in the home is a ruthless use of shame. The child is made to feel the humiliation of his errors and to believe that whenever he fails in meeting the appropriate standards of behavior others will look down on him.[7]

It is in the frequent and widespread use of shame by parents that we find the dynamic origins of the sentiments about humiliation and its relationship to anger. The general cultural willingness to wallow in humiliation coincides with the childhood experience that it is better to yield and admit to faults than to fight back; but, as we have observed, modern politics is a great improvement and release from the pains of humiliation, for in politics one can give vent to all

[6] John H. Weakland, "The Organization of Action in Chinese Culture," *Psychiatry, 13* (1950), 361–370; Weston la Barre, "Some Observations on Character Structure in the Orient: II, The Chinese," *Psychiatry, 9* (1946), 215–237.

[7] Martha Wolfenstein, "Some Variants in Moral Training of Children," in Margaret Mead and Martha Wolfenstein, eds., *Childhood in Contemporary Cultures* (Chicago, Ill.: The University of Chicago Press, 1955).

the hostility and anger that one could not express in childhood.

Anthropologists have put much stress on the differences between shame cultures and guilt cultures, and the Chinese are generally acknowledged to have almost the model example of a shame culture.[8] Whatever the merits of such a distinction, it would be wrong to believe that the Chinese psychic reaction to shame is somehow more superficial and less deeply felt than what is usually meant by guilt. Shame is a manifestly disturbing experience; and the Chinese parent applies great vigor and wit to ensure that it continues to be so, because he is horrified at the prospect of his child ever becoming shameless. To be shameless is to be uncontrollable, and hence an outcast from both the family and the culture. When the Chinese child experiences shame and humiliation he wants to disappear from sight, to fall through the floor, to shrivel up and be inconspicuous, to hide his face, indeed, to feel the loss of his face. To give expression to the emotions that accompany humiliation is "to stand up," to be conspicuous, to be reckoned with, and above all, to exude hate and anger; in short, just what Mao Tse-tung wants China to do. It is thus the legitimacy of anger that can turn shame upside down.

Returning to the dynamics of the socialization process, we must observe that closely associated with the need to control emotions is the equally central factor that in the Chinese personality there is little room for ambiguity. Since every relationship has its correct form, the total system of relationships must fit together to form a perfect design. As long as one acts according to the rules of proper conduct, everything is supposed to be clear-cut and well defined. The child is thus made to be hypersensitive to the judgments of others, to look to the social situation for cues to guide his own actions, and to be cautious about initiatives and in-

[8] Hu Hsien-chin, "The Chinese Concept of Face," *American Anthropologist, 46* (1944), 45–64; Francis L. K. Hsu, *Americans and Chinese: Two Ways of Life* (New York: Henry Schuman, 1953).

novations. Here is the basis for the powerful mechanisms of conformity that dominate Chinese society. Whether they are reactionary traditionalists or revolutionary modernizers, the Chinese are above all conformists. If one has to be conspicuous, it is best to receive the conventional esteem of the group, to be a model member, and to be looked up to as one who embodies all the group ideals. The young Chinese Communist student who says that he thrills at the prospect of being a dutiful student of the thoughts of Mao Tse-tung is probably telling the truth; conformity has an element of excitement since it gives him the opportunity to prove self-mastery and to gain a sense of self-efficacy under terms that are not too demanding and may be highly rewarding.[9]

The Chinese child therefore learns early from both exhortation and experience that security comes from self-discipline. A rational decision to conform to vividly defined standards of behavior can reduce tensions and provide a sense of well-being. On the other hand, any display of emotion, any uninhibitedly spontaneous act, can cause great grief. It is necessary always to control emotions, particularly if they are likely to appear hostile or aggressive. The ultimate goal of socialization is perfect politeness, the ability to act according to an elaborate set of manners — but manners must be separated from sentiment, for they represent the ideals of self-discipline. Also, however, since self-discipline may break down, there is a constant need for external authority. The self-discipline of the individual is intimately dependent upon the existence of some form of authority, and the absence of authority is thus peculiarly threatening to the personality.

The Horror of Confusion

To overstate slightly, we may say that two central impressions come out of the early socialization process: first,

[9] Warner Muensterberger, "Orality and Dependence: Characteristics of Southern Chinese," *Psychoanalysis and the Social Sciences, 3,* (1951), 37–69.

that authority is monopolistic, and second, that there should be precision and rigidity in role relationships. When these two central props of human relations do not exist, there is diffuse anxiety. Confusion is dangerous, and chaos is the ultimate horror.

However, this does not mean that the individual Chinese, either in the past or in modern times, found complete satisfaction in a familial setting in which the father monopolized authority and in which every acknowledged relationship had its particularistic content. On the contrary, there is considerable evidence that real tensions existed, and the very severity of the sanctions used to enforce the idealized pattern suggests that the socialization process did not customarily proceed without some opposition by the individual.

There was apparently little warmth toward and considerable fear of the father. Children were made to feel that there was something profoundly wrong if they experienced even the slightest opposition to or withdrawal from their father; but adult Chinese confess that in their childhood they generally felt a bit uncomfortable in his presence and often had a strong sense of relief whenever he left the house.

Fear of the father was traditionally modified by the latter's highly predictable behavior as the head of the household. The child was suppressed but according to very set and stable rules. This situation stands in sharp contrast to that, for example, in the Indian family in which powerful parental authority is coupled with strong demands for affective and emotionally charged relationships. The Indian father wants to be loved by his sons, and both father and sons can hope for outbursts of affection even though constantly inhibited by the demands of convention. The situation differs also from the Burmese pattern in which the feared father tends to behave erratically, with much vacillation between the extremes of warm informality and cold authority. In China there was such a high degree of stability and routinization that at best the child could hope to influence authority only by pleasing the parent through conformity to well-established patterns of behavior. Eventually the child would take his place and would act in terms of well-defined roles in the larger pattern of social relationships within the extended family and clan. In this sense the son had a clearer basis for self-identity in China than he did, say, in the Indian or Burmese family where there could be only unending subservience to the father.

The mother wielded power in the household but had no legitimate authority, thus the Chinese child was not given the feeling, as the American child is, that the different functions of the father and mother produced different sources of authority and that these, if not competing, could at least to some degree be played off against each other. In particular, the son could not expect to enlist his mother as an open ally in opposing the wishes of his father, for the mother too had to display at all times a complete acceptance of male authority. At best the child could hope only to "scheme" and "plot" with the mother on the possibilities of circumventing the one authority in the household.

As we have already observed, the lack of affective paternal support during the Oedipal period, the stress on ideals of behavior, and the craving for self-esteem that was generated during the earlier phase of infant omnipotence have contributed to a narcissistic strand in the Chinese character. The child develops a strong need to appear praiseworthy in the eyes of others, but when this is not possible he can still gain self-esteem by finding satisfaction in suffering at the hands of an unjust world. As an ultimate consequence of this need for narcissistic support the Chinese tend to separate the passions of moral ideals from the need to be unemotionally submissive before the dictates of circumstance.

Guarded Emotions and Exposed Sentiments:
The Separation of Passion and Action

The importance of stable and orderly interpersonal relations is matched by the ideal of inner orderliness, which is based on self-discipline. An outstanding characteristic of the Chinese socialization process is the intensity with which it instills an ordered self-discipline and the need for absolute self-control at all times. There is a fair degree of permissiveness in the early years, but once the child has reached the age of awareness he is taught that controlled behavior is more likely than emotional outbursts to bring results and rewards. Increasingly over the years pressure is brought to bear to make him inhibit all emotional displays and to understand that correct conduct is affectively neutral. The ideal of the socialization process has been to produce people who are capable of guarding their emotions at all times and who know that when sentiment must be expressed there are correct forms and ritualized ways of doing it.[10]

The critical distinction between a child and an adult is that a child acts in direct response to his emotions and an adult acts without any apparent emotion. Childlike behavior involves the direct coupling of passion and action, while in adult behavior these are separated. The Chinese child is not only taught explicitly that self-discipline means the control of emotions; he is also in numerous little ways taught indirectly to separate feelings from actions. We have already observed, most importantly, that the child is taught never to reveal his true feelings about his parents but to adhere strictly to the manifest principles of filial piety.

A second indirect method is through the widespread practice of teasing, which is often carried so far by parents that the child cries and has a temper tantrum. Parents, and adults generally, find both amusement and a certain fascination in observing the emotional outbursts of children who have been teased. The child gradually learns that if he can control his feelings he can escape such torment. Teasing thus becomes a highly effective method for instilling self-control and for teaching children to be on guard against any display of emotion.

[10] John H. Weakland, *op. cit.*

Since the prime restraint in the Chinese socialization process is to ensure that there will be no spontaneous expression of any form of emotion, it is dangerous, and most unmanly, to allow emotions to determine behavior. Man is supposed to be able to calculate in detail what act is rationally and ritualistically appropriate to the situation. Then, only after a clearheaded decision, can emotions be allowed to enter in to serve primarily as a means of reinforcing or binding the decision. A decision about marriage, for example, is supposed to be made rationally and without the interference of unsettling romantic sentiments. Clearheaded judgment is needed to determine the appropriateness of the match that will so greatly influence the individual's life. Only after the commitment to marriage comes the time for emotional expression, and thus love and affection must wait upon intelligence and intellectual choice.

Obviously the Chinese are not capable of complete control and of making only ritualized expressions of sentiment, but their emotions are not usually closely geared to action, and the former do not generally mirror the latter. Action can occur with few cues about the submerged feelings; and the sudden expression of emotion does not provide a reliable guide for predicting probable behavior.

In politics this has meant a gap between choice and passion. Emotions are not the guiding force leading the Chinese to take particular positions. Rather, they make their decisions on the basis of calculations as to the advantages of the moment, and then, once the decision has been made, the expression of emotion becomes appropriate as a means of proclaiming their choice and of identifying for others where their loyalties now lie.

It is this connection between the expression of emotions and the identification of loyalties that makes Chinese politics seem so passionately partisan and so apparently supercharged with emotions. People must constantly be proclaiming their

101

support of the one and their hatred of the other to prove that they have maintained a consistent position.

The Suppression of Aggression and the Ideal of Friendship

Without undue oversimplification we may suggest that while the Chinese socialization process has placed the greatest explicit emphasis upon filial piety and correct manners, that is, upon authority and role relations, the central problem of the Chinese family has been the overpowering need to suppress and deny all forms of aggression. In no way could legitimacy be given to any expression of aggressive sentiments, and all forms of conflict and competition were seen as a breakdown in order and, hence, were the cause for great anxieties.

Although it is dangerous to try to characterize a culture in terms of any particular personality dimension, it may be useful to think of the Chinese attempts to suppress aggression as being analogous to the American culture's traditional attempt to suppress sex. The puritan tradition, with its rejection of more explicit recognition of the realities of sexuality in human nature, has instilled a pattern of suppression of sex but has not eliminated it; on the contrary, sex creeps out in all manner of unexpected places and colors much of American behavior. In the same fashion the Chinese have been puritans about aggression, seeking to deny its legitimacy, but it constantly creeps into personal relations; hence, the constant undertone of bickering and indirect warfare in the family and in most small-group relations; hence, also, the traditional interest in torture and in hurting others while demonstrating complete control over one's own emotions.

Traditionally, in the Chinese culture the well-cultivated official could prove that he was in complete control of any feelings of aggression by adhering to the cult of effortlessness. The relaxed mandarin idly watching fish swim about while he

102

sat under a tree and got happily drunk with his bosom companion is possibly the extreme example of the ideal that a man of power should display not a trace of aggression. The Communists have rejected this approach and have instead latched on to the other Chinese ideal of the task-oriented individual who displays perfect self-control as he channels his aggressive impulses into a single-minded course of routinized action.

The central quality of the problems raised can be seen in the extraordinary importance that the Chinese attach to friendship. While in the West the suppression of sexuality has led to a great emphasis upon romantic love and to anxieties about the realization of and the permanence of heterosexual relations, the Chinese have had almost exactly the same concern with friendship. Chinese poetry has stressed the value of friendship, the joys of relaxed companionship, and the sweet sorrows of separation. Yet there has always been a subsurface tension because friendship has been so rare; the best of friends might part, and highly delicate relationships could be easily shattered. Indeed separation, which has been such a conspicuous theme in Chinese poetry, can provide security to friendships because by being apart the friends cannot commit any aggressive acts toward each other — and the friendship will only weaken if they fail to reaffirm its absolute quality. By imposing upon the boy a need to suppress all aggression the socialization process has set him off on a lifetime search for the perfect relationship in which suppressed aggressive emotions may never break through and relations can be as safe and innocent as they should ideally be.

The Joys of Childhood

In light of the heavy demands made upon the Chinese child it might seem amazing that the vast majority of Chinese remain utterly convinced that childhood provided the happiest days of their lives.

When asked to articulate their reasons for the joys of child-

103

hood, they tend to give two general explanations. The first is that everyone is willing to be helpful to a child and to teach him what he needs to learn. He can have complete trust in the motives of others because the weaknesses of childhood do not leave him exposed to being cheated by them. There is no need to be constantly on his guard against the scheming forces of the adult world. In short, in childhood one can enjoy the pure bliss of dependency and not feel threatened. [11]

The second general reason commonly given for the happiness of childhood is that a child has no worries or pressing problems, because he has no responsibilities. Since the Chinese feel very acutely the awesome burdens of having to be fully accountable for their decisions and completely responsible for the consequences of their actions, they see childhood as the golden period when one does not have to calculate carefully what one should do at every turn.

The joy of childhood dependency is closely related to the importance of authority. It has been observed [12] that the Chinese manifest a very striking form of oral dependency in which authority is seen as a nurturing force, anxious to provide food, and always ready to soothe the disturbed by feeding them. This dependency leaves the Chinese with a basically happy memory of childhood and with a permanent need for the comforting reassurance that only a strong external authority can provide. It also leads to forms of "oral" aggression, or the imagery of "people eating people," if they are not kept in check by authority.

These are very powerful psychological reasons why the Chinese maintain their belief in the bliss of childhood. To these must be added, however, the negative restraint that nothing should ever be said that might be construed as critical or unkind toward one's parents. It would be sinful even

[11] Warner Muensterberger, op. cit.
[12] See Richard H. Solomon, "The Chinese Revolution and the Politics of Dependency," Ph.D. dissertation, Department of Political Science, Massachusetts Institute of Technology, 1966.

to admit that one's parents had made childhood unbearable. Historically the effect of the socialization process has been to produce individuals with a strong sense of the advantage of order, discipline, propriety, and competence. Above all, the process has taught the individual that he could be threatened by his surrounding world, that he could experience great pain and humiliation if he did the wrong things or failed to perform as others expected, and that he should never display hostile sentiments toward those who have had authority over him.

All the passion and resentment that come from having to sacrifice the self in favor of the authority-dominated collectivity are supposed to be ignored and the emotions suppressed. Instead, anger and resentment toward superiors are supposed to make the individual work harder to achieve the objectively defined standards of behavior that can bring universal praise. One has to work out one's anger by being a model of social propriety.

Thus, behind the complex patterns of social manners and convention that the Chinese built up through their elaborate socialization process, there were strong emotional forces that compelled the individual toward uniformity, even though he may have developed resentments toward the forms of authority that enforced such standards on him. Yet there was always a constructive outcome as long as the stable social order existed, because the individual did, and rather early in life, find a distinct social niche. Hard as it was to learn all that was expected of him, the individual could always achieve some social successes. He was his father's son, but he also had his own place as elder or younger brother or as head of a new family. He himself in turn could become an absolute and monopolistic form of authority. Thus there was a sense of justice in the complete repression of aggression and anger toward the world.

But the sense of justice vanished when modernization broke down the structure of the traditional social order and the individuals socialized to one kind of life were left to cope with quite a different set of circumstances.[13] We must now turn to an examination of what has happened to the Chinese concern about authority under the stresses of social change.

[13] For discussion of the way in which the Chinese have tended to adjust to variations in normative demands see N. N. Shen, "The Changing Chinese Social Mind," *Chinese Social and Political Science Review*, 8 (1924), 68–87, and 125–166; Liu Chiang, "Contrasts between Chinese and American Social Codes," *Forum of Applied Sociology*, 10 (1925–1926), 41–45; K. L. Wu, "Japanese Bushido and Chinese Sincerity," *China Forum* (1938), pp. 270–274.

BROKEN FATHERS
AND THE BITTER SEARCH
FOR NEW AUTHORITIES

In characterizing Chinese socialization patterns we have tended to stress many elements of the traditional order. The decades of social change and of war and revolution have of course challenged, disrupted, and in numerous ways compromised the traditional Chinese family pattern. But there is substantial evidence that while the adult institution has been considerably weakened, the basic processes of socialization, especially of the early years, have not been greatly changed. Memories of the old have been well preserved, for all Chinese still know how they should behave when dealing with the older generation, but there has been an increasing uncertainty about what should properly be expected in the conduct of the young. The confusion of Chinese parents gives a vivid microscopic picture of the confusion of China as a civilization in the modern era. In the end, however, since the only thing parents have been able to do is to act according to their own natures, they have generally conveyed to their children much of what they themselves have learned.

We are now prepared to advance our key hypothesis that the psychological intensity of the Chinese authority crisis has its roots in the fact that the initial and earliest socialization process is still dominated by traditional sentiments about authority, order, and the control of emotions; however, the young Chinese, as he grows older, becomes increasingly aware that the realities of authority both in his home and in the larger society do not meet his expectations. The contradictions between his deepest psychological expectations and the realities he perceives in later political socialization create tensions that tend to dominate much of his subsequent political behavior.

These tensions are further heightened by the universal tension between fathers and sons. The result, however, has been a strikingly ambivalent spirit of revolt against parental and other forms of authority. On the one hand there are powerful psychological anxieties about challenging authority, first, because of the cultural heritage of filial piety, and second, because of the individual's basic need for dependency on authority and order. On the other hand, these very pressures on the individual can create deep feelings of hostility that cannot safely be expressed, especially toward the closest symbols of authority. A need for authority is combined with resentment over the failings of authority.

In looking now at the various patterns of revolt and the craving for more complete authority, we must begin with the general observation that the spirit of rebellion of the younger generation has been characterized by a remarkable degree of moderation. During the first decades of this century the younger generation, in a timorous and somewhat charming manner, sought to make their rebellion against traditional conventions appear as a plea for mere common sense. In calling for new social practices the modernizers could pretend that all they were opposing was ignorance, superstition, and foolishness.

Within the family context the modernizing generation claimed that in their search for greater freedom they were in fact aiming to bring respectability and honor to their families. The general practice was for children to deny that they were rebelling against parental authority and to claim instead that they were asserting a higher form of morality than appeared in the decadence of conventional social practices.[1] In the broad challenge to planned marriages there was a striking quality of sweet reasonableness, of virginal innocence: The young could self-righteously demand the rights of freer social contacts, because in their minds they knew that if boys could meet girls freely nothing in fact would happen. The rebellion for greater freedom of choice in sexual matters was not inspired by a desire for illicit relations or even for a serious modification of the institution of marriage and the family. It was a rebellion in the name of higher ideals for marriage, which the young thought should also inspire their parents. This was the spirit that permeated the modernization movement among students in the 1930's; it is also to be found today in the personal relations among the Red Guards.

Instead of rebelling directly against parental authority in favor of a contrary ethic, the modernizing Chinese sought to establish warmer and more sympathetic relationships with their parents. The ethic they championed was so innocent that, if understood by their parents, it could only make the latter proud. The significance of this pattern of revolt is that Chinese youth generally have steadfastly denied, under great provocation, any hostile feelings toward their parents in spite

[1] In a study of family relations as revealed through short stories written (1) during the modernist revolt of the 1920's and 1930's, (2) under the Communist regime, and (3) on Taiwan, Ai-li Chin substantially documents the call for purification of the family as a main inspiration of the early reform movement. Similarly, during the first years of the Communist regime the dominant theme was that youth would have to show the way to a higher morality. What is interesting and exceedingly significant is that after the failures of the Great Leap there was a sharp reversal, and to a degree unique both in China and in world literature the family was viewed largely from a perspective sympathetic to the parents! Suddenly the Communists seemed anxious for everyone to appreciate the problem of authority and leadership. The short stories produced on Taiwan tend to reflect world cultural fashions, in which the theme of the family no longer has much relevance and boy meets girl without matrimony in mind. This degree of emancipation is equally shocking to the spirit of the 1920 reformers and to the current puritans of Communist China. (Chin, *op. cit.*)

of the tremendous demands of filial piety. Their need to speak of the goodness of parents has been an almost absolute imperative, which in turn reflects the intensity and completeness with which they have learned to repress their emotions of hostility and aggression.

The difficulties of even the modernizing generation to violate the Confucian demands of filial piety and to express criticism and hostility toward their parents has meant that they have had to blur the distinction between good and evil in immediate personal relations. Compelled to see merit in the very areas in which their parents have damaged them, they have been inhibited from recognizing the specifics of good and bad in reality. Consequently, they have tended to grasp for absolute standards in more abstract or distant considerations; hence, the sharp divide between friend and foe in political situations, between those who can be legitimately declared good and those who can be declared bad.

This strange confusion of good and bad in the perception of parental authority has been further compounded by the continuing limitations on the realization of psychic comforts from the open expression of affection. Even within the modernizing family there has been little overt reliance upon affection between generations, husbands and wives have continued to maintain a degree of emotional distance, and husbands have asserted elements of absolute authority. Even the most modernized husband has had to maintain at all times some sense of his presumed competence and authority. In this respect the Chinese male is a permanent prisoner of the need for reserve and dignity, and he does not have the releases permitted, for example, to the Japanese male, who, precisely because he is a male, can find escape from the demands of his role by seeking the legitimate support and comfort of women.

For the Chinese the greatest possibility for easy affection has been within the actual or the re-enacted brother-sister relationship. As a balance against filial restraints and the obligations in the brother-to-brother relationships, the Chinese have tended to find great emotional comfort in the less demanding relations between brother and sister. In this relationship, which uniquely recognizes a male role but does not demand any proof of his competence, it is possible to let a shared sense of humiliation and shame become the basis for mutual sympathy and admiration. In this relationship the very refusal to display emotion or hostility over acknowledged sufferings becomes the cause for gaining honor and admiration. From this blend of sympathy and admiration the male can actually achieve a sense of being stronger than the threatening and unreasonable father. The ideal of male authority and competence has thus been maintained.[2]

As the process of social change has allowed the denial of explicit criticism of parental authority to turn into a search for a self-sacrificing, pure, and innocent, but heroic, claim to respectability, the Chinese have shown increasingly a need to strike out aggressively at other forms of authority. As their social world became confused and disrupted in the 1930's and 1940's, feelings of bitterness and resentment, particularly toward the failings of public authorities, became more and more prevalent. The stage was thus set for aggression to become explicitly mobilized in politics.

With this generalized picture of the trends in social change during the last several decades in mind, let us now examine in greater detail some of the more typical patterns of reaction, all of which have contributed to the rising intensity of hostility in the political culture and to the growing ambivalence between the desire for revolt and the craving for a more perfect authority.

[2] The best analysis of the ideals of each of the paired relationships among family members is Marion J. Levy's classic study, *The Family Revolution in Modern China* (Cambridge, Mass.: Harvard University Press, 1949). On the changes in the family under communism see C. K. Yang, *The Chinese Family in the Communist Revolution* (Cambridge, Mass.: The M.I.T. Press, 1959). The best source, however, for the spirit and emotional qualities of Chinese family relations is probably to be found in the large number of novels about the Chinese family.

111

Strike at All Surrogate Forms of Authority

During the first stages in the weakening of the family system, when the demands of filial piety were still strong but the more rigid patterns of social relations were beginning to give way, the most typical pattern of revolt among the young was the expression of hostility toward distant and less threatening forms of authority, but authorities *to which their fathers still felt bound.* Many outbursts of student aggression that were taken as examples of political awakening were in reality expressions of youthful hostility within the sharply prescribed limits of family life.

The significance of this pattern of revolt was that it brought to Chinese politics a degree of emotionalism and hostility that was out of proportion to the intensity of the political issues involved. In challenging, criticizing, and demonstrating against political authorities the youth were expressing emotions far more intense than their understanding of politics would justify. Passion and politics were thus unconsciously married and, in time, became ritualized and standardized. Anyone going into political action was expected to display a massive outpouring of sentiment that could be genuine only if it were coupled with internal tensions.

It should be noted that when the revolt of youth is not against real parents but against those *in loco parentis,* or against more distant symbols of authority, the result is almost inevitably antidemocratic. This has been true in a wide variety of political cultures, from Germany and Latin America through the Middle East to Japan. There seems to be a genuine need in such situations to strengthen the sentiments of solidarity and, oddly enough, to minimize any sense of the uniqueness of the self. But when the search for individual identity has to be played out on the stage of a collective movement of revolt, the result is an artificial one that makes it even more difficult for the individual to face up to his real psychological problems as an individual.

By participating in a collective effort of revolt the young Chinese were shying away from their very genuine personal crises of identity in relation to their parents. Thus, just as their fascination for idealized versions of democracy could become a substitute for acceptance of the realities necessary for achieving political democracy, so their acceptance of revolt against distant authority became a substitute for the real need to establish autonomy from their parents. The dynamics of this revolt therefore strengthened the already strong antidemocratic tendencies in the political culture in spite of the fact that democratic symbols and slogans were used to articulate them.

Since the possibility of catharsis from the expression of aggression against surrogate forms of authority made it easier for sons to remain filial within the family context, attacks on political authority were consistent with remarkably docile acceptance of traditional parental authority. For this generation of Chinese there was often a lack of symmetry between attacks upon the lingering hold of tradition on society and politics and a general acceptance of tradition within the home.

Seeming Compliance and Cynical Acceptance

Another way in which the youth could make an oblique attack on parental authority was by following quite consciously a strategy of compliance while at the same time finding new areas for the expression of personality development beyond parental control. Parental authority could be accepted fully so long as this meant little more than adherence to the rituals of deference within the home. Outside of the household the young Chinese felt free to seek a new world, and in doing so he told his parent little about what he discovered.

This did not always entail a sharp conflict, for the individ-

113

ual could feel that he was complying with his old master even as he accepted new taskmasters. The young might turn to Western knowledge, something about which his father knew little, and believe, and make his father believe, that by becoming a dedicated physicist or modern scientist he was in fact bringing greater glory and honor to his family. By moving into a world completely removed the individual was able to escape from the tensions of parental control while claiming to be still respectful of traditional authority.

It is noteworthy that this manner of handling the problem of traditional authority encouraged young and bright Chinese to escape into modern professions and provided them with a psychological and emotional stimulus to excel.

Through success in modern pursuits they were merely, in a sense, proving again their inherent superiority as rational men. For them, success was what counted rather than the preservation of particular life patterns. In this respect the Chinese are quite different from most other transitional peoples, who even when they excel in modern pursuits often fear that they are rejecting their own cultural identities and violating their traditional roots. Other Asians often question whether they should be devoting themselves to success as measured by Western standards and feel that they must compensate somehow and assert their Asian heritage. Indians, for example, are afraid that they may be denying their cultural identity by wholeheartedly working in modern professions; thus the Indian intellectual can endlessly talk about his "rootlessness" and his "tragic alienation" from his own culture. The Chinese has few such doubts; it is enough for him to prove his cultural greatness by excelling in any area, whether traditional or modern.

It should also be noted that when this strategy of escape takes the form of career satisfaction, all the compulsive tendencies of the personality can be combined and given an even more intense emotional form through the individual's striving to remove himself from his father's real authority. The result is an extreme form of dedication and a great capacity for hard work. The individual can find release from tension in such work and is not hampered and inhibited by feelings of conflict. Success in new avenues of endeavor makes the practice of compliance with parental authority more tolerable and easy to live with.

The strategy of seeming compliance has not, however, been worked out only though professional career pursuits. Frequently it has been recognized by the whole family that conditions have changed, and that it will be necessary for the son to learn how to cope with new social and economic realities. Father and son continue to pretend that nothing need compromise the traditional basis of their relationship even though both act in terms of the realities of new circumstances. In all ritual forms the father assumes complete authority, and the son seemingly complies with the forms of filial piety at the same time that he copes with the greater imperatives of his life outside the family.

The modern Chinese are among the world's greatest masters of the art of coping. The breakdown of the highly structured system of role relations of old China has brought in its wake a compelling need to be situationally oriented, to be highly sensitive to opportunities hidden in every unfolding circumstance.

To carry out the pretense the son needs the cooperation of his father, a cooperation that can be coerced out of the father's fear of not being able to control the situation but that can also be articulated on the basis that everyone agrees on the need to be "realistic." The concern for "realism" opens the door to a form of fiction that in turn heightens the justification for opportunism.

In developing the ability for seeming compliance with paternal authority the Chinese have also learned to divert emotional commitment from the forms of action. If one is to be guided only by logic and see clearly the potentialities of each new situation one must be able to separate feeling from action and to recognize that there can be the appearance of emotion without the passions of sentiment. As we have already observed, the earlier experiences of socialization have prepared the ground for this form of separation. The irony, however, is that in the first years of life it was necessary because of the absoluteness of parental authority but now it is legitimized because of the weakness of parents.

The strategy of seeming compliance with parental authority therefore prepares the young to pretend to be more passionately involved in politics than in fact they are. This may help to explain the ability of the Chinese to sustain what appear to be strong emotions in politics for long periods of time. The apparent expression of passions does not always mean that an outlet has been found for real emotions.

This capacity for pretense is apparently now infuriating the leaders in Peking, who sense that their subjects may be only pretending to their enthusiasm for the revolution and the thoughts of Mao Tse-tung. The Communist leaders have fallen into the frustrating trap of believing in the ultimate importance of willpower and human passion while at the same time being fully aware that there is nothing easier than the pretense of emotions. These effects of the socialization process often mean that individuals are not sure where their emotions really lie, and they are content to leave well enough alone and to look for security in the potentially more orderly world of their own private lives.

The Broken Father and the Search for New Authorities

In more recent years the pressures of external events have been so overwhelming that it has been impossible for the young to play out the tactic of apparent compliance. The process of social change outside the household has made it clear to all that the father is no longer an omnipotent source of authority; the very suggestion of traditional standards of paternal power serves only to emphasize what a weak and helpless man the father, as a representative of the older generation, has become. Precisely because the Chinese value the ability to cope with situations, the father can only lose respect in the eyes of his son for his inability to be more successful in the modern world. At the same time the son, who was taught to believe in the absolute powers of his father, may feel distaste and repugnance at now seeing the latter's weakness.

The inherent tension in the relationship with paternal authority becomes compounded by resentment at the weakness of what was supposed to be supreme strength and results in a seething form of humiliation. It can produce at times an identification with the "aggressor" that has destroyed the parental authority, and the son may become a passionate champion of ever more "modernization" for Chinese society. If he advocates that all fathers who followed the old pattern of authority should be shown up for what they are, he is no longer alone in his humiliation. The shame of young Chinese at having weak and incompetent fathers is in a sense equated with their humiliation for China as a nation. For these Chinese there is an impatient need to make up for the weaknesses of their fathers' generation.

In the dynamics of this pattern of reaction the final outcome may be a desire by the son to assert himself as the new and more effective form of authority. Even if this is not the case, there is a need for some new authority, and the search is, paradoxically, for an even more omnipotent, more monopolistic form of authority than that of the parent against whom the individual was initially in revolt. Here again is the distinctive feeling that the weakness of authority is the father's crime and not the son's chance for "freedom," that the crumbling of national as well as parental authority is a cause for shame and not an opportunity for achieving greater individual freedom.

117

Direct Confrontations and Anxious Memories

Politically the patterns of reaction to the persisting traditions of Confucian family authority are extremely important in explaining the basic tone of the followers of the Chinese revolutionaries. They give both meaning and passion to the emerging political activists who struggle to destroy old forms of authority for being too restrictive while they anxiously accept more totalitarian forms as desirable. These young people have demonstrated their continuing need for dependency in their intense desire to overthrow all forms of political authority that have shown weakness and to saddle themselves with more repressive rulers, all in the name of greater self-dignity.

They have needed leaders who can speak the language of revolution and who in their own lives are capable of carrying the spirit of revolt against parental authority to the point of direct confrontation. It is significant that a disproportionate number of the top leaders of Communist China had violent and even traumatic confrontations with their fathers. Out of their experiences they seem to have internalized a spirit that has legitimized their leadership. Yet the trauma of their experiences has left scars that have compromised their own understanding of change once they have become the symbols of authority.

These individuals did not necessarily make a direct break with parental values but willfully adhered to activities that were in violent opposition to them.[3] Chu Teh cites as one of the most vivid memories of childhood his father's violent de-

[3] Agnes Smedley, in *The Great Road: The Life and Times of Chu Teh* (New York: Monthly Review Press, 1956), quotes Chu Teh as saying, "I loved my mother, but I feared and hated my father. . . . I could never understand why my father was so cruel." Significantly in a later Chinese edition of the book the phrase "and hated my father" was deleted.

nunciations of a group of soldiers who passed by the house. In choosing a military career Chu Teh seems to have been striking back against a father he could not rebel against directly. When he insisted upon enrolling in a school of physical education he again defied his father's wishes in a peculiarly aggressive manner. Given the traditional sentiments about the inappropriateness of physical exertion on the part of educated people and the belief that a son's body belonged to his family and should be treasured as the vital link of family continuity, an interest in physical education did represent a psychological challenge to the deepest meaning of family authority.

P'eng Teh-huai's story is extraordinarily traumatic. His mother died when he was six, his stepmother soon displayed a strong dislike for him, and his father gave no protection and was indifferent to his fate. At school he struck back at his teacher, who frequently beat him, and he had to be sent away to his uncle's home where his grandmother, an opium addict, lived. One night P'eng kicked a pan of his grandmother's opium from the stove, and the old lady demanded a clan meeting at which P'eng was "sentenced" to death by drowning for his unfilial act. All agreed, including P'eng's father, but an uncle interceded and the penalty was changed to banishment for the nine-year-old boy. For seven years the boy had to make out as best he could before he was accepted in the home of the uncle who had saved his life. This relationship soon broke down, but by then P'eng was old enough to join the army and find the kind of security, order, and comradeship he needed.

The story of Mao Tse-tung's emotionally violent revolt against his father was frequently narrated during the 1930's and 1940's, but significantly, since the cult of Mao's personality began after Stalin's death, little mention has been made of the fact that he was stubborn and willful in defying his father's wishes.

We can touch only briefly upon the main features of Mao's

119

childhood struggle with his father.[4] Mao was born into a family that had known poverty but was rising in the little community of Shao Shan as a consequence of the single-minded determination of his father. It may have been symbolic for Mao Tse-tung, whose rise to power came in no small measure out of his appreciation of the use of armies in politics, that his father also found an escape from poverty by joining the army. Mao Shun-sheng returned from his army experience with enough capital to elevate himself to the level of a "middle" peasant with fifteen *mou* of land, and soon he had a growing business of trading rice and lending money to poorer peasants. Mao Shun-sheng was a stern and demanding father who wanted his son to apply all of his energies to the family enterprise; he invested in a tutor and expected young Mao to keep the family books as soon as he had learned a few characters. As Mao later said of his father, "He was a severe taskmaster. He hated to see me idle, and if there were no books to be kept, he put me to work at farm tasks.[5]

As Mao grew older the conflicts with his father became more intense. When he was thirteen he was denounced by his father before a group of neighbors for being lazy and useless. In a fit of fury he went to a nearby pond and threatened to jump in, and thus employed against his father the classic Chinese threat of shaming another through self-destruction.

---

[4] In spite of the campaigns to build up "the cult of the personality" in China and the large number of books that contain his name in the title, we have relatively little information on Mao's early life. The principal source is still his autobiographical discussion with Edgar Snow reported in *Red Star Over China* (New York: Random House, 1938). Other sources include Siao-Yu, *Mao Tse-tung and I Were Beggars* (Syracuse, N.Y.: Syracuse University Press, 1956); George Paloczi-Horvath, *Mao Tse-tung: Emperor of the Blue Ants* (New York: Doubleday, 1963); Emi Siao, *Mao Tse-tung, his Childhood and Youth* (Bombay, 1953); Robert Payne, *Mao Tse-tung: Ruler of Red China* (New York: Henry Schuman, 1950); Jerome Ch'en, *Mao and the Chinese Revolution* (New York: Oxford University Press, 1965).

[5] Edgar Snow, *Red Star Over China* (New York: Random House, 1938), p. 114.

After this incident his rebellion became more aggressive. His father persisted in believing that Mao was willfully determined to amount to nothing because of his hatred for physical labor and his constant reading of historical novels and romances instead of classical literature.[6] Finally, the crisis came when Mao was sixteen years old, and in an act of cold anger he collected a few clothes and three of his favorite books and left his home without saying goodbye. He never returned to Shao Shan to see his father, nor do we have evidence that he ever communicated with him again.

Mao, on his own, then forced his way into the primary school at Tungshan. He was a big strapping lad, large for his age, and over six years older than any of his classmates. Those who remember him at this period picture a youth who could not deal easily with his equals, who was always challenging his teachers, and who displayed all the aggressive bullying tactics of his father. It is interesting that Mao has always been remarkably insignificant as a subordinate dealing with peers and that in his leadership roles he has always been distant, with no equals, and always the "older" figure.

It is psychologically noteworthy that the principal charges Mao's father made against him were that he was lazy — lacking in willpower — and that his interest in books was of an impractical nature. It may not be too unreasonable to speculate that in an unconscious way Mao has been seeking ever since to prove his father wrong. Certainly, the latter-day Mao of the Cultural Revolution and the Red Guards seems obses-

---

[6] It is, of course, impossible to obtain an objective picture of this relationship, since everything we know comes from the son. We can question, however, whether the demands of the father were particularly excessive in terms of the poverty of that Honan village. Indeed, even according to Mao's account the physical demands for labor seem to be modest by Chinese standards for poor peasants and are severe only by the standards for richer peasants. To understand the situation, it may be appropriate to keep in mind the excruciating pains of an adolescent American boy whose father tries to nag him to mow the lawn and to do other chores that require exertion when he is preoccupied with his own growth.

sively determined to prove that he values above all else the powers of the human spirit. Moreover, he has been equally determined to show that his understanding of the power of the book and the word is not in the slightest impractical. On one hand he has been vigorously anti-intellectual, on the other, he has sought to demonstrate that by "merely grasping a little red book" the Red Guards have found a powerful source for action.

Over the years Mao has also sought to justify his revolt against his father by depicting him not only as harsh and cruel but also as a "rich peasant." By identifying his father with what to communism is an evil class, Mao has been able to give legitimacy to his own behavior that violated the deepest rules and to give emotional meaning to the abstract evil of "landlord" and "rich peasant." Mao's intense experience may thus have contributed to his practice of depicting the landlord class as immoral and personally despicable. We can at least speculate that the strength of Mao's feelings against "rich peasants" has been fed in part by the need to justify his own violent and intemperate revolt against his father. We may also speculate that his experiences have left him with an exaggerated expectation of the willingness of others to revolt against their parental authority if they are presented with a legitimate basis for doing so. However, he must have doubts whether others are in fact capable of doing the ultimately bold thing that he did when he denounced his own father.

Significantly, over the years Mao has sought increasingly to personify in himself the strong but understanding figure of authority that he felt his father was not; in a sense he has set himself to become an even greater father figure. Given this pattern of reaction, it is likely that Mao was profoundly and intimately disturbed when he discovered during the Hundred Flowers period that those who apparently had fully accepted his benign rule were prepared to revolt against him. Nothing can disturb a son who has revolted against paternal

authority more than the discovery that his own sons are prepared to do the same against him.

The Meaning for Politics and Nation Building

Thus the culture that has made the most of filial piety
and the dutifulness of sons has, with modernization, been
the most troubled about achieving strong authorities. In a
larger political sense, recent generations have dreamed of
idealized forms of authority that, miraculously, would solve
all problems and put China at the forefront of a new order
of nations. The expectation that pure authority has the capacity to change everything has made the Chinese peculiarly
prone to throw in their lot with any emerging authority that
has seemed in any way efficient. Thus with every change in
regime in modern times the Chinese have responded with
initial enthusiasm and a childlike optimism, each time hoping
against hope that all their problems would be solved but fear-
ful that once again they would be disillusioned.

Yet, anxious as they have been for the magic of authority,
they have continually resented all the authorities they have
had. They have been prone to see malice in those with power,
suspecting that they themselves will probably not be treated
with justice. They accept completely the need for order, but
their deep awareness of the self makes them project to those
with power the same aggressive tendencies.

These deep personal reactions have brought about profound changes in the basic style of politics. In the traditional
Confucian order there was a tolerable respect for hypocrisy
because all knew that authority had to be shrewd and calculating at the same time that it defended conventional morality.
What is striking in the recent generations of political activists
is not so much their addiction to revolutionary language as
their drive toward puritan morality and complete denial of
the legitimacy of compromise and accommodation. Their

123

rigid, very self-righteous, and priggishly moralistic manner, so much a part of the Chinese revolutionary spirit, seems to be directly related to the psychology of adolescent revolt. Modern Chinese politics, reaching a climax under communism, has dramatically institutionalized a distinctive set of attitudes that is related directly to the struggle of youth against the weakening Confucian family structure. The mixture of past innocence, shrill self-righteousness, and violent aggressiveness provides the basic elements in this pattern.

WILLPOWER AND MORALITY:
THE DYNAMICS OF ACTION

So far in our analysis we have been dwelling on the dynamic historical and psychological factors that have contributed to the emotional tone of modern Chinese politics and its ritualized language of assertive aggressiveness. There remain the implications of the authority crisis for the capacity of the Chinese to act and to create and effectively manage the kinds of organizations and institutions that are essential for successful modernization. In many transitional societies that are plagued with identity crises there is paralysis both on the level of conceptualizing the future of the society and in overcoming internal psychological inhibitions to action. In these societies people often find it difficult to work effectively together, and there is widespread uncertainty over what can and should be done to advance national development.

In China, the basic question we must ask is whether the authority crisis has been of such a nature that it can be resolved by the establishment of a new and strong central authority or whether it has deeper dimensions that will continue to affect large numbers of Chinese both in their capacity for action and in their behavior in organizations.

In this chapter we shall consider the rather elusive subject

125

of Chinese attitudes toward effort, willpower, and human energy. We already had a hint of that relationship to the authority crisis when we noted how anxious Mao's father was about his son's laziness and lack of willpower and how Mao himself has become so obsessed with the importance of maintaining revolutionary enthusiasm in the youth of Communist China.

Since it is central to our hypothesis that their culture has repressed aggression to an extreme degree, it follows that the Chinese are likely to have very complicated and extremely ambivalent feelings about everything closely related to the force of aggression and the mechanisms for the control of aggression. That is, they are likely to see the dynamics of human behavior as governed above all by the forces of purposeful willpower and physical energy, not the forces of love and idealism, aspiration and longing, which dominate in the cultures that accentuate the need to control sexuality. Since the meaning of action in the Chinese culture is closely associated with the repression of aggression, we would expect that there would be a strong tendency to attach both mysticism and morality to the concept of willpower.

Yet at the same time the demonstration of willpower can come dangerously close to being no more than an expression of aggression, and hence, the powerful drive toward passivity in the culture. There is a dynamic tension underlying the Chinese approach toward effort, willpower, and human energy that in some respects Mao Tse-tung has tapped successfully; but it may also prove to be an uncertain basis to the motivation for modernizing Chinese society. Before turning to the psychological dimensions of this problem we need to note the historical attitude toward social change and human effort. We shall have to explore the ambivalence of the Chinese which at times has made for their passivity and at others had led to their faith that demonstrations of willpower can easily change history. What is the relationship between the outbursts of emotionalism that have characterized the mass campaign of the Communists and the quiet purposefulness of action that has marked the traditionally industrious Chinese?

Faith in History and the Cycles of Change

First, we must observe that traditionally the Chinese have had a somewhat mystical faith in the powers of history to bring about change. Time alone, and not man's will, produces cycles, and cycles bring about the rise and fall of all things, including the greatness of nations and the stability of empires. Traditionally the Chinese have tended to be passive before history.

This basic sentiment has in modern times made the Chinese ambivalent about the role of effort in bringing about modernization. Employing their mystical-historical persepective, they have often been able to convince themselves that it was purely an accident of history that brought a confrontation between China and the West at a time when the Chinese civilization was at a low point in its cycle. Merely with the passage of time cycles would change, and China could expect to rise again to its position of acknowledged historical greatness.

This basic outlook has made the Chinese talk not about programs of modernization but about the need for "revitalizing" life and about the arrival of a "Chinese renaissance." Hence, they have tended to be slow in adopting the programmatic approach toward economic and political development that has swept all the ex-colonial countries. Development planning and programming have been foreign to their thinking. Historically, they have believed that limited demonstrational or educational programs should be adequate to trigger the latent capabilities of the people to re-establish their greatness.

The importance of effort has always been qualified by a deep faith in the inevitability of China's greatness. Beyond anything that effort can hope to bring about lie the

127

beneficial powers of time and history. With each decade, planning has become increasingly more important, but the Chinese have not lost their capacity for faith in history. Chiang Kai-shek can still believe in the miracle of a return to the mainland which involves far more than what human planning and effort can accomplish. Mao Tse-tung similarly believes that by recapturing the spirit of the rural guerrillas he can ensure that the Revolution will achieve undreamed-of successes. All the goals of modern Chinese politics have exceeded the limits of rational planning, and all have rested in the last analysis upon an extraordinarily optimistic faith in history.

This faith has been further sustained by a powerful and essentially mystical belief that moral uprightness and ethical correctness on the part of rulers is enough to determine the fate of empires. It is perhaps natural for the Chinese to see magic in morality because this is what has provided solutions to the most central problem of their culture, the control of aggression.

Thus although the cyclical view of history has been open to powers of moral force, the traditional belief in political cause and effect has not been seen as a closed system in which all the levels of force or energy should be accountable. The magical quality of energy has been that great things could come out of nothing while great efforts might yield little. The universe is not lawlike, it all depends upon who you are.

For the Chinese the payoff of events can always hopefully exceed the amount of purposeful effort exerted, and it is desirable to be the kind of person for whom this happens most frequently. Luck, therefore, is important; moreover, it is necessary to test one's luck frequently, for it would be tragic not to know how it is running at any time. This basic quality of trust, of optimism about the self, that comes from being born into a nurturing environment and from knowing the protective comforts of dependency can produce intensive, if not compulsive, gamblers.

Lethargic Officials and Diligent Masses

In turning to the role of effort in Chinese politics we confront an odd but persistent contradiction between ideology and behavior. Traditionally the upper classes adhered to a creed of action in Confucianism but in practice cultivated effortlessness, while the masses accepted the creed of nonaction in Taoism but behaved entirely in the spirit of diligent purposefulness. Mandarins in government spoke in terms of the puritan Confucian ethic while dreaming of retirement, of long leaves of two or three years to bury their parents, and of leisurely sessions of tea and wine drinking. In contrast the masses found comfort in their Taoist religion, which suggested that all could be accomplished through non-effort, while developing the compulsive capacity for work that we now associate with the long hours and single-mindedness of Chinese laundrymen.

Historically the tempo of Chinese politics was lethargic and cautious. The picture one has of imperial offices and *yamen* is one of slow-moving and heavily clad officials, the only bustle of activity coming from the purposeful but anxious movements of flunkies, who, however, could not be a part of politics precisely because they were so active. The more important the man, the slower his pace. The arrival of the Republic brought a more dynamic vocabulary to politics, but the rhythm of decision making in vast reaches of provincial offices remained the same as ever, and life in the national offices and ministries did not appreciably quicken.

Authority was always slow moving, somewhat deliberate, but never conspicuously purposeful. Greatness went with grandeur, and grandeur for the Chinese had a heavy spirit.

Yet, the sensation of life in Chinese society was always one of potential energy. Of all the adjectives that have commonly been used to describe the Chinese, the one that sets them apart the most from their neighbors in Asia is "ener-

129

getic." Whatever might have been said about the sluggishness of the political system, it was generally agreed that the Chinese as a people were almost universally hard-working and industrious. In their family life and in their struggle to make a living, the Chinese could always act with determined purposefulness. It is true that the activity of individuals on the move has often been more noise than accomplishment, but the culture has always been a distinctively high-decibel one; the Chinese happily surround themselves with noise and are almost impervious to the possibility that their own noises can disturb the privacy, even indeed the sleep, of others.

Since action, movement, and purpose are highly valued in personal behavior, a central feature of the Chinese socialization process has always been the effort to instill into youth the need for action and a fear of laziness. Parents have always tended to be extremely sensitive to the frightening danger that their offspring might drift, if not constantly checked, into slovenly ways. For man was supposed to be purposeful as well as rational.

Thus we have a contrast between the lethargic tempo of public life and the vigorous rhythm of private life. Visits to the world of officialdom during the decades from 1911 to the end of the 1940's could be excruciating experiences for anyone who valued time. The contrast that existed between inside laxity and outside straining suggested often to foreigners that Chinese officials were uniquely incompetent, ineffectual, and lacking in decision and purposefulness. Yet for the Chinese the contrast was a reminder that the capacity to delay others was the ultimate mark of power and authority. He who had to step faster at the words of another was clearly the subordinate, and he who could bide his time in the face of another's impatience was clearly the superior. This was how parents could behave in the face of the impatience of youth. It would not be too great a caricature of the gradually modernizing Chinese political culture to say that there has been a direct and firm correlation between the degree of authority and the degree of inactivity. This has caused China a great deal of trouble, especially since it has been combined with the equally important practice of centralizing all decision making. Decisions can be made only by superiors, so that quantitatively most decisions have always had to be made at the top; but the sign of power is its capacity to move slowly, so that the top must always take the most time in making a decision. If one were too efficient, how would people know how important one was? For efficiency leads to inconspicuousness, and to be inconspicuous in politics is to be irrelevant. Hence, even when the Chinese are successfully accomplishing their objectives in public life, they feel compelled to proceed with great fanfare.

It might seem that with the arrival of the Communists there would have been a profound revolution in this aspect of the political culture. Certainly the contemporary world of commissars and cadres has not been lacking in movement and energy. The gross image of the China of the Great Leap is one of frantic, if not mad, activity. And it is this spirit of compulsive "leaping," or "soaring," as the Chinese now call it, of massive assaults, that best characterizes the Chinese Communist style in trying to get things done. It is this spirit of action which inspires the charge that Mao Tse-tung is a romantic revolutionary.

Yet strangely enough there still seems to be an element of the old China in the movements of Communist officials. High officials still move slowly, and it is not just age that keeps them out of sight. One of the most striking impressions of a British editor on visiting government and industrial offices in mainland China was how unbusy the officials seemed to be and how unaware the people were that the rest of the modern world worked at a much more intense pace. He sensed that the Chinese believed they were busy when following the leisurely pace of an era long past in the West. Interviews during office hours with high government officials or industrial managers could last for hours — when everywhere else in the world they would customarily be measured in minutes. A glance at the daily schedules of high officials and key industrial plant managers suggested that their daily quota of conferences, meetings, and individual office visitors would be a shock to, and the envy of, Western executives. This British editor, as well as other Western visitors, noted that Chinese officials, in arranging what they honestly believed to be "busy schedules" and "full days" for their visitors' conducted tours of China, usually left the Western (and even more the Japanese) visitor frustrated that precious time was being wasted. The tempo of life that is taken as acceptable or "normal" is usually so unhurried as to make others feel that the Chinese must be "holding back" and refusing to be fully cooperative.[1]

Other evidence suggests that the pace of governmental life is not as intense as might be expected considering that the country proclaims so emphatically that it is in a hurry. From what we know about the structure of communications, the Chinese do not seem to have the facilities essential to the intensive patterns of interaction common to modern industrial life. The telephone is becoming a more prominent feature of offices, but officials still seem to have far less need to use the airplane than officials of most countries. In the main, communication and decision making continue to rely almost entirely upon the pace at which reports can be drafted and papers moved about. The weakness of internal governmental communication can be seen from the way in which the Chinese must depend upon announcements within the public press to pass on the word about policy decisions.[2]

[1] This conflict in the tempo of daily life clearly comes through in the letters of C. H. G. Oldham in the reports of the Institute of Current World Affairs of 1965. As an Englishman who has waited years for the opportunity for even a brief visit to the forbidden land of China, Oldham clearly could not bear to see a moment of his visit wasted; so possibly he was excessively impatient with the inherent slowness of the Chinese.

[2] In all societies the press helps to facilitate the communication of high governmental decisions not only to the public but to subordinate

In spite of these important qualifications about the pace of governmental life, it is nevertheless true that the tempo of Communist politics has greatly accelerated compared to that of earlier regimes. In a sense, as the scope of political life has expanded, many patterns of behavior that characterized the more energetic tempo of private life have been incorporated into the realm of political activities. Cadres and lower officials often act with the compulsive purposefulness once common only among private citizens engaged in personal pursuits. The industry of the Chinese in general has now been incorporated into the behavior of at least low- and middle-range officials. As a result government gives the impression of being a dynamic and purposeful force.

This change in tempo has helped to highlight a traditional Chinese distinction between public and private life. Traditionally, powerful officials moved slowly not just because this was the proper style of action of authority. They did so also because in applying a form of "cost-benefit analysis" they believed that the correct strategy in public affairs was to minimize effort; in private affairs they were somewhat more prone to apply a profit-maximizing approach. That is to say, in government matters they tended to worry about how to get the most for the least effort while in private affairs they tended to want to make the most regardless of effort.

Historically in the West modernization has called for the profit-maximizing approach: People have been prepared to discount costs if the returns increased with greater effort. For the Chinese the objective even in national development has usually been to discover the optimal level of perform-

---

members of the government itself; in most modern governments, however, officials are restrained from formal action until they receive official communications about the precise nature of such higher decisions. In the Soviet Union, mass media in the form of official newspapers have been heavily relied upon for explicit official communications. The Chinese, however, seem to go even further, for often cadres receive no further instructions than those they can deduce from the public press.

ance at which the minimum input of effort will give either a satisfactory or even the highest proportional return. To the extent that an explicit rationale has been behind the Chinese cult of effortlessness, this is it.

At present there appears to be considerable doubt whether either profit maximization or effort minimization is the right approach. In their search for enthusiasm and in their belief in the potentialities of willpower the Chinese Communists seem to act as though it were no longer important to calculate the expenditure of human energy. On the other hand, the tradition still persists that leadership should be wise, philosophical, and slightly withdrawn from day-to-day activities.

Since the increase in the tempo of public affairs has affected mainly the cadres and not so much the life style of the highest decision makers, it has resulted in a unique form of tension: The lower cadres, in response to general directives, have consistently tended to display inordinate zeal and have often left the higher officials far behind. This was most dramatically demonstrated during the period of the Great Leap and again during the Cultural Revolution, the era of the Red Guards, and the purges of 1966 when, time and again, ridiculous excesses could be traced to the commands and actions of local authorities and not necessarily to the intentions of the highest officials in Peking.

There is a fundamental pattern of rule and policy implementation in Communist China: Peking indicates with relatively limited cues that a new campaign or program should be initiated, and then the local authorities race ahead in executing the policy; when events reach a point of excess, Peking calls for exaggerated efforts in the other direction, which then produce a return to a form of equilibrium. There are, of course, many contributing factors to this pattern of behavior — including the inadequacy of trained personnel and imperfect communications systems — but among them is the difference in tempo of those in high authority and those in lower positions.

Since the quickening pace of low-level governmental behavior appears to be similar in many respects to conventional private behavior, it is appropriate to examine further the dynamics of action and discover why the Chinese without high responsibilities may be more effective than other transitional peoples in overcoming social inertia and working for change.

Conquering Inertia Through Compulsive Behavior

A striking characteristic of Chinese social behavior outside of politics has been that inertia and procrastination have played such small roles in the routine patterns of life. It is true that with the beginnings of modernization novelty often produced endless waiting and great uncertainty, and many activities seemed to take forever to be accomplished, but not because people were inactive. Within the set patterns of the different occupations and rounds of life people did what had to be done with little hesitation.

We have already observed that the Chinese socialization process tends to stress the rewards of routinized behavior. The child is made to believe that there are correct ways of acting that can bring security, praise, and a degree of parental warmth. Whenever action accords with set norms the individual is remarkably free of uncertainties, self-doubts, and anxieties.

Therefore the gap between desire and action is small in Chinese culture — that is, so long as the particular act fits set patterns. Once circumstances unambiguously call for a certain action, the only question is that of the artistry with which it is executed. And artistry is usually associated with alacrity and decisiveness. For example, in art the skilled practitioner usually knows at the outset exactly what he

135

plans to paint, and the test of his ability is in large measure the speed with which he can execute the necessary strokes. Once the painting has been started, there is no room for revision or replanning; the entire painting is supposed to follow directly and inexorably from the first stroke. The practice of teachers is usually to make the first stroke on a piece of paper and then expect the student to understand and execute the entire picture that should properly follow.

Above all, the consummation of an activity is assumed to be contained in its initiation. Once something is started, the expectation is that it will be completed. The wish of the master readily becomes the completed act of the servant, and when high political authority indicates a proper course, lower authorities need only respond without further thought.

Thus, as long as an activity conforms to a recognized pattern of behavior, there is little inertia either in translating a wish into initial action or in moving from the first step to the last. This pattern of behavior contrasts sharply with the hesitation and vacillation, the moods of lethargy and the appearance of laziness, so manifest in some other Asian cultures. In contrast to the Indians, for example, who will start an enterprise with great enthusiasm but little expectation of fulfillment, the Chinese tend to believe that anything started seriously will produce serious outcomes. Less hobbled by inhibitions and inner tensions than the Indians, they are not only emotionally capable of action but are usually more afraid of inaction.

The expectation that initiation assumes consummation affects all forecasts of the future and often leads in the political realm to a tendency to jump to conclusions. When the logic of a situation calls for certain acts on the part of others, the Chinese are quick to assume that the latter will carry through the chain to its "self-evident" conclusion. Thus they easily convinced themselves that the Americans after crossing the thirty-eighth parallel in Korea would certainly go on into Manchuria. Similarly, Ch'en Yi, in 1966, said that the Chinese "were growing old and white haired" awaiting the American attack, and he made the point that it was not the Chinese but the Americans who were delaying in doing the self-evident. In the Sino-Indian border clashes the Chinese interpreted Indian probes as designed to achieve major objectives, while their own refusal to complete what was started was to them a dramatic example of self-control.

The same pattern is to be found in the Chinese propensity to believe that when a project is started it should not be laid aside until it is completely realized. Thus the Communists continue to pretend they are still following every policy they have ever initiated even though it is apparent that they cannot reach their goals. This is true of policy failures ranging from the "liberation of Taiwan" to the pretense that the essence of agricultural policy is still the building of the communes.

In the same spirit the Communists tend in their propaganda to stress the wonders of immediate conditions in China rather than to talk of a protracted process of working toward distant ideals. The application of the "Thoughts of Mao Tse-tung" to any problem supposedly leads directly to immediate solutions. The wish becomes the act, and the act brings the consummation. And since they expect things to work this way, propagandists tend to dwell on results being achieved and not on the intervening processes by which intentions eventually become consequences.

The Dangers of Laziness
and the Potency of Willpower

The fact that Chinese behavior tends to be compulsive but purposeful has its roots in many features of the socialization process. First, there has been the extraordinary awareness of the extent to which children could be systematically molded and trained. So much seemed to rest upon the assumption of responsibilities by the parents that there could be little room

137

for irrelevancies; too much depended upon conscious effort to leave much to chance, and thus parents were anxious to guide and criticize, to prod and scold. Second, the underlying spirit that has justified such intense efforts at civilizing children has been a deep cultural belief that in every individual there was an inherent desire to be moral and to do good. Children, then, should want to be trained.

For the Chinese parent it is never too early to implant in children adult virtues and to worry about signs of adult vices. They have had an overriding concern that their children might yield to laziness, for this would suggest that they lacked willpower. The demand that children should display respect and filial piety was usually coupled with the desire that they should be diligent in everything they did. A theme that appears in numerous Chinese autobiographies concerns the fury of a father at the laziness and lack of purpose of his son. As we saw in the adolescent struggle between Mao Tse-tung and his father, the underlying issue was the father's feeling that young Mao was indolent and incapable of hard work, that he idled his time away in meaningless pursuits and the reading of useless novels. Ultimately the only way that Mao could strike back at his father was to perform feats of physical labor that exceeded the father's highest demands.

In the fascinating letters that Tseng Kuo-fan, the great nineteenth-century Chinese official, wrote to his family he frequently cautioned his parents and his brothers to be on the alert for any symptoms of laziness and arrogance among the youngsters.

> Since all of you [brothers] are at home, you must teach the nephews and your children to be respectful and diligent. Since I am an official and have power and prestige, our nephews will be prone to be arrogant and lazy. These two qualities inevitably lead a family to ruin. You must guard every minute against our nephews going near arrogance and laziness.[3]

[3] Chao Jung-chi, ed., *Tseng Wen-Tseng-Kung chia-shu* (Tseng Kuo-fan's Letters to Home) (Kweilin: Nan-kuang shu-tien), p. 26. The danger of "arrogance" needs no further elaboration here since it is

The need for children to be both diligent and respectful was a practical imperative in the traditional culture, since parents had to count upon their children to provide for them in old age. A lazy and indolent son could not be truly filial. The pressures against laziness were inspired, however, by more than just utilitarian considerations. They were supported by powerful psychological concerns because they were fundamentally linked to anxieties about death and hopes for immortality. The continuity of family life was a guiding consideration in Chinese cultural behavior, and the test of continuity was more than just biological; it required that sons realize an ideal of proper behavior. The drive to train and socialize children was thus linked to more than just the urge for conformity and the meeting of social responsibilities. All the most elemental anxieties about death and the possible extermination of individual identity were brought into play. The one comforting hope was that if the transition of generations could be properly managed the absoluteness of death could be modified.

Anxieties about death and the meaningfulness of life, were channeled in the West into the search for individual salvation and served as a driving force behind economic and, eventually, industrial development; they were focussed in China upon the socialization of children with respect to both moral standards and ideals of action. So tremendous was the force behind parental demands that it would be hard to exaggerate the pressures that were applied. Permissiveness was unthinkable.

It has always been assumed in China that the young can be trained easily. The Communist stress on socialization is thus not a new development. But the traditional view, like the Communist view, was not that training was possible because human nature was infinitely pliable. On the contrary,

---

related so closely to the question of whether a child has the capacity for "shame," and hence "humiliation," that we have already discussed at some length.

they adopted a more positive view of the legitimacy of powerful socialization methods by convincing themselves that fundamentally all children wanted to be made good. Parents could justify their high demands on children, and possibly assuage any latent anxieties of being excessively harsh, by believing that children were so constituted as to be naturally desirous of achieving the proper ideals of conduct. Formal Chinese philosophy, from at least the time of Mencius, has held that man's nature is good and that education and training ensure that the basic urges are given their proper expression. Thus parental authority and education were not employed to tame wild spirits, civilize destructive forces, or control the id as they are in the West.

Since it has been assumed that the child wants to be assisted in achieving adult ideals, the Chinese notion of frustration is an ambiguous one. While at times it is recognized that a child can rebel against the guidance of adults, it is' also expected that he will be disturbed if he is not given adequate direction. For example, Tseng Kuo-fan, whose views on child rearing we just quoted, made the following interesting observation about why his younger brother was causing so much difficulty:

> Our sixth brother is an unusual man. His will cannot be strengthened nor his mind broadened in an isolated village. His youthful spirit should not be thwarted too long. That he was not admitted to school has already frustrated him. He was again frustrated when I refused to bring him to the capital to study. If he is not permitted to go to study in the provincial capital, will not his frustration be unbearable? [4]

The Chinese believe that from a very early age people are inclined toward purposeful behavior; that behind purpose lie reason and willpower; and that reason can be cultivated and even taught but that willpower is a more tenuous matter. Assumptions about human nature all point to the vital importance of willpower, for it is the presumed existence of

[4] *Ibid.*, p. 1.

140

such an element in the make-up of the individual that reassures the Chinese of the child's desire to be properly socialized. Yet in the socialization practices there is little to suggest that others can give willpower to a child. Chinese parents are acutely sensitive to the differences between willpower and willfulness, and they are prepared to do much to counteract all signs of stubbornness. All that a parent can do is to encourage and exhort his child to demonstrate his will to do right.

In making a sharp distinction between willpower and willfulness or stubbornness, and in giving primacy and legitimacy to the former and denying completely the propriety of the latter, the Chinese deny to the child a sense of individual identity that can come only from the experience of opposition. They would not even consider that the child had any legitimate desire to oppose authority. He can only have willpower, which is the purposeful desire to become what others expect of him. The fear that willpower may be replaced by willfulness is so great that parents hold back from having any interest in the actual feelings and sentiments of their children, the latter need only separate feelings from actions and make their actions conform to what is expected.

Children are thus made to feel that in spite of constant harassment and criticism they can still demonstrate their ultimate worth by showing that they are not lacking in the vital ingredient of willpower. They are fed a constant stream of stories of the single-minded determination of heroes who persevered in gaining their set goals. To demonstrate correct desires to act purposefully so as to reveal one's willpower is thus the most assured way that the Chinese child has of proving his worth to others. It is also the way to demonstrate dutiful compliance with authority and to receive the emotional rewards of security.

Conversely, failure in conduct is readily linked to a lack of will. When individuals do not realize the goals set by their elders it is commonly understood that the will was either insufficient or was confused and addled. Others can assist in trying to clarify purpose and to define the proper standards of behavior. The individual alone, however, is responsible for having the necessary willpower.

Thus there is a peculiar interrelationship between efficacy in action, moral behavior, which represents the basic content of all socialization, and willpower, which is the unique quality of the individual. This triad occupies a central place in the political culture. Traditionally it appeared in the basic assumption that there was an automatic connection between the morality of rulers, the character of their will and desire, and the actual effectiveness of their rule. In the Communist culture it appears in the inordinate emphasis that Mao places on voluntarism, on the ability of the spirit to overcome all obstacles to ensure effectiveness, and on the importance of correct behavior and outlook among the cadres in guaranteeing the effective performance of the entire political and economic system.[5]

The manner in which the socialization process uniquely links efficacy, morality, and willpower suggests the basic psychological mechanism by which aggression is repressed

[5] The interrelationship of efficacy, morality, and willpower is also tied to the importance of self-discipline and the need for external authority in the personality. The oral-dependent character of the personality provides the basis for the fear that overindulgence is a real danger whenever anyone is in a position to provide unlimited oral gratification. There is a well-based expectation in the culture that if hard-working and industrious people become rich, it is they and not necessarily their children who will quickly seek to recapture the pleasures of their dependency in infancy and thus dissipate the family fortune. Chinese folklore is full of stories of the ups and downs of family fortunes that are governed entirely by vacillations between frugality and dissipation. If self-discipline is compromised by the seductive pleasures of dependency and oral gratification, then control will disappear and all can be lost. The extent to which the Chinese display oral dependency and oral aggressiveness has been documented by Richard H. Solomon, "The Chinese Revolution and the Politics of Dependency," Ph.D. dissertation, Department of Political Science, Massachusetts Institute of Technology, 1966. See also Warner Muensterberger, "Orality and Dependence: Characteristics of Southern Chinese," *Psycholoanalysis and the Social Sciences, 3* (1951), 37–69.

and becomes the powerful sublimated force providing energy for the quest for acceptance. The separation of willfulness from willpower, the divorce of emotion from action, and the acceptance of authority all converge to ensure that the individual will hold in check any feelings of aggression.

Infinite Willpower but Finite Energy

In the modernization of China the relationship between efficacy, morality, and willpower has been critical in attracting people to the tasks necessary to the building of this new society. With the Communists these tasks have been recognized explicitly in the call for physical exertion. Thus in discussing the pattern of action and inertia in the political culture it is appropriate for us to explore briefly Chinese sentiments about human energy. This is particularly relevant for an understanding of the problems of the Peking government because there have been so many reports that the people have been exhausted and are now apathetic as a result of the demands made upon their energies.

In noting the traditional antipathy toward youthful laziness we observed that the ideals for behavior were diligence and purposeful action, but this did not imply any glorification of physical exertion. The mandarin abhorred all forms of physical exertion, and in his dress and in the cultivation of long fingernails sought to demonstrate in every possible way that he did not have to work with his hands. It is, therefore, unnecessary for us to elaborate on the powerful class feelings that the Chinese had about the demeaning character of physical labor. The Communists, of course, have been struggling valiantly to break down these "feudal" views about manual labor, but, if the attitudes of refugees are any guide, they still have a long way to go.

For our purposes, however, it is significant that beneath these obvious class attitudes the Chinese have deeper psychological feelings about the nature of human energy which are probably more firmly ingrained. Specifically, they have traditionally taken the view that the energy at the disposal of an individual was finite, that it could be wasted, and that it could not readily be replenished. Wisdom in life involved knowing the precise pace at which one could properly expend one's exhaustible supply of energy. Almost entirely missing in the traditional culture was the idea that one could easily replenish or expand one's resources of strength, and above all, there was little feeling for the concept of expending energy to build up one's strength.

Thus, danger lay at the two extremes of laziness and overexertion, while health and general well-being were identified with the golden mean. To the extent that parents were in a position to do so, they were inclined to err on the side of overprotecting their children from the dangers of exertion even more than from those of laziness. For children to dissipate their strength and risk exhausting their bodies was seen as dangerously unfilial and a possible threat to family continuity.

To a large degree these attitudes can be traced to beliefs about the weakening effect on men of sexual intercourse. The Chinese have a concept of limited virility. Young men need to be cautioned against more than the minimum necessary sexual activity, otherwise their power will not last into the later years. The concept of impotency is almost entirely associated with the effects of old age and the consequences of earlier excesses. In sex as in life man has only so much initial energy, and any reckless expending of it will lead to tragic consequences.

Socially these concerns about the limits of energy were expressed in the extraordinarily rigid standards or norms of acceptable work loads for almost every occupation. Men in different types of jobs should properly be called upon to work only at certain levels of intensity. The lower the occupation, of course, the higher the norms; this conforms with the beliefs that the lower the occupation the less life is valued and the more physically demanding the job the shorter the life expectancy.

Thus each occupation had its proper tempo, and any demands to exceed the accepted tempo were resisted strongly. For example, in the field of transportation Chinese muleteers and camel train drivers set quotas for the distances to be traveled each day, and any attempt to urge upon them greater distances was stoutly resisted even if accompanied by the offer of significantly higher pay. When new occupations or industries were introduced, it was possible to establish high norms of work, and the Chinese accepted the concept of pay for piece work; but once the standards were established there tended to be strong resistance to any efforts to raise the daily quotas.

There was thus a delicate balance between views about the potency of willpower and anxieties about the limits of energy. As long as the manifestation of willpower called only for diligence, purposefulness, and disciplined behavior, and not great exertion of physical energy, there was no problem. Scholars, mandarins, and the upper classes could demonstrate their proper possession of willpower while following sedentary pursuits.[6] Lower-class people, on the other hand, could demonstrate the dangers inherent in the finite character of human energy. There was a form of division of anxieties in traditional China that complemented the division of labor. The upper classes could be concerned with the problem of willpower and the lower classes with that of energy, and each could in some degree appreciate and respect the others' problem. Here ideology and class ethos matched well, with

[6] It is, however, noteworthy that Chinese parents had little sense of placing limits on their children's need to study long and hard, and the dangers of physical overexertion were in no way matched by fear of the dangers of mental overwork. To falter mentally was a sign of inadequate willpower and not of energy. At the same time, the Chinese did see danger to the will in excessive contemplation, which, however, was quite a different thing from studying, for in contemplation there was no telling where the mind might wander, while in studying there was complete discipline and usually rote memorization.

Confucianism and its concern for willpower belonging to the upper classes and Taoism and its concern for energy with the lower classes.

This distinction according to class also appeared in the socialization process. The rich were generally overindulgent with their young, making little or no demands upon their physical energies and encouraging levels of laziness that could not be tolerated by the poor. The rich could so act, however, because they were confident that all was right as long as their sons displayed willpower and were headstrong, and even haughty, toward subordinates.

In modern China, however, and particularly under the Communists, the problem has become intensified because the concepts of willpower and energy can no longer be so readily separated. The demands of the Peking rulers for action and their assertions of the primacy of the human spirit call for high levels of physical exertion. The most dramatic characteristic of Communist rule has been the ability of the regime to mount tremendous campaigns and drives that have called for massive outpourings of energy. The climax of such demands for the popular expenditure of energies came with the Great Leap, but the Communists still have almost unlimited confidence in the powers of enthusiasm.

It is significant that one emotion-laden issue of modernization has been the interest of the youth in physical education. Young Chinese in the early decades of the century found enough tension in mere physical exertion to be enthusiastic about calisthenics and mass drills, and they did not have to carry their experiments with what their parents considered "sins" to the extent of indulging in competitive sports that might bring either bodily contact or actual exhaustion. Numerous Chinese were inclined to express their rebellion against the old China by taking up an interest in physical education. One of Mao Tse-tung's first articles was entitled "A Study of Physical Education"; and Chu Teh horrified his family by seeking a degree in physical education.[7] It is also significant that young Chinese so readily related physical education to the martial spirit and feelings of aggression. The Communists have merely been following the modern trend in emphasizing mass exercise and the sense of collective identity that the Chinese seem so able to realize from noncompetitive physical exertion.

Insofar as the Communists have stressed the importance of desire and willpower, of enthusiasm and purposefulness,

[7] Stuart R. Schram has translated Mao's interesting article into French in Mao Ze-dong, *Une étude de l'éducation physique* (La Haye-Paris: Mouton, 1962); and has translated excerpts into English in Stuart R. Schram, ed., *The Political Thoughts of Mao Tse-tung* (New York: Frederick A. Praeger, 1963).

Since this article, which first appeared in *Hsin Ch'ing-nien* in April 1917, is so revealing of Mao's pre-Leninist views and also so relevant for many of the points in our analysis, it is appropriate to quote here excerpts from Schram's English translation. (The italics appeared in Mao's original.)

Our nation is wanting in strength. The military spirit has not been encouraged. The physical condition of the population deteriorates daily. This is an extremely disturbing phenomenon. . . .

If we wish to make physical education effective, we must influence people's subjective attitudes and stimulate them to become conscious of physical education. . . .

. . . When one's decision is made in his heart, then all parts of the body obey its orders. Fortune and misfortune are of our own seeking. "I wish to be virtuous and lo, virtue is at hand." [From the Confucian *Analects*] How much more this is true of physical education! If we do not have the will to act, then even though the exterior and the objective are perfect, they still cannot benefit us. *Hence, when we speak of physical education we should begin with individual initiative.* . . .

Physical education not only enhances knowledge, it also harmonizes the sentiments. The power of the sentiments is extremely great. . . . We often observe that the weak are enslaved by their sentiments and are incapable of mastering them. . . .

Physical education not only harmonizes the emotions, it also strengthens the will. . . . *The will is the antecedent of a man's career.* . . .

The superior man's deportment is cultivated and agreeable, but one cannot say this about exercise. Exercise should be savage and rude. . . .

There are three things to which we must pay attention in exercise: (1) perseverance, (2) concentration of all our strength, (3) that it be savage and rude. . . .

147

they have conformed to traditional expectations about intelligent and reasonable behavior. But with the inordinate demands that they have made on will and intentions they have inevitably extended their claims into the area of physical exertion; and thus they have had to challenge the traditional belief in the exhaustibility of human energy. I would hypothesize that in their taxing campaigns, such as the Great Leap, the magnitude of the party's call for action had to be inordinately large to overcome the traditional beliefs. I would further suggest that much of the frantic excitement of such efforts came precisely from the fact that the people sensed that they would be doing something dangerous and traumatic.

The corollary to the concern about undue expenditure of energy is the sensitivity to tiredness. The Chinese have a vivid understanding of all the symptoms of tiredness, a great concern for rest, and deep anxiety about the state of exhaustion. Politically it is striking how much direct and indirect reference has been made to the sensation of tiredness ever since the excesses of the Great Leap. The damaging effects of the Great Leap involved the waste of scarce material resources and the destruction of the Communist myth of magical solutions to China's problems, but the people themselves continue to mention the effects of exhaustion even years after the event. It seems that the decision makers have become more rather than less sensitive to the border line between willpower and the exhaustion of energy.

The Dangers of Introspection but the Importance of Feelings of Well-being

The ambivalent approach to the expenditure of physical energy and the contrasting sentiments about willpower and energy help to establish the general considerations that govern the relationship between emotion and action. They also point to some even more complex cultural attitudes that

148

lie at the basis of the Chinese style of regulating the relationship between the inner self and manifest behavior. From our discussion it should be apparent that the Chinese have strong concerns about the importance of the inner person. Yet, as we have also observed, they strive to separate passion from action and to discipline their emotions out of existence. This suggests another central ambivalence that greatly affects the character of action.

On the one hand, the Chinese have a very strong feeling for the relationship between inner, essentially psychic, well-being and general physical well-being. On the other hand, they have an equally strong concern for the control of emotions, and this concern produces a fundamental antipathy toward extensive introspection. Their ambivalence creates considerable tension, which in turn strengthens both the anxieties about introspection and the concern with emotions. This tension is often resolved by being highly sensitive to the reality of emotions, in the self as well as in others, while not examining deeply what lies behind them. The inner self is thus important but it should not be examined too directly. Above all, it is assumed that the cause of emotions lies outside the individual.

In many dimensions of Chinese culture we find this strange appreciation of the importance of emotions but the denial of the propriety of detailed inner self-examination. Literature, for example, focuses on actions and emotional responses, not upon the subjective realm. Objective reality is explicitly discussed, and often in great detail, but the subjective is at best alluded to only in passing.

In concentrating so strongly on the objective bases for emotions the Chinese culture differs noticeably from its neighbors in Asia. The Japanese, from the time of the *Tales of Genji* to the present-day psychological novelists, have had a much greater fascination with the inner dynamics of human sentiments and conflicts. Indian culture is rich in the treatment of the subjective realms, and in Southeast Asia both

Indonesians and the Burmese are extremely sensitive to the nuances of their inner worlds.[8]

In modern times, the Chinese have proved to be singularly uninterested in psychiatry and, especially, in psychoanalysis. Only a handful of Chinese have ever been trained in psychiatry, and, as far as it has been possible to determine, not a single Chinese has ever tried to practice psychoanalysis in a Chinese culture area.

When the Chinese must deal directly with emotions, their approach is usually strangely wooden and even mechanistic. Emotions tend to be seen as absolute states with only gross gradations. More important, the emotions are thought to have almost physical characteristics and to be a prime determinant of people's physical health.

This is most dramatically illustrated by the theories of traditional Chinese medicine, which the Communists are sanctioning and supporting at the present time. At the risk of seeming to digress from the strict course of our analysis we shall examine rather extensively some key features of Chinese medical doctrines, particularly those that have received the Communist stamp of approval. We shall do so partly because these doctrines help to explain attitudes about the relationship between action and subjective consideration, partly because they provide striking illustrations of Chinese patterns of reasoning, partly because they remind us that contemporary China, like all transitional societies, abounds in anomalies of old and new knowledge and that it is peculiarly difficult to study the patterns of thought of people who are simultaneously exploring nuclear power and accepting prescientific theories of medicine.[9]

[8] For an examination of the importance of the subjective in Indonesian culture see Clifford Geertz, *The Religion of Java* (New York: The Free Press of Glencoe, 1960); for Burma, see Lucian W. Pye, *Politics, Personality, and Nation Building* (New Haven, Conn.: Yale University Press, 1962), Chapter 14.

[9] The fate of Chinese medicine in the modern world is a fascinating subject, for it is the only body of quasi-scientific knowledge from a

At the center of Chinese medical thinking are the three key concepts of *ch'in,* the inner substance that is the material base of physical energy, *ch'i,* the gas or air that is both general to the body and specific to the separate vital organs, and *sung,* the spirit that governs the complexion and general appearance of well-being. To illuminate these concepts, as well as the close relationship the Chinese see between emotion and physical well-being, it is useful to quote fairly extensively from *A General Introduction to Chinese Medicine,* which the Peking regime published in 1958 as their main textbook in the field of approved traditional medicine.[10] We may begin with a summary statement of the interrelationship of the three concepts:

> The ancients regarded *ch'in, ch'i,* and *sung* as the three treasures of human life. The relationship among them is intimate. *Ch'in* originates from the kidneys' assimilation of watery energy; this is the material base of human activity. *Ch'i* originates from the combination of *ch'in,* or the watery energy's essence, and the air breathed in; this is the biological function of human life. Thus we see the intimate relationship between *ch'in* and *ch'i. Ch'in* gives birth to *ch'i,* and the manifestation of *ch'i* is *sung.* That is why when one's *ch'in* is full, his *sung* must be

traditional culture that has been able in any degree to maintain its claims to technical competence in the face of Western scientific knowledge.

Initially Chinese reformers, in championing the introduction of modern and scientific Western knowledge, attacked Chinese medicine as unscientific and as a compound of superstitions. Later, however, as some Chinese herbs and other treatments were found to be efficacious, and as the modernists became more anxious to root some of their identity in features of the culture, the reformers proposed that traditional medicine should be examined scientifically and that whatever passed the test should be incorporated into general modern medicine.

The amazing position of the Chinese Communists has been to state that it is improper to pick and choose among features of traditional medicine; in accepting any part of traditional medicine it is essential to accept the entire system, including the strange theories we are about to discuss.

[10] *Chung-yi-hsüeh kai-lun* (A General Introduction to Chinese Medicine), compiled by the *Nan-ching Chung-yi hsüeh-yüan* (Nanking Chinese Medicine Academy) (Peking: 1958).

strong too. On the other hand, weak *sung* reflects insufficient *ch'in*. Because of their chain connection, excessive consumption of *ch'in* weakens the birth of *ch'i*, excessive harming of *ch'i* also weakens the transformation of *ch'in* [into *ch'i*], and all will contribute to the sagging of *sung*. Though *sung* (spirit) originates from the combination of *ch'in* and *ch'i* excessive *sung* activities will hurt both *ch'in* and *ch'i* and then the body.[11]

Although it would be hard to explain the nature of Chinese logic and causality, we can get a slightly better understanding of the process from the separate definitions of the three kinds of spirits. *Ch'in* is apparently related to what happens to food and its transference into energy, and it is associated most directly to the kidneys and the marrow of bones. The essential point is that *ch'in* becomes *ch'i*, which is vitality or energy of both a general and a specific nature as it is related to the particular *ch'i* of each vital organ. Our Communist textbook tells us that the general *ch'i*, which means gas or air and also vitality or energy, is of two natures:

> *Sun Wen* [an ancient text on Chinese medicine] says:
> "The heavenly *ch'i* comes through the lungs, the earthly *ch'i* comes through the throat." This means that human *ch'i* is taken into the throat through eating. *Lin Chu* [another ancient text] says: "The true *ch'i* is made of the *ch'i* from the heaven and the earth that fills the body." So the content of "true *ch'i*" is the combination of earthly and heavenly *ch'i*'s whose functions are to cultivate and fill the body with energy.[12]

The problem of terminology is greatly confused by the employment of a somewhat similar, but to the Western mind logically different, combination of the earthly or material and the heavenly or gaseous elements to comprise the energy of the various organs of the body; thus every inner part of the body (the material) has its own *ch'i* (gas), so that there is blood air or gas (*hsüeh ch'i*), kidney air (*sun ch'i*), heart air (*hsin ch'i*), and so forth. Each of these is in turn con-

[11] *Ibid.*, p. 71.
[12] *Ibid.*, p. 64.

nected to a particular manifestation of *sung,* which covers both the complexion and attitudes of well-being.

> *Sung* is the synthesis and realization of one's mental state, one's consciousness; and all other activities of being alive. It is an abstract term. *Sung* just as life, originates from the combination of parents' blood. When the embryo is being formed, the spirit of *sung* is also cultivated. *Lin Chu says* . . . two *ch'ins* entangle and *sung* is made.[13]

When all the sub-*ch'is* are in equilibrium and there is adequate, but not too much, general *ch'i,* we have health. When the equilibrium is disturbed, sickness follows, but the cause of disease is specifically related to particular emotions. Again our textbook makes this most explicit:

> The inner causes of diseases consist of seven types of emotion. The seven types are gladness, anger, worry, contemplation, sadness, fear, and shock. They are the results of human contacts with the outside world. They are the materialization of human mentality, they vary according to different objects and environments. For example, when a baby is born he knows nothing but crying. After he gets a little older, he begins to smile when he is glad and he will suffer shock if he suddenly hears a loud noise. After he becomes an adult his contact with objective events expands and he begins to contemplate because of either nostalgia or idealizing the future. And if he loses touch with reality he cannot achieve his goals, and so he worries.[14] When worry is carried one step forward, it becomes sadness. When one worries about getting and losing things, one fears. Living within the universe, a human being is bound to have contacts with the surrounding environment. One's mind changes continuously. But if the changes are within regulated bounds, then no harm is done. But if one overacts, then the mind is excited, and this will affect one's physical condition and the result will be sickness. *Su Wen* says: When one is angry, *ch'i* rises up. When one is glad, *ch'i* relaxes. When one is sad,

---

[13] *Ibid.,* p. 70.
[14] We are compelled to note this typically Chinese statement in which it is taken as self-evident that realism is the basis for effective action and that failure to be effective is the source of human worry and anxiety.

ch'i dissipates. When one is frightened, *ch'i* descends. When one is shocked, *ch'i* is confused. When one contemplates, *ch'i* is entangled. *Yin Yang Hsiang Ta Lun* [*On the Manifestations of the Yin and Yang*] also mentions that "gladness hurts the heart," "anger hurts the liver," "contemplation hurts the kidneys." All these speak of the effects of the seven types of emotions on the human body. Though the seven types of emotions can hurt the eleven viscera [heart, heart cyst, liver, spleen, lungs, kidney, gall, stomach, bowels, bladder, thorax] and cause sickness, they hurt the heart inevitably because the heart is the basis of all the viscera. *Lin Chu* says: "Sadness and worry cause disturbance of the heart. When the heart is disturbed, all the eleven viscera are disturbed." [15]

We cannot here examine all the complex interrelationships that the Chinese recognize among the states of emotions, physical well-being, and human energy. We can only illustrate these relationships by quoting the text on three of the seven recognized emotions.

Anger: Those whose blood and *ch'i* are rich will burst into anger when they encounter an unreasonable thing. *Su Wen* says, "The rising up of *ch'i* and blood causes anger." It also says: "When there is a surplus of blood, anger results." This means that those whose blood and *ch'i* are rich will easily become angry. On the other hand, violent anger will also exhaust the blood. Therefore, *Su Wen* says: "violent anger hurts the *yin*." [16] When the *yin* blood is consumed too much, naturally the liver fire becomes stronger. Hence one spark will cause violent anger. But anger can also be caused by other inner parts of the body. For example, Chang Chin-Yueh said, "Originally anger comes from the liver. But it is said that the gall can also cause anger because the liver is related to the gall. So when the *ch'i* of the liver is strong, the gall follows in strength." [17]

Worry: Worry is the stagnation of one's emotions and will. If one's worry is excessive, the *ch'i* will be affected. *Lin Chu* says: "worry means that one's *ch'i* is blocked." *Ch'i* is based on the

[15] *Ibid.*, pp. 125–126.
[16] In Chinese metaphysics blood is said to belong to the element of *yin*.
[17] *Ibid.*, p. 126.

lungs. So when *ch'i* is blocked, the lung is also affected, and hurt. So *Su Wen* says: "Worry hurts the lungs." But worry can also hurt the spleen. . . . Chang Chin-yueh said: "Worry originates in the lungs. The reason for the spleen's being also hurt is because when you hurt the mother you also hurt the son." [18]

Gladness: Gladness is a reflection of one's happiness. When one is glad, the *ch'i* relaxes. This is the sign of health. But if gladness is excessive, the *ch'i* in one's heart proceeds from relaxation to dissipation. Thus *Lin Chu* says: "When glad, one's *sung ch'i* dissipates and the body loses its vital forces, and one no longer has any purpose." [19]

The Denial of the Subjective and the Stress on the Objective

This has been a rather long excursion into the esoteric and bizarre world of Chinese medicine, but hopefully it has been useful in giving us an appreciation of the basic beliefs about the nature of emotions. We can now see that the Chinese place emphasis on the reality of emotions but do not examine them introspectively. By giving them such clearly substantive and mechanistic qualities the Chinese are still employing a form of defense mechanism to avoid a full confrontation; they accept the reality of emotions by attributing them to the outside environment, and thus their concern tends to make them look outward rather than inward.

In this sense the Chinese are truly "realists." Even though they have great concern about the importance of willpower, the preciousness of human energy, and the physical nature of emotions, they strive to deny the importance of any separate subjective world that might have its own autonomous dynamics capable of controlling the individual's behavior. Reality is to the Chinese the objective, and particularly the social, environment. We could go on to examine how this view is reflected in their approach to religion, but here we

[18] *Ibid.*, p. 127.
[19] *Ibid.*, p. 127.

need point out only that the Chinese have been less inclined, particularly compared with other Eastern peoples, to look for and expect mystical experiences in religion. Their approach is "secular," rather pragmatic, and based upon calculations about the significance of rituals for the preservation of social order. In short, the Chinese cannot even be atheists with vigor because if they were they would create the insecurity and dangers of social disorder.

In placing the cause of emotions entirely outside of the self the Chinese give extraordinary importance to what they take as the social realities of their situations. Their perception of reality is heavily influenced by this bias, and as a consequence they tend to have exaggerated ideas about how the environment can influence and control them. As realists and as people who look to the objective world, the Chinese are peculiarly sensitive to all the dangers and threats to the self that can lie in the environment.

This has meant that even though the Chinese have been far less encumbered by otherworldly and mystical inhibitions than any other Asian peoples in becoming a part of the modern world, they have established a somewhat different, but functionally equivalent, set of inhibitions. They have tended to attach so much importance to "reality" that they have felt powerless to act against it. Also, and even more important, they have known that if their emotions were aroused, their condition could not have been self-induced but had to be the work of others. The individual should never properly seek self-stimulation, and, therefore, if one does feel the reality of one's emotions, the respectable assumption is that others have in fact been doing something to the self. In this manner the practice of denying the subjective and stressing the objective has the strange consequence of producing hypersensitive "realists," manifesting seemingly paranoid behavior but with a great capacity for action whenever the cues are well defined.

156

Avoiding Choices and Denying Responsibilities by Perceiving No Alternatives

This brings us to a frequently observed feature of Chinese culture: the degree to which behavior is oriented to surrounding circumstances. Francis L. K. Hsu has gone the furthest of any anthropologist in elaborating the extent to which Chinese behavior is "situation oriented" in the sense that the child is taught from early years to regulate his actions according to what is assumed to be objective social reality.[20] The Chinese are taught to take the cues for their behavior from an unemotional reading of the circumstances and they are encouraged to discount their own internal sentiments and not allow themselves to be blinded by emotions.

It may be significant that among a group of Chinese who were formerly members of the Malayan Communist Party it was precisely these features of behavior that made them quite different from former members of the American, British, French, and Italian Communist parties.[21] It was discovered, for example, that the Chinese adamantly rejected any suggestion that they might have been emotionally influenced by the propaganda appeals of the party. They took the very suggestion as an affront to their dignity as human beings. In contrast, the American and European ex-Communists were quite ready to admit that they had been emotionally affected by the appeals of the party, and indeed often took pride in the fact that they had "acted without

[20] See his *Americans and Chinese: Two Ways of Life* (New York: Abelard-Schuman, 1953); *Under the Ancestor's Shadow* (New York: Columbia University Press, 1948); and *Clan, Caste and Club* (Princeton, N.J.: Van Nostrand, 1963).

[21] The Malayan Chinese data are reported in my *Guerrilla Communism in Malaya* (Princeton, N.J.: Princeton University Press, 1956); and the American and European data appear in Gabriel A. Almond, *The Appeals of Communism* (Princeton, N.J.: Princeton University Press, 1954).

calculations" and in response only to their deep inner feelings. Vulnerability to sentiment has a degree of respectability, or at least acceptability, in Western cultures but appears to be only degrading to the Chinese.

On the other hand, most of the Chinese in the Malayan Communist Party suggested that the logic of the situation, or circumstances in general, had left them with no option but to do what they had. They constantly declared that they had had no choice, that they had had to accept reality, and that anyone in their circumstances would have done the same. In contrast, the Americans and Europeans took pride in being masters of their fate, and they would probably have considered the Chinese respondents as degradingly opportunistic. To the Westerner, man should have the inner resources to stand up against mere circumstance, while to the Chinese, the quality of man is a common capacity to share a rational appreciation of reality.

In part, acceptance of the dictates of circumstance is no more than the typical response of tradition-oriented peoples. That is to say, in the more stable order of traditional China individuals might expect that all social situations could be foreseen and that for each situation there would be a correct mode of behavior. Socialization stressed the learning of manners and customs that represented ritualistic ways of coping with relatively standardized situations. Security lay in knowing the correct formulas of social behavior.

This search for ritualized behavior is closely related to the compulsive concern for order and the anxieties about disorder and unpredictability. As we have already observed, these anxieties in the Chinese culture appear to encourage a very constricted view of reality and a great capacity to ignore everything that may threaten the sense of order. This means that there is a tendency to deny whenever possible the existence of choice and to suggest that the self has no alternatives. The result is a freedom from inhibitions, but not in the direction of spontaneity. Without the burden of having to make constant choices, the individual can freely seek security through disciplined, and what may seem to be almost instinctive, responses to socially given cues.

The expectation that there is probably only one correct response in any situation is consistent with the belief that one is free only when one has learned the correct answer. This, of course, is also the spirit of communism.

The sum effect of this analysis is to suggest that action is relatively easy in the Chinese culture because responsibility is not closely linked to choice but rather to the manner of behavior. The individual need not be held personally accountable for the consequences of all his actions; what he can be responsible for is knowing how he ought to act in recognized situations and then effectively doing precisely that. Confronted with any kind of uncertainty or complexity, the individual tends to reduce the problem to manageable proportions by ignoring the disturbing aspects of reality and concentrating on what is familiar, and for which there are recognized responses, and then all energy can be poured into action.

In interpersonal relations, if the individual feels that he is in a dependent relationship, and thus absolved of responsibility, he is freed of inhibitions and capable of compulsive action. The role of the subordinate is always that of the activist. This was true, as we have already noted, in the contrasting tempo of movement of low and high officials in traditional Chinese politics. And it is still found in the manner in which the Communist cadres seek vigorously to carry out national decisions.

Implications for the Political Culture

This pattern of interrelationships between capacity for action and protection from anxieties about responsibility suggests that the excesses of the last few years, such as those of the Great Leap, the Cultural Revolution, and the numerous mass campaigns and propaganda drives involved more than just the decisions of a few national leaders. Although fanaticism may have characterized the leaders of the Long March generation, they could not possibly have instilled a comparably fanatical style on the great masses of the Chinese people. Nor could they have coerced them into such extremes of behavior, even though coercion is exceedingly important in Chinese totalitarianism. There had to be something in the culture that encouraged such widespread single-mindedness, and this something seems to have been the basic capacity of the Chinese to escape into actions that are uncompromised by doubts.

Similiarly, even if the top rulers were to learn from experience and were to change some of their ways, compulsive behavior might still characterize much of public life. The excesses of the system have been less related to patterns of decision making at the highest levels than to a style of avoiding choices and responsibilities among subordinates.

The basic expectation of the subordinate is that his conduct will be appropriate, correct, and rewarding if he adheres to the proper rituals and forms and responds to all commands with alacrity. His focus is always on the correctness of his actions in the smallest details, and his assumption is that if he so acts in the small issues, then the larger ones will be taken care of automatically. This is the same as the socialization process, in which the child learns to expect security and the satisfactory realization of his ultimate destiny if he is diligent and conscientious about the details of manners and customs. It is this capacity to find purpose and meaning in the single act or the routine procedure and not in the raising of larger issues about the propriety of larger goals that gives the appearances of fanaticism: Energies are poured into actions for which the ultimate purpose has been forgotten or never really understood.

We have suggested that the dynamics of such behavior are associated largely with subordinate roles, yet in the

160

Communist political culture there has been a strange shrink-
age in the numbers of the politically responsible and an ex-
pansion of those who feel that they are free to act without
serious concern for the consequences. This is partly because of the Communist fetish that identifies all national
decisions as coming from the spontaneous demands of the
masses and partly because of the leaders' wish not to appear
as the isolated elite that they are. Even relatively high-ranking
officials can abandon a posture of responsibility and seek
compulsively to carry out the national policies with the same
single-mindedness as everyone else. With officials stumbling
over themselves to be identified with the people, there is
no one left to worry about the utility of presumably correct
decisions. Responsibility is abdicated to the spirit of action.

Equally important, however, is the role of ideology in
forecasting history and thus relieving the decision maker of
anxieties about the consequences of his actions. The more
determined history appears, the freer the individual is of
responsibility for his decisions. In Communist China both
subordinates and decision makers are in search of formulas
that will leave them free to act. It is extremely significant
that the Russian Communists have been less the prisoners
of this form of ideological determinism because they have
had a profound sensitivity for the uncertainty of the short
run. For the Russians, even though ultimate history was
predictable, all effort has had to be poured into mastery of
the unpredictable short run. The Chinese Communists do
not seem to have any such uncertainty about the short run;
rather, as we have seen, their propensity is to jump to conclusions and to go directly from initiation to consummation.

There are also certain pragmatic reasons inherent in the
operations of the Communist system that contribute toward
excess in action. Subordinate cadres, for example, have
learned that it is always safer to err on the side of excessive
enthusiasm than to be accused of dragging their feet. Cadres
are wise enough in the workings of communism to ap-

preciate that although those who establish the party line may be subsequently charged with "adventurism" and "left deviation" these are not sins of the subordinate. On the other hand, any cadre can be charged with the very serious crime of being a "rightist," of having "bourgeois tendencies," and of being an "enemy of the revolution."

In the ranks of the leadership, similar tendencies contribute to the bias toward excessive action. In some of the early campaigns and drives the leaders seem to have pushed the rank and file to excesses at the initial phase and then later called for a more judicious pursuit of goals. This tactic of leadership has meant that the rank and file could be blamed for all that went wrong. Thus the "bad features" of the land reform campaigns, the Great Leap, and the Cultural Revolution that were identified later were all attributed to the excessive zeal of cadres. At the same time the very act of pulling back from an extreme policy position makes the leadership seem more reasonable, and this in turn apparently gives a degree of legitimacy to what is left of the basic policy after extremism has been officially rejected. After the public has been exposed to an extreme version of a policy, a modified, but still inherently radical, version can seem to be both more reasonable and more tolerable.

In the larger perspective of modernization, it is apparent that the Communists have been able to tap to a unique degree the Chinese potential for action. In one sense this has been a great achievement, for the energies of the people have been the most vital ingredient in all the Communist accomplishments. On the other hand, there has never been any question about the industriousness and capacity for hard work of the Chinese. In other developing societies the leadership has the problem of shaking people out of their lethargic and impotent ways. But this has not been the problem in China. Yet the Chinese leaders above all others have incessantly demanded that the people should work harder and have had, apparently, an unlimited determination to prod. In doing this, however, the Communists, just like Chinese fathers, have had little sense of imposing their own wills upon the wills of their subjects; from their faith in the role of willpower in human nature they have derived the arrogance to believe that people want to be helped to become more effective and more acceptable citizens.

Although their society has been spared the problems of lethargy and psychic paralysis, the Chinese still do have a problem of action that has become more acute with modernization and that must be resolved if they are to be more successful in all forms of development. This is the problem of relating action to creativity and of giving more scope to imagination. In time the Chinese must learn how to cope with the prospects of an increasing variety of choices, for modernization cannot be built upon actions uncompromised by doubts.

The Communist concern with maximizing compulsive behavior and with ensuring that all acts fit set patterns has tended to emphasize traditional deficiencies and has not set the stage for the spontaneity essential to effective modernization. These tendencies have given to the Communists the appearance, but not always the substance, of effective development and are present in the patterns of political organization, the subject we must turn to next.

ORGANIZATIONAL BEHAVIOR
AND THE MARTIAL SPIRIT

Although there are many perspectives from which to view the processes of modernization and political development, almost all, in the last analysis, must postulate as a fundamental element of successful development the capacity to create and maintain the complex organizations that are basic to all aspects of modern life. The power that comes from the creation of adaptive and purposeful organizations is the most decisive technological advance that distinguishes modern institutions from more traditional ones. The test of development is thus the capacity to organize in all aspects of life, whether it is the establishment of a vigorous civil bureaucracy or the creation of a system of education, whether it is the establishment of industries and distribution systems or the building of universities and research facilities.

From our analysis of their authority crisis we should expect that the Chinese would have deeply ambivalent sentiments and uniquely mixed capabilities with respect to this ultimate test of modernization. On the one hand, their concern for order and dependency upon authority would make them welcome the orderly and predictable qualities of hierarchical organizations, on the other, the intensity of human relations essential to any dynamic organization might tap their basic anxieties about aggression.

In this chapter we shall seek to explore some paradoxes about Chinese organizations and the expectations of the Chinese when they find themselves in institutional settings. We shall start by observing the ease with which they establish formal groups and how readily they seem to adapt to hierarchical arrangements. Then we shall note, however, how frustrating such arrangements often are and how frequently the spirit of organizational life is filled with bickering, hurt feelings, and sensitivity to injustices. Finally, we shall observe the basic trend of Chinese political organizations to move in the direction of the military prototype.

At the outset it is important to note that many Chinese tend to sympathize with Mao Tse-tung's basic assumption that there is a conflict between emotional commitment and routinized organizational performance. In the West it is usually assumed that the smoother and more effectively an organization performs, the higher will be the morale and the greater the spirit of commitment. Yet we find that Mao, for example, has become powerfully distrustful of both the Chinese Communist Party and the governmental bureaucracy as these two organizations have become increasingly institutionalized. For Mao, as for many Chinese, there is a basic contradiction between emotional enthusiasm and ritualized behavior, which seems to be related to the fundamental Chinese quality of the separation of emotion and action. Thus, the expectation is that ritualized or standardized behavior tends to drain away affect and emotion. Rituals are introduced so as to limit and control emotions. In the West, however, rituals are used as an effective device for appealing to emotions and reinforcing deeper sentiments. Hence, in the West there is less sense of a conflict between routinized behavior and effective emotional commitments to the performance of organizations.

Be this as it may, it is clear that in Chinese politics there has been considerable ambivalence about the relationship between organizational development and the capacity to mobilize collective efforts. At one moment the Chinese seem anxious to construct bureaucratic organizations and at the next they seem set on tearing down or ignoring what they have built up. In a sense, Chinese political organizations are in the spirit of Chinese magic. What seem to be firm and resilient institutions or movements are suddenly conjured up out of nothing, and just as suddenly they dissolve into nothing. New organizations and movements can spring into being with an instantaneous climax of enthusiasm, for the high point of excitement and loyalty for the Chinese is generally at the beginning of things. The process of erosion may then be gradual but the end is usually swift, and when all is over there are few sentimental memories. Of course many organizations do not entirely disappear; they only prove to be hollow shells where once they seemed to be of profound significance.

The imperial bureaucracy appeared even at the end of the nineteenth century to be a stolid and massive institution, possibly too given to inertia to accomplish much, yet, by the same token, too weighty a structure to disappear from history; but disappear it did in the aftermath of the rather gentle and unprovocative revolution of 1911. Then came the appearance and disappearance of warlord armies and governments, and the rise and fall of the phantom republic at the capital in Peking. After that the Kuomintang appeared as a powerful force — for good in the eyes of some and for evil in the eyes of others — but it too proved to be a hollow shell.

Once the Communists came to power they too followed the tradition by rapidly creating structures that appeared more solid than they eventually proved to be. Administrations based on regional authorities appeared and then disappeared. In almost frantic restlessness the institutions of the countryside — the mutual production teams, the lower-level cooperatives, the higher cooperatives, the production brigades, and the communes — appeared full-blown, were organized and reorganized, and then as suddenly disappeared or proved to be only paper structures. Each one of the numerous campaigns and drives — which have been the very essence of Chinese Communist rule — has called for its own forms of mass mobilization, and these have then dissolved as easily as they took shape.

Even now that the Communists have been unquestionably in control of the entire countryside for nearly two decades, there is some question about how institutionalized their government really is. Is the formal government of the Chinese People's Republic in fact capable of managing the day-to-day affairs of the society? Or do the rulers in Peking have to rule through the party apparatus and through directives and public communications to the party cadres? There is even the question of how solid the Chinese Communist Party is. Why has it been so necessary to preach the virtues of the People's Liberation Army, to rely upon the army for many tasks even before Marshal Lin Piao was picked as Mao's probable successor? Above all, how do we explain the appearance of the Red Guards, apparently organized out of nothing more than adolescent enthusiasm and thoughtlessness, who have taken over command of tasks that might be expected to fall to the party?

Elsewhere in Chinese society institutions have tended to be highly deceptive. The extended family once appeared to be an immutable force capable of obstructing all modernization; and then it proved to be shockingly fragile in resisting the advance of communism. In numerous aspects of social life the same pattern is repeated: Apparently unshakable loyalties can suddenly give way to unmalicious opportunism, and then when circumstances change, the old loyalties can be reasserted as though nothing had happened.

*A Sense of the Dramatic and
the Appreciation of Formalism*

One explanation for the speed and ease with which the Communists have created a succession of organizations is to be found in the peculiar Chinese appreciation for both dramatic and formalistic behavior. There is a strong pull in much of Chinese life toward the theatrical, and for the Chinese the essence of the theater is movement with style, flair, and discipline — that is, formalistic movement. Thus spontaneous political acts are often acts of drama in which there is a calculated concern with pretensions, and in Chinese politics people have generally been prepared to place great store on the manner and the form of actions and not just to look for substance.

The Chinese appreciation of drama and theater is reflected in many aspects of life, ranging from the central place of the theater and opera in the culture to the style and mannerisms that accompany so much of the day-to-day activities of individuals. The link with politics is even more conspicuous, for in no other political culture has use of the theater been so widespread and intensive. Strip away the dance teams, the theatrical groups, the mass parades, and the gymnastic formations, and one of the most distinctive features of the Chinese brand of communism would disappear. Even more basic is the fact that modern Chinese political history would be without much of its dynamic quality if it were not for the endless use that the leaders have made of the theatrical gesture. With the warlords there were the innumerable heroic declarations about fighting to the last man — on the eve of shameless capitulation. Both the Nationalists and the Communists have made their interminable grandiose promises that were followed by modest, if not downright humble, achievements, and both have constantly used slogans as though the mere chanting in unison of words could bring down enemies. From the May Fourth Movement through the Cultural Revolution and the Red Guards, the youth of China have not lost faith in the efficacy of demonstration.

The dramatic act is not entirely for the beholder; it is also intended to satisfy the actor. The grand displays and parades in Peking are only partly staged to impress outside viewers; on occasions, for example, when the Red Guards first appeared, foreigners were excluded from parades in Tienanmen Square. Chinese soldiers in Korea and the Chinese of the Malayan Communist Party before going into combat regularly engaged in a ritual of standing up before their fellows and boasting dramatically about how bravely they were going to fight; from those who participated we know that these were rituals in which the speakers impressed themselves more than their comrades.

In these situations we can note a connection between the sense of the theatrical and the narcissistic strand in the Chinese character which encourages their almost universal propensity to speak aloud to themselves in uninhibitedly vigorous and dramatic tones. In playing out in vivid form their unceasing psychic struggle between the virtuous but helpless self and evil and oppressive circumstances, the Chinese readily indulge in the fantasies of endless morality plays. The result is the strange spirit of adolescent heroics, breast beating, and elementary moralism that is so much a part of the Chinese political drama. Even when the political theatrics are not performed by adolescents the quality is seemingly adolescent.

The connection has been made between the sense of the theatrical and the Chinese concern with "face." Arthur Smith in the first chapter of his classic, *Chinese Characteristics,* begins his discussion of "face" by describing the Chinese dramatic instinct; he suggests that it served as a means of gaining greater respectability and prestige in the eyes of others and of protecting the self from harsh and realistic evaluations.[1] We have already noted the stress on pretensions in the political culture that has led so easily to hurt feelings.

The combination of a dramatic sense and an appreciation for formalism makes it natural for the Chinese to act as though they have established more orderly, neatly arranged, and clearly defined sets of relationships than in fact they have. Historically they unhesitatingly idealized the structures of government that supposedly existed at the dawn of their civilization, and throughout their history they have been predisposed to suggest that they have had tidy and symmetrical institutions. The dynastic histories have all tended to give a glorified picture of bureaucratic order and an exaggerated sense of formalistic precision in governmental affairs. Traditionally when the Chinese spoke about what was best in their government, when government was at its best, they invariably provided descriptions of formal bureaucracies that were almost Weberian in spirit.

Another manifestation of this basic characteristic is found in the propensity to exaggerate the element of precision in programs and policies. With the Communists this has taken the form of a love for numbers: the three-anti's and the five-anti's, the six-this's and the eight-that's, in which the urge for formalism and precision takes on the form of pseudo-distinctions.

Thus in the political culture there has always been a strong appreciation of the value of having organizations and institutions appear to be orderly, disciplined, and effective. It would be most uncommon for the Chinese to praise an organization by suggesting that it was based on informal and imprecise arrangements. No group has been too weak to pretend to being disciplined, and any party that is strong will pretend to an absolute degree of organization.

Although some of the first founders of the Chinese Com-

[1] Arthur H. Smith, *Chinese Characteristics* (New York: Fleming H. Revell, 1894).

munist Party were more attracted to the Marxian vision of history than to the Leninist concept of party organization, it is striking how quickly, thoroughly, and naturally the Chinese comrades came to accept the spirit of the completely disciplined party organization. They learned to do this first in language and more gradually in practice. To this day Chinese pretensions about the orderliness and completeness of their party organization have steadily exceeded reality. Partly because they have known so little order in public life in modern times, all Chinese governments have sought to give the appearance of being more organized than in fact they were. Even the Communist regime, which has achieved the most complete degree of control known in Chinese history, has shown this same tendency to exaggerate the precision and thoroughness of its organization.

The Primacy of Personal Relations

To understand the form and dynamics of Chinese organizations, and particularly the speed and ease with which the Chinese can create the appearances of having an organization, it is necessary to go beyond the tendency to pretension and come to an appreciation of the rich meaning that personal relations have for them. Few other cultures attach so much importance to interpersonal relations. From their formal philosophy at one extreme to their day-to-day practices at the other, the Chinese have steadfastly emphasized the problems of getting along with each other and of managing human relationships. The definition of one's "situation" or "circumstances" is invariably the particular set of human relationships in which an individual finds himself at the moment. There is thus a solid sense of reality in personal relationships that the Chinese tend to assume is apparent to everyone. Relationships form a powerful web that holds a person in place and gives him a basic orientation in life.

At the same time the attitude of the Chinese seems to

171

make them peculiarly insensitive to the extent that human relationships are a delicate or fragile matter. Historically theirs was a culture that could oddly value personal associations without stressing empathy and the need to appreciate the inner feelings of others. There is a solid and "objective" quality to human relationships that permits the identification of a wide range of gradations and even complexities but not of subtle hidden sentiments. Although the critical axis in classifying relationships is that which runs from friend to foe, and the Chinese greatly stress the value of a friend, they are capable of stripping affect completely from their characterization of relationships. Moreover, they tend to employ an exceedingly concrete and unemotional vocabulary in describing them. They can talk quite candidly and objectively about their particular sets of associations.

There is thus a high degree of propriety in Chinese culture in calculating the value of particular relationships and in describing them in terms of reliability and steadfastness. The measure of friendship does not have to be purely psychic satisfaction; it can be seen quite openly in material terms.

This primacy of personal relations is relevant for the building of political organizations, because the Chinese, by being so quick to attach significance and to give substantial form and structure to any set of human relationships in which they are involved, are uniquely capable of making any set of extended human contacts appear as a potential if not an actual organization.

There has, in a sense, been a caricaturing of role theory; in any situation the Chinese instantly appreciate that there are roles to be played, and they are usually prepared to throw themselves into the playing of whatever role is assigned to them.

Whenever groups of Chinese are brought together they seem quickly to form themselves into structural organizations. In their overseas communities the Chinese have tended to sort themselves into their various associations, their *huis* and their *tongs*. It is entirely consistent with their culture that the Chinese prisoners of war in Korea did not become the apathetic mass of demoralized individuals that prisoners usually are, but they quickly and almost spontaneously became intensely organized political groups; leaders emerged overnight and the vast majority soon formed themselves into solid hierarchical structures.

What we are hypothesizing, therefore, is that in Chinese culture there is a spontaneous tendency toward organization building. The propensity to appreciate the concept and spirit of social roles means that relationships once established tend to take on a formal quality, and even the most personal relationships have a strange impersonality about them. The result is the distinctive Chinese blend of affect and impersonality, a denial of the importance of expressing emotion and yet a placing of great emphasis upon the sentiments of human relationships. For example, the Chinese tend to treat in a most impersonal and highly formalistic fashion the relationships within the family circle, which in Western and most other cultures are expected to be extremely intimate and intensely charged with emotion. Here again they highly prize subtlety in calculating and manipulating personal associations and yet have little sensitivity for the subtleties in people's emotional reactions. On the other hand, relationships that are customarily seen as more formal and impersonal in other cultures, such as those between employee and employer, or teacher and student, can easily become highly infused with affect and the norms of friendship. Affect and emotion, however, only follow the lines of direct personal associations and are not easily related to abstractions.

Personal relationships are also important for Chinese political behavior because they are accepted as providing the focal point for most of the cause-and-effect relationships in society. The Chinese tend to see the manipulation of human relationships as the natural and normal approach for accomplishing most things in life. This also means that by perceiving society

173

as a web of human relationships and associations the Chinese are highly alert to the importance of being skilled in manipulation. Precisely because personal relations bulk so large there is a tendency to exaggerate all that can be accomplished through the management of such relationships and to undervalue the potency of impersonal policies or programs. As a consequence, any particular pattern of personal relationships tends to become an organization that can properly be utilized in a purposeful manner.

All of this is to say that the Chinese tend more than is common among most transitional people to think and act in essentially organizational terms. In many other societies the process of modernization has been greatly impeded because people for one reason or another resist or are basically incapable of acting in ways consistent with the building of large organizations. The Chinese also have their problems with maintaining trust and avoiding damaged feelings within any kind of formal organization, but they readily take to and expect a great deal of any organization because of all that they tend to expect from personal association.

The Search for Security as the Motivation for Building Organizations

There is more, however, to the Chinese capacity for political institution building; there is also their compulsive need to avoid disorder and confusion, to seek predictability and the comforts of dependency, and to accept the importance of authority. Their craving for order, which has been intensified by the disruptions of social life in modern times, has seemingly made them anxious to seek out any acceptable basis for orderly human relationships. Thus the restless, driving search of modern Chinese for personal security has frequently been the motive force behind their marked desire to belong to stable and protecting groups. This is the drive that has been mobilized in the creation of organizations —

174

and it is also the source of so much disillusionment with politics when the search for security proves ineffectual.

History has taught the Chinese that politics is inherently dangerous, something to be avoided by timid people, but also potentially bountiful. In modern times there has always been high personal risk in active political participation — yet also the possibility of breathtaking rewards. This sense of risk has tended to make those who have ventured to enter politics expect and demand substantial rewards, which frequently have been material but also psychological. The fact that politics can be dangerous and that prudent people should seek to avoid involvement as much as possible has given a degree of legitimacy to the use of politics for personal gratification.

Before the Communists, it was widely expected and generally accepted that this search for security would customarily involve material benefits. Now, under the Communists, material rewards are officially frowned upon and are therefore more muted, more subtle. Instead the search is more explicitly psychological; people strive for group acceptance, seek unashamedly to be admired and respected by others, and hope that power and status will give security. The puritan spirit of the Communists has not reduced in the slightest the need for achievement; on the contrary, the denial of the propriety of being materially acquisitive has only intensified the drive to obtain success and recognition by being well accepted by those in high positions.

Thus we see that the predispositions already observed in this study — the propensity to fear disorder and to seek predictability, the drive for conformity and the comfort of well-defined norms, the great capacity for energetic activities and the desire to avoid the risks of personal responsibility in decision making, the belief in hierarchic authority and the fears about conflicting authorities — all combine to make the Chinese enthusiastic and effective participants in organizations that are hierarchic in form.

175

If group norms are reasonably clear and the system of rewards and punishments well defined, the stage is set for the Chinese to perform at their best. These at least are the conditions that the Chinese themselves believe are desirable or, rather, necessary for effective social action. The very essence of Confucianism was the establishment of clear norms and a belief in the inestimable benefits to be derived if everyone followed his own well-defined role. Both the Kuomintang and the Communists have sought in their separate ways to give the Chinese people clear standards for their conduct and thus, hopefully, have satisfied a basic need.

Stability, Promotions, and Opportunism

Historically, the desire to belong to a group and to adhere to recognized norms has been coupled with the expectation of social stability. The individual worked desperately not to advance himself but to be fully and securely accepted in his role. The reward for effort was security — not change or greater responsibilities. Subordinate clerks and office managers were remarkably content with their lot in life and were willing to perform their tasks faithfully without the slightest thought that advancement might be possible.

In modern times the decline in the stability of Chinese society has produced a widespread appreciation of the importance of being alert for opportunities, of always looking for ways to get ahead, and of being sensitive to any cues that might signal one's big chance. It has thus tended to produce a more and more urbanized, quick-witted, and calculating population.

To a considerably lesser degree it has ignited the hope that an increase in one's own efforts might bring about a predictable improvement in one's status and well-being. In modern times, whenever Chinese have been placed in situations in which effort was rewarded with promotion and advancement, they have generally responded in an enthusiastic manner.

But these situations have been rare. More frequently modernization has meant quasi-promotional situations in which advancement is exceedingly slow. In these circumstances the Chinese have generally tended to display a remarkable degree of patience; the prospect of promotion or advancement has not been a necessary incentive to ensure hard work; just the vaguest prospect has usually been quite enough.

In short, we are suggesting that in seeking out group identification in political life the modern Chinese have often tended to be highly opportunistic in pursuing career advancement, but once within an organization they have remained remarkably contented and satisfied with relatively static arrangements. The rewards of security and the comforts of predictability are generally enough to ensure consistent and disciplined behavior that suggests high loyalty and even blind commitment.

This is a pattern that we have seen repeatedly in modern Chinese politics: The warlords, in spite of their unsavory reputations, could easily recruit all the young and ambitious talent they needed; when the Kuomintang came to power, a generation of young Chinese flocked to the service of a national government and party; and once Mao and his associates had established their regime, there was a tremendous growth of the Communist Party. Out of the provincial schools and from lowly and dispossessed families came the millions of ambitious Chinese who swelled the ranks of the CCP. Their enthusiasm in welcoming the new order was coupled with the belief that in the ordered world of communism they would be able to find a basic form of personal security and a more just world — in which their outpourings of energy and effort would be appropriately rewarded.

The disciplined structure of communism, with its clear standards of correct behavior and its doctrine that those who want to do right are destined to inherit power, offered countless Chinese their first and only opportunity to become part of a system in which, in theory, their loyal and dedicated

177

behavior could lead to indefinite possibilities for advancement. People who were not born to power and status could now think the unthinkable — they could advance themselves over the heads of those who had always been their betters.

Yet what is striking about the structure of the Chinese Communist Party is that over the years there has been relatively little mobility and yet considerable contentment in the prolonged holding of the same office. It has been widely recognized that the top Chinese Communist leadership has been remarkably stable over the decades, and until the purges of the Cultural Revolution that accompanied the elevation of Lin Piao to the post of heir apparent there was relatively little turnover. What has been less well appreciated, but is possibly more significant, is the amazing stability of the personnel of the lower and middle cadres throughout the countryside. Probably no other political party or government over the last decade has had such a frozen personnel structure. Neither effort nor duration of service has greatly affected the status of the cadres, who generally have the same standards of living and the same burden of duties that they had a decade and more ago. More important, the lack of regular advancement and of opportunities to move into positions of greater responsibilities and honors has not apparently influenced their morale or their work habits. Although the regime constantly decries all the dangers of bureaucratization and routinelike behavior, the careers of the cadres advance at a snail's pace. Even when shunted about from place to place, their basic status remains relatively constant. And over the years punishment rather than reward has been more decisive in determining any changes. Advancement has come when others have been purged or "sent down" for "thought reform."

Both at the top reaches of the party hierarchy and at the rural outposts men have been remarkably content to adhere to their assigned roles as long as the system seemed stable. All the evidence we have suggests that those in higher offices have had almost no pressure from people below stepping on

178

their heels. The impetus for change has always come from above.

Yet, if our interpretation is correct, once the orderly stability of the system is rocked by a purge or by crises of succession, the apparently placid pattern of relationships may give way dramatically and uncertainty will communicate the need for opportunism and for gambling on the relative strength of one's chain of personal relations. Because the Chinese see so vividly that political power is ultimately based upon a linking of personal associations, any break in personal relationships implies the prospect of significant shifts in power and, hence, the need to readjust individual relationships. This adjustment must be made because, as all Chinese know, intelligent people must cope with circumstance and not ignore reality. Communism has intensified rather than modified the basic Chinese tendency to believe that real politics is hidden from view and that people must read between the lines and appreciate isolated clues and cues in responding to events.

This is why the remarkable stability of the Chinese leadership during most of the years of Mao's reign is not a reliable indicator of what may happen once he leaves the scene. Much as the traditional extended family was able to contain all manner of tensions under a placid surface while the grandfather symbolically ruled, but would suddenly break up upon his death, so the Chinese Communist Party has given a false picture of enduring stability under Mao's control. The tendency to swing from the extremes of placidity to turbulence is heightened by the feelings about authority and competition that we have already noted — the desire for monolithic authority, the fear of confusion, the anxieties about competition, all of which make it difficult to manage and contain conflict situations.

The Need for Identification
and the Personal Rewards of Loyalty

The potential for creating organizations has been heightened during periods of social disruption because more and more people have felt the need to find personal security through identification with others. It is noteworthy that although the family has traditionally been the prime unit of social organization, most Chinese families have not had adequate resources to meet crisis situations, and it has been commonly recognized that when "times are hard" and "conditions uncertain" everyone will have to look outside the family for possible means of help. In traditional China, disorder and natural calamities always brought a rise in membership of secret societies, bandit bands, and other forms of fraternal and quasi-political association.

In more recent times much of the attraction for active participation in politics has sprung from this basic need for identification and association with powerful peer groups, a need that has been stimulated by the widespread feelings of insecurity and uncertainty caused by the breakdown of the old order and by the persisting anxieties over social confusion. The individual Chinese seeks identification with others who will give him the positive feelings about security that he craves.

As we have already observed, the psychological effect of the Western impact on China has not produced the kind of identity crisis typical of most transitional societies. Instead, the Chinese have had a problem with efficacy; since the issue for them has been how they can effectively be what they are supposed to be, the focus of their quest has been on the associational arrangements that will provide the sense of efficacy and power that they assume should follow from being responsive but dependent members of society.

We have said that in modern times there has been considerable opportunism and calculation in the manner in which Chinese have sought to find the security of group association. This initial pragmatic approach to political loyalties apparently tends to strengthen rather than qualify the intensity of later idealistic and emotional commitments. This is possibly because the very style of relating choice and emotion is to limit the play of emotion until after decisions have been made, and to associate the demonstration of emotion with the proclamation of loyalties — much as the American student decides with pragmatic calculation what college he should attend and only later manifests any sense of school spirit.

The care and calculation with which the Chinese make decisions of political identification are appropriate because of the tremendous importance they attach to the value of loyalty in all political relationships. All Chinese political leaders have recognized that it is loyalty that gives the basic form and structure to political life. To champion an ideology, or a version of an ideology, is all good and well, but the ultimate significance of any ideology is that it belongs to a particular group to which individuals can show loyalty.

The decline of the family and the weakening of other parochial institutions have intensified the meaning of political loyalties for the young Chinese; and, once committed, they have generally displayed a strong willingness to maintain these loyalties as long as possible. Even during the period of the warlords there was a remarkable degree of unquestioning loyalty on the part of subordinates toward superiors and of disciples toward their mentors. Younger officers developed strong filial attachments to their sponsoring superiors, and many of these associations endured long after the warlord period.

Loyalty in Chinese political culture has been largely of an organizational or hierarchic nature. Thus the Chinese have had great difficulties in maintaining stable relations among political equals, and the alliances and coalitions among semiautonomous power figures have always been fragile and un-reliable. In contrast, there has been little movement of individuals from one organization to another. Thus, for example, the disintegration of the Kuomintang armies and of political authority on the mainland was not accompanied by a mass of individual decisions to break with a faltering regime and to seek terms with the Communists. The desertion rate was remarkably low. What happened was that superior commanders, often acting with some slight regard for the welfare of their troops, made a decision for the entire unit.

In modern Chinese politics there has been a general recognition that circumstances may compel people to break their bonds of association and establish new ones; but the Chinese suspect those who make such shifts, and leaders distrust those who once had loyalties to others, for it is commonly believed that if circumstances changed, the old bonds of loyalty might quickly be re-established. Suspicions about the enduring powers of friendship and loyalty inject unrealistic expectations into politics. From the time of Sun Yat-sen, aspiring political leaders in China have steadfastly believed that a change in position of only a very limited number of power holders could bring about ground-swell changes in all of Chinese politics. Today the Chinese on Taiwan and aspiring leaders of "third forces" in Hong Kong believe that if the Peking regime were weakened by a serious crisis the Chinese masses would quickly revert to old patterns of loyalty. The Communists have acted in the same spirit and have consistently discriminated against those who once held positions in the old regime as people whose class background has made them permanently suspect. To a degree unknown before in communism the Chinese act as though the son can never eradicate his father's class taint.

Thus, paradoxically, the very quality of loyalty that is presumed to give stability often operates to make the Chinese believe that their political systems are no more than houses of cards and can be easily destroyed. Usually, and not surprisingly, it is when the Chinese estimate the power of other cliques and groups that they are most appreciative of the possible fragility of temporary relationships and the strength of older fundamental loyalties. When they calculate the power of their own groups they like to see all relationships as expressions of ultimate loyalties and to discount any possibility for reshuffling. Yet it is striking that regimes that have been in such complete control as the one in Peking and the other on Taiwan remain oddly nervous about the dangers of disintegration. Since all power is somehow fragile there can never be enough power.

There is considerable evidence that, contrary to the beliefs of Chinese power holders, ordinary Chinese do have the capacity to make decisive changes in their loyalties if they feel that they are compelled by circumstances. Those Chinese who defected from the Malayan Communist Party were quite prepared to make an absolute change and to see their old comrades as their new mortal enemies. Similarly, among the refugees in Hong Kong it is possible to find people who had sincerely wished to be accepted by the Communist regime but who were persistently rebuffed and discriminated against because of previous associations and were driven eventually, much against their wills, to change their allegiances.

The emotional and moral importance of political and organizational loyalty is further confirmed by the justifications that the Chinese tend to use when explaining any change in their loyalties. More often than not they suggest that even though circumstances compelled them to act as they did they were justified because of mistreatment by their former superiors. Thus, since the Chinese concept of mistreatment usually involves a failure to provide sustenance, security, and general protection, their feelings about loyalty and identification with organizations tend in the last analysis to be very close to their feelings about authority. They expect of loyalty the same qualities they want to find in their relations with authority. Just as with authority, they expect more than is possible and tend to be persistently dissatisfied with what they must accept.

This appreciation of the importance of loyalties, of the fragility of human ties, and of the close links between loyalty and authority manifests itself whenever a succession problem arises. While a leader is still alive and commands authority there is a strong taboo against speculation about what will happen once he dies. No one except the leader himself can give the slightest hint. Reflections about the future can be only of a highly formalistic nature, stressing constitutional and customary proprieties, which everyone assumes will in practice be irrelevant. The very fact that the Chinese feel so inhibited in speculating about the power and loyalty relations that will follow the death of either Mao or Chiang leads us to speculate that neither regime is likely to handle this problem with skill.

The Search for Dependency and the Welcoming of Helpful Criticism

The apparent facility in building organizations is further encouraged by the intense responsiveness of most Chinese to the cues for conformity which may be related to their basic search for the security of dependency. They believe that when they join any kind of organization, group, or association they should adjust their personal behavior to reflect the fact of their new membership. In looking for cues to guide their own behavior they are predisposed to support anyone who can assert authority. They generally expect that if they do all in their power to adjust to group standards, the group will look with favor upon them and support their interests.

One of the most dramatic expressions of this characteristic was provided by the Chinese prisoners of war in Korea. Historically the almost universal experience in wars is that prisoners tend to show little capacity for self-organization. Even when apathy is not complete, spirited behavior tends

184

to be highly individualistic, and only a single man, or a small and select group of men, will plot an escape. Among the Chinese prisoners, however, there was a startling collective effort to form organizations. The mass of them acted as though it was quite natural and proper for them to join one or another faction in the camps, and the leaders of both the pro-Communist and the anti-Communist factions often turned out to be men without formal rank or previous experience in leadership positions. It was apparently inconceivable that such large numbers of people could be brought together without everybody being organized into some form of group structure. The American authorities on the other hand were profoundly surprised that both politics and organization should have taken place in the camps.

Wherever Chinese in numbers have gone overseas they have invariably tended to create tightly structured organizations. The history of the Chinese in Southeast Asia can be told largely in terms of the stories of their secret societies, their benevolent associations, and their clan and provincial organizations. A striking characteristic of the overseas Chinese is their unquestioning expectation, on arriving in a strange setting, that they will gain security and support if they adhere to the norms of some group or organization.

It is this kind of expectation that helps to explain why the Chinese have apparently welcomed some practices of the Communist Party that one would think might be highly repugnant to them. The self-criticism and mutual criticism meetings have not been nearly as disturbing to many Chinese as might have been expected, considering that they can put an individual in the exceedingly threatening situation of "losing face" before both peers and representatives of higher authorities. It is true, we have innumerable reports of how traumatic and even "personality shattering" such sessions have been for the more sensitive and politically vulnerable Chinese. Yet what is more interesting is the remarkable extent to which the people have accepted not only the practice

185

but the rationale for self-criticism and mutual criticism. In a rather innocent and compliant manner refugees and former Communists talk about how helpful and good it was of the Communist Party to go to the effort of trying to assist them in improving their conduct and thought.

Peasants and workers have been willing to accept the idea that the Communist leadership was being constructive and trying to help them to become better citizens in a Communist world, and in return they have often felt a sense of obligation to improve their ways. At least, this is the spirit in which many Chinese embarked on the experiences with self-criticism and mutual criticism, and frequently it was only after considerable exposure to such meetings that they began to appreciate the differences between their own and the party's interests. By then, however, their concern for getting on well with the Communists had changed from a positive desire to an operational necessity. As happens so often with the Chinese Communists, what is useful and effective is carried to the extreme degree, and the ultimate effect is self-defeating.

Rituals and Feigned Sentiments

The combination of searching for security through group identification and of believing that one can best cope with authority by adhering to expected standards of behavior tends to focus considerable attention upon the appropriate day-to-day behavior of political activists. The Communists have hit upon a style of politics that accentuates to a unique degree the basic Chinese belief in the importance of personal conduct in determining larger matters. The Communist notion that it is necessary to work hard at learning to be a good revolutionary conforms to the traditional Chinese expectation that those with influence must engage in self-cultivation and the disciplined learning of correct procedures.

This self-conscious concern has tended, however, to encourage a drift toward ritualized behavior. Rank-and-file members of the party have learned that particular cues and signals from the leaders call for specific behavioral responses. Once the correct responses are learned, they can be tireless in repeating what they feel is expected of them. The result is a widespread tendency to standardize and ritualize all forms of learned behavior. The chanting of lurid slogans, the proclaiming of extreme demands, and the protesting of the sins of the non-Chinese world would all require greater expenditures of emotional energy in other cultures than they seem to in China.

Thus we can begin to observe a pattern in Chinese politics: the quick, and even eager, formation of groups and organizations, followed by great and somewhat dramatic outbursts of enthusiasm and emotion, which, however, soon become ritualized and easily repeated with little sign of boredom.

For example, mass actions, particularly those involving students, have been a constant feature of Chinese politics from the time that the first modern generation of students protested the Versailles settlement to the sudden appearance of the Red Guards. The same exhilaration that once went with denouncements of Japanese and British imperialism is now to be found in the protests against Russian revisionism and American imperialism. In each situation, collective action, although never truly spontaneous, was rapidly formed; but then in time the expression of emotions became ritualized. As a consequence of this pattern, a perennial question in Chinese politics is whether people are expressing genuine or feigned sentiments. Leaders in particular are always uncertain whether their supporters are indeed as loyal and sincere as they pretend to be. The situation is complicated because the traditional test of "sincerity" in Chinese culture has been the willingness of individuals to expend great care in meeting the requirements of convention. In short, sincerity has traditionally demanded ritualized behavior.

In modern times the Chinese have in general continued to appreciate ritualized acts; however, as we have noted from the beginning, a cardinal feature of contemporary China has been the belief that politics is coterminous with the violent expression of emotions. But here we have a dilemma: Leaders constantly demand a greater expression of emotion than the people are capable of, and as a result the people have to ritualize their actions, which in turn makes the leaders increasingly anxious. Thus the demand for even greater demonstrations of sentiments is stepped up, but this only increases the tendency toward ritualized behavior. This is the vicious circle that has been frustrating Mao Tse-tung in the evening of his life.

The problem has become much more intense for the Communists, because the Chinese propensity for ritualizing conduct is now peculiarly provocative to the new elite, which has strong feelings about the virtues of shared sentiments between leaders and followers. Historically it was reassuring to the psychologically secure Chinese leaders that a gap in sentiment and behavior existed between elite and masses — how could one know that one rightfully belonged to the elite except by contrasting one's feelings and behavior with those of the common mass? At present the Communist leaders consider any evidence of a difference between elite and mass sentiments as the source of genuine anxiety. The result is the endless searching for reassurances of the sort Mao has carried out in his probes to discover the intensity of sentiments behind the ritualized behavior.

The Frustrations of Participation

From our analysis so far, it might seem that the modern, politically active Chinese are essentially organizational men. Although recognizing the high risks of political participation, they have been anxious to identify themselves with groups. Once they have joined any association or party, they are predisposed to work hard and adapt to the collective norms; they truly want to be loyal, and even as they ritualize their participation they are prepared to go along with the leadership. Yet this picture is clearly incomplete, for the larger history of the ups and downs of parties and associations in modern China is evidence of far greater uncertainty than such a description of individual organizational behavior would suggest. The spirit of large-scale modern organization in China has been overwhelmingly one of internal tension, endless bickering, gossiping, and mutual recriminations. Instead of being uniquely effective, modern organizations have been peculiarly adapted to bruising and damaging sensitivities and causing all manner of mental anguish.

It has been only in the small and highly paternalistic organizations that individual behavior, conforming very much to our description, has provided the basis for stable and relatively tension-free relationships. Under these conditions, which at times can be realized also in small cells and subdivisions of larger organizations, the pattern of face-to-face relationships seems to provide the necessary balance between the need for authority and the need for self-efficacy.

Larger and more impersonal organizations, on the other hand, cannot generally provide the rewards of security that the Chinese seem to want and expect when they make a commitment of identification with a group. In this sense the Chinese expect too much of the mere act of joining, and as a result of their inevitable disappointment they are often quick to find fault in the way others have treated them. Since the spirit of dependency is so directly related to the expected element of security, it is not surprising that the typical reaction to unsatisfactory experiences in large organizations has mainly to do with being mistreated, slighted, ignored, overworked, or generally unjustly treated.

The frustrations with organizations are, however, not all related to the problem of dealing with authority. Peer relationships, and general difficulties in dealing with equals, are just as important. Here again the pattern is one of high expectations being shattered by reality. The great value that the Chinese place on the ideals of friendship leads them to hope that membership in any organization will produce personal acceptance, warm relationships, and the unquestioning trust of friendship. A common theme in the accounts of former Communists is that initially they welcomed the spirit of comradeship that appeared to be the essence of life within the party. To be called "comrade" by everyone, to be treated as a brother, and to have the possibility of frank and genuine communication was exciting. This would be particularly appealing because in most of life the Chinese realize that they must be on their guard in personal relations, they must be careful not to be cheated, and they must constantly remember that all people who are not "like brothers" will have little regard for their interests.

In joining groups the Chinese demand a great deal of the tone and spirit of interpersonal relations, and when their ideals are not realized they see their peers as dangerous threats who have personally, and therefore with calculated malice, let them down. Here we touch again upon the basic theme of the problem of aggression in Chinese culture. We need only add to our earlier analysis the observation that while formalism, etiquette, and strict adherence to proper manners have generally provided the prime method for handling aggression, a second approach, and highly idealized because it is so rare, is through complete and guileless intimacy. This is the romantic theme of Chinese culture — the dream of having a bosom companion with whom one can drink freely and, therefore, from whom no secrets need to be kept. What is significant is that when the second technique is tried and fails, the Chinese tend to return to the first, but with considerable moral fervor, so that formalism becomes completely entangled with issues of rights and justice. This, in turn, evokes complex and quite ambivalent feelings about justice in brotherly relations. Few relations are recognized as more important in Chinese culture, but at the same time there is a peculiar basic contradiction in this particular sibling rela-

tionship. Although the relationship is recognized as absolute
— the elder brother will always be the superior and the
younger brother always somewhat the dependent — it is also,
in part, enveloped in the ethic of equality. For example, there
is no principle of primogeniture, and in many respects all
children are supposed to be treated equally or according to
the personal whim and pleasure of the parents. The relationship is thus usually surrounded with considerable tension. Although the Chinese constantly idealize the relationship between brothers, they generally have some difficulty with it in
practice, especially when they try to apply its spirit to non-
familial situations.

In short, when the Chinese have enthusiastically characterized a relationship as a brotherly one — and this to the
Chinese means an elder brother–younger brother relationship
— it has often been soured with strong feelings of personal
misuse and exploitation. We have already noted the significant
fact that the family relationship in which the Chinese obviously find the greatest happiness, satisfaction, and comfort,
that of brother and sister, is rarely idealized and never suggested as the proper model for any other relationship. This
is a peculiarly tension-free relationship because the roles are
so manifestly differentiated. There can be no disturbing suggestion of competition, each can in different ways find dependency, and neither has to meet harsh standards of performance. Moreover, the relationship is comfortable because it is
sexually safe and contains no disturbing overtones of power
and potency, only innocent teasing and the mutual admiration
of pure youth in which the stress is upon the promise of future
performance and in which there can be no serious anxieties
about failure.

Given the nature of the Chinese personality, it is quite
understandable that the brother-sister relationship is much
too precious to be alluded to in the context of other relationships. Instead great emphasis is given to all the basic tensions
of the association between brothers. A key to an understand-

ing can be found in the fact that behind this latter relationship there is always the sense of a powerful superior authority, either the father in actuality or his spirit and the spirit of his ancestors. It is viable just because of this vital addition of an arbitrary outside authority. Brothers are not supposed to be able to work out their difficulties, and the details of their relationship are always defined for them by the wishes of the father. Thus, although the Chinese like to idealize its pure and completely self-contained comradeship, brotherhood usually implies some guiding hand, some role for authority.

What this means for large organizations is that tensions among peer relationships are assumed to be properly brought to the attention of superior authorities. When things do not go well with equals, all parties concerned anxiously seek to gain the ear of their superior in order to reach "justice," protect their innocence, and hopefully see that others are punished.

These patterns of tension and frustration in Chinese organizational life deserve special attention because the principle motive behind participation in politics has been the hope of direct rewards from membership identification rather than from the expected benefits of the policy objectives of the group. The Chinese participate in political associations more because of the psychic satisfactions of belonging than because of their belief in policy matters.

Since their followers are not attached to them by feelings of commitment toward limited policy objectives, leaders have generally had great freedom in changing their strategy and tactics. It is noteworthy that shifts in the party line have not caused crises among the rank and file of the Chinese Communist Party. As long as general success is likely and no direct personal interest is threatened, there is a readiness to have complete faith in the wisdom and judgments of the leadership. We can go even further and say that because so little is attached to nonleadership judgments about policy, it is psychologically reassuring to believe that the leadership has complete wisdom and that there is magic in the "Thoughts of Mao Tse-tung."

Chinese leaders do, however, have to pay a price for their freedom in external policy making: They have to face potentially explosive internal relationships. Since the more limited and specific goals of the group or party are not as personally important to the membership as the realities of their personal relations, problems of morale cannot easily be satisfied by particular accomplishments of the group as a whole. Such limited value is attached to specific policy goals that there is little willingness to trade group successes off against the personal frustrations of group membership.

This is why modern Chinese who have broken with either the Nationalists or the Communists have tended to explain or justify their disillusionment by stressing either their initial belief in the ultimate success of the party or the way in which they were treated personally. The tendency has been to discount the intermediate level of substantive policies — which provide the essence of politics in most political cultures. Such policies are important only to the extent that their attempted implementation introduces doubts about ultimate success or introduces personal problems for the individual in his relations with the group. Thus the almost universal story of the politically disillusioned Chinese has been: At first I was not too sure of them, but after I joined them I was completely for them and had no doubts. Then they mistreated me and I realized that I had been misled, and I decided then that they would fail in the end.

The Military Model

From this analysis of personal behavior in organizations we can discern significant psychological reasons for the Chinese tendency to favor military-type organizations. There are strong historical reasons for the prevalence of armies in shaping modern Chinese politics. As we have already ob-

193

served, once the basic Confucian-bureaucratic structure of imperial politics was shattered, the only group that could command was the military, which alone had the necessary capacity for building significant organizations. From the days of the warlords to the succession crisis in Communist China, military power and the reality of armies have been constant and dominant elements within Chinese politics. When the confusions and disruptions of the Cultural Revolution and the Red Guards had put into disarray the party apparatus, the pattern, as always in the past, was an instinctive turning to the army to rule society. Military power has been the basic currency of modern Chinese politics, and when Mao Tse-tung speaks of "power as coming from the barrel of a gun" he is speaking both as a Chinese realist and as a Communist.

It is equally significant that all organizations tend quickly to become militarized, and the spirit of military organization finds its way into all manner of governmental and political organizations. In most developing countries, public organizations usually take on the qualities of the dominant institution. For example, in many former colonial countries the formal, legalistic, and hierarchic characteristics of the civil service administration are found in most other groupings such as political parties, trade unions, and peasant associations. In China the model has generally been the army, and the cultural ideal of the well-organized group stresses the essentially military qualities of discipline, order, vigor, loyalty, and obedience.

The Communists have carried this tendency to new extremes. From the organization of the land-reform drives, through the countless mobilization campaigns, to the "Learn from the People's Liberation Army" drive and the Red Guards, the trend has been increasingly to exploit the assumed advantages of military organization and procedures. In this process two rather distinctive styles have emerged.

The first occurs when a quick surge to action is needed,

and the cadres are instructed to mobilize large numbers of people to carry out the particular campaign in a spirit of enthusiasm. The martial spirit appears in the call for people to put aside all calculations of personal reward, to rejoice in the ultimate dream of victory, and to excel in bravery and sacrifice.

The second style is related to the operations of more permanent enterprises, in which the emphasis is largely upon the military virtues of discipline, the instant response to authority, and the appearance of efficiency. This approach is to be seen in the way the Chinese believe a railroad should be run, a factory organized, and a government ministry managed. Here the emphasis is upon reducing all ambiguities in relations, establishing behavior that is as routinized as possible, and eliminating all possible cross-pressures or sources of confusion.

One style stresses emotionalism, the other professionalism, and it is significant that the problem of combining these two qualities of behavior has given the Chinese Communists the greatest difficulty in all their organizational efforts. Running throughout the Communist political culture is the problem of combining, balancing, and reconciling emotionalism and professionalism, enthusiasm and rationalism, or, as they call it, the problem of "red and expert."

From what we have observed earlier it is easy to appreciate why this problem of emotionalism and professionalism should be a most perplexing one for the Chinese. It tends to become even more acute not only because of the obvious stresses that Communist ideology imposes upon the regulation of behavior but because of the tendency to emphasize military organizational forms. A universal problem of armies is that of reconciling the intense emotions of loyalty and sacrifice with the need for professional calculation and skill.

The prospects for modernization and development are very much bound up in the ways in which the Chinese work out this basic organizational problem. It is significant that the organizational trend is constantly in the direction of highly rigid and routinized behavior. As long as the function of the organization is best served by extremely disciplined and routinized behavior, the Chinese can be expected to excel. For example, it is not surprising that the post office and railroad systems have been among the most effective organizations in the modernizing of China. In most industrial societies these kinds of organization have difficulties in attracting imaginative talent, and the energies of creative people are to be found in other forms of organization that call for more diversified, innovating, and flexible behavior. So far the only way in which the Communists have been able to solve the problem of flexibility has been to create new organizations or campaigns for each new task. This is no real solution. The illusion of progress and accomplishment is there, but reality must lag behind until the Chinese can develop more flexible and responsive organizational forms.

In other developing countries the breakdown of civilian institutions and the frustrations with the modernization process have produced tendencies to turn to military rule, and in many respects armies do have the ability to make a country appear as though it were surmounting indecision and getting on with the tasks of development. In a sense, Communist rule in China has been the functional and historical equivalent to army rule in many developing countries. With their reliance upon militarized organizations the Communists have given the same impression of providing solutions to development problems as have the ruling armies of other countries. Yet with time it has become clear that army rule is not a panacea and it must be greatly modified if progress in modernization is to take place.

THE DYNAMICS OF CHINESE POLITICS

To this point our analysis has been general and theoretical, moving back and forth in the history of Chinese politics and the life cycle of the individual to identify the characteristics of thought, sentiment, and behavior that may help illuminate the political problems of the Chinese as they seek to modernize. In order to appreciate how the spirit of Chinese political culture plays out in the realm of action, we need to focus on the dynamics of Chinese politics, which are to a large extent concentrated in the uneasy tension between, on the one hand, the public imperative of consensus, conformity, order, and orthodoxy imposed by the leadership and, on the other hand, the private search of cadres for security in their factional groupings and their particularistic ties of *guanxi*. To a man the leaders will declare that factions are a curse and *guanxi* an abomination. Yet, with only a few exceptions, all politically active figures have personal ties to other cadres.

This contradiction has been a driving force in every phase of Chinese communism. The supreme importance of consensus, conformity, and agreement requires a standardized denial of conflicts and unresolved disagreements, but beneath the surface show of conformity, tensions, feuding, and factional conflicts abound. Although Chinese politics has historically

197

vacillated between elite solidarity and factional struggle, the two tendencies have always been present, and possibly the most significant characteristic of Chinese politics has been the ceaseless tension between them. This tension seems to be basic to the culture, which has traditionally demanded both conformity and self-assertion, both humble self-effacement (or self-sacrifice) and a constant striving to be exceptional, distinguished, and superior.

Although politics is done in the name of the "people" and the "masses," the citizenry in fact have no voice or independent means of participation; routine Chinese politics is exclusively a matter of relations among cadres and officials. The docility of the public, like that of the lesser officials, comes in part from the culture. The tradition of respect for superiors and deference to authority helps establish the virtue of conformity. To be out of step is not just dangerous but also foolish. The level of fear is well below that of terror, but high enough that prudence commands compliance in form and a continuing search for the added insurance of trusted personal ties. People are aware of the labor camps, the harsh penalties for "spreading counter-revolutionary propaganda," and the arbitrary intervention by Public Security forces into everyone's private affairs. The officials follow the public's practice of knowing where the lines are drawn as to what can be said and done in different kinds of situations. Even governors of provinces who may have profound differences with Beijing's policies never speak out as Boris Yeltsin has done in his disagreements with Mikhail Gorbachev.

Politically, the cultural need for conformity contributes to a deep craving for order and propriety to the extent of creating a profound fear of *luan,* or disorder. The general expectation is that life is better when agreement is widespread, nonconformity has been rectified, and stability prevails. The rule is consensus for the sake of consensus, and therefore the orthodoxy of the moment can be based on dogmas that, except for being

198

officially proclaimed, would probably command little respect. No one challenges Premier Li Peng's pronouncement that "socialism is superior to all other systems" any more than people questioned Mao's dictum that with the Great Leap Forward China was about to achieve the blessed state of communism. For most Chinese, the imperatives of political stability and of orderly social life require a denial of individualistic self-interest. Ideally, the collectivity should take care of all its members, so no one should need to assert his or her individual rights.

Yet at the same time, individuals—especially when experiencing anxiety—are predictably inclined to do something, to act to remove the source of trouble, or at least to reduce its consequences. Simply professing loyalty to the consensus is not enough to guarantee security, especially for those caught up in power relationships. They feel a compelling need to get more protection than is afforded by merely mouthing the slogans of the day; they are generally driven to seek more personal protection. One can believe in the virtues of conformity, but for one's own fate it can be too impersonal; therefore, one needs to act in terms of a more particularistic calculus. Action usually means striving to manipulate social relations, which for the Chinese are not abstractions but very concrete personal ties and associations that are palpably measurable. One tries to share one's innocence of any wrongdoing, place blame elsewhere, and generally make others aware of one's misfortunes. Most Chinese do not believe that troubles will go away if one ignores them or pretends that they do not exist.

The taboo against individualism rules out effective norms for controlling private relationships. The idea that *guanxi* is improper, indeed essentially immoral, means that those who turn to particularistic ties often are primed to be unscrupulous. From early childhood Chinese are taught that individualism is evil because it is no different from pure selfishness, and that security can be found only by sticking to their assigned roles in the collectivity. Therefore, they are aware of the impropriety of even semisecret relations; hence, when they enter a realm where it is assumed that morality does not reign, they often act in quite unethical ways.

The awareness that such personal behavior is widespread creates a pervasive suspicion that corruption is commonplace and that the "backdoor" is being routinely used by others. It takes only a few examples of sons and daughters of high officials cashing in on their connections for personal gain to convince people that the families of most officials are taking advantage of their positions. Among the cadres themselves the need to rely upon personal ties produces the cliques and factions that are the key units of elite politics. But it is also to their advantage to mask such behavior. Hence the continuing stress on the importance of pretended consensus and formalized conformity.

The gaps between words and actions make it relatively easy to maintain a veneer of consensus even while acting in accordance with the realities of the cliques and factions. Yet the need to preserve a symbolic veneer has profound consequences for the dynamics of Chinese politics. Above all it establishes a universal understanding that throughout the system subordinates will feel compelled to feign compliance, to give lip service to the orders of the highest authorities while pursuing their own personal interests. The highest authorities, knowing that this is taking place and unwilling to acknowledge their impotence publicly, go along with the make-believe, confident that only foreigners will be taken in by the pretense.

The Price of Consensus

The contradiction between words and actions has certain other fundamental consequences in Chinese politics. It reinforces, for example, the profound taboo against the articula-

200

tion of particular interests. The consensus supposedly supports the interests of the collectivity, and in politics this means the nation. The result is that the rhetoric of Chinese politics is filled with lofty sentiments of patriotism. Anyone who gives voice to particular interests is regarded as selfish and therefore unpatriotic. As a result there can be no open process of politics in which interests compete to attract attention and trade-offs can be reasonably discussed.

The iron law of consensus also affects the nature of Chinese leadership by operating as a critical factor in determining the type of people who reach the top. The rule tips the balance in favor of people who always appear to support the consensus even as they excel in their assigned tasks. It is not just that creative and somewhat idiosyncratic people are generally screened out. But significantly, few of those who do rise to prominent positions have developed oratorical or debater's skills; therefore, they have little ability to mobilize the public for new adventures. Operating throughout their careers in the context of orthodoxy, their strengths lie in administrative battling under a cloak of anonymity, not in publicly articulating new visions. Although it has become common to suggest that the Chinese leadership is caught up in policy debate, the debates, if that is the proper word, are exceedingly muted, discernible only to skilled analysts. Therefore, the participants can only quietly and indirectly press forward any innovative ideas. Leadership in a framework of hierarchical consensus produces colorless people. This is true for both traditional and contemporary China and helps explain why the founders of dynasties, like Mao in the People's Republic, could be larger-than-life leaders, but their successors become ever more nondescript. Deng Xiaoping's successor will probably be several degrees less the public figure than Deng was in comparison to Mao.

In supporting conformity the aspiring cadres are often driven to trying to outdo each other in proclaiming the orthodoxy, a situation that encourages hyperbole. The need for exaggeration also stems in part from the troublesome fact that realistic statements would fail to provide a satisfactory test of political loyalties. Subordinates need to demonstrate their enthusiasm for their leaders. Exaggerated rhetoric provides a symbolic dimension to politics. In this context people can clearly reveal that they are supporting particular spokesmen by repeating statements that are often at odds with common sense or reality. (This practice is also observable in the way the Chinese extend the logic of their factional loyalty testing to foreigners, classifying those who unquestioningly accept Chinese exaggerations as "friends" of China while treating skeptics not as unimaginative realists but as people to be distrusted.)

Respect for consensus requires public discussions of policy to be elliptical and to use code words without identifying people and positions. However, informal communication among cadres must be even more circumspect than public statements for fear of suggesting the existence of cliques based on self-interest. It is dangerous for officials to try to change policies by seeking confidential channels of communication to gain potential allies. The only safe approach is to hint cryptically through the mass media at the direction of a possible new policy, making it seem to be part of the consensus and hoping that other officials will pick up the signal and demonstrate their sympathy by repeating the new code words.

The avoidance of straightforward public rhetoric that the rule of consensus demands is reinforced by the culture's veneration of authority. Knowing that the public is prepared to attribute omnipotence to authority, high officials wisely hesitate to expose more of their thinking to public scrutiny than is absolutely necessary for fear of shattering the illusion of their presumed magical powers. Mao could write a lot because it was well established that his words required careful "study" and therefore could not be as simpleminded as they appeared to be. Deng has been able to strengthen his authority from time to time by merely spreading rumors of his own cryptic quotations. Although top Chinese leaders are expected to attend large public meetings, such as sessions of the National People's Congress, to give four- or five-hour talks that usually leave much unsaid. Not called upon to answer public criticisms, Chinese leaders have no need to defend in detail their actions or to spell out their policy proposals. Both Mao and Deng operated as oracles, giving only hints of their real designs, thereby allowing people to rely upon their own wishful thinking.

The dynamics of factional politics thus encourages extensive use of symbolic language, which furthers the tendency toward exaggerated rhetoric. The underlying objective—to mobilize favorable elements and neutralize the opposition— produces the earnest treatment of make-believe. Farfetched statements, such as that foreign governments have a carefully planned strategy to overthrow Chinese socialism by "peaceful evolution," have the same practical purpose: the mobilizing of factional support for fundamental power alignments. Thus the dynamics of factional mobilization can, on the one hand, impart great urgency and inordinate attention to ritualized formulations about matters that otherwise might seem trivial— for example, the need to "find truth from facts," or U.S. policy has "hurt the feelings of one billion Chinese." On the other hand, the same dynamics can trivialize what, if taken literally, would be world-shaking events—for example, the startling idea that "the bourgeoisie is right in the middle of the party," or that "world war is imminent and conditions are excellent."

In the administrative realm, the veneer of consensus effectively operates to impede initiatives from below. Changes in formal policy come from grand pronouncements by the top leaders, with at times little regard for the day-to-day operations of government. Once such dictums are issued, lesser

203

officials must scurry about to try to implement them by figuring out how they can be administered. The obligation to maintain the consensus inhibits the bureaucracy from pushing demands for decisions and policy changes to the top. Minority views can rarely surface, and any faction can usually veto activist policies sought by others.

These rules of consensus, when combined with the Chinese belief in the need to advance one's interests through particularistic relationships, contribute to a very acute need to be alert and shrewd in dealing with social and political situations. The knowledge that beneath the layer of consensus there must be personal calculation and planning reinforces the necessity to mask one's own actions while trying to unmask the private intentions of others. Hence the extraordinary emphasis in both social and political relationships on designing and executing ploys, stratagems, and game-playing tactics—many of which rely upon deception because of the assumed inevitable gap between appearance and reality.

The anthropologist Chien Chiao has argued that "social and political strategies form a highly enduring tradition in Chinese culture," and that both quantitatively and qualitatively the Chinese use of social stratagems exceeds the American. He has identified some two dozen categories of Chinese strategies. Some of the classic stratagems include: "Besiege Wei in order to save Zhao" (save one party by attacking another); "Loot the house while it's on fire" (take advantage of chaos for private gain); "Watch the fire from across the river" (from a safe vantage point watch others destroy themselves—a version of "Watch the tigers fight from the mountain top"); "Befriend distant states while attacking the nearby"; "Put Zhang's hat on Li's head" (attribute something to the wrong person in order to gain benefit); "Avoid the important and dwell on the trivial" (keep silent about major mistakes and confess to minor ones); "Kill the chicken to frighten the monkey" (punish the weak in order to warn others); "Point at the mulberry and abuse the locust" (point at one while abusing another); "Take away the ladder after climbing into the chamber" (don't give those behind you a chance); and "Drop stones on someone who has fallen into the well."

On the basis of his collection of Chinese strategies, Chien Chiao has produced "a sketch of a fine Chinese strategist" in social relations:

> He waits patiently for the right opportunity with full alert, constant observation and investigation of the situation. When he moves, his actions tend to be deceitful and indirect, and often he tries to achieve his goal by making use of a third party. He may exaggerate or fabricate occasionally, but he always feigns. He does his best to stop his opponent's advance. He may allure, prod and warn his opponent, but unless it is absolutely necessary, he will not have a real direct confrontation with him. If he has to, he will move fast and try to quickly put his opponent under his control. He is always ready to abandon or withdraw, for that is only a step from coming back.[1]

Swings from Wishful Thinking to Despondency

The consensus-compelled rhetoric contributes to the tendency of Chinese politics to vacillate between periods of unbounded wishful thinking and phases of despondency, between enthusiastic optimism and a pessimism that is heavily flavored with suspicion. Since public rhetoric is routinely taken as being less descriptive of current realities and more a statement of hope, it is not normal to scrutinize the words of leaders for their accuracy. Moreover, given the culture's fantasies about the omnipotence of authority, it is natural for the people to give the leaders the benefit of any doubt. In the process the distinction between future and present becomes confused, especially since the leaders usually dwell only on

[1] Chien Chiao, "Chinese Strategic Behaviors: A Preliminary List," in *Proceedings of the International Conference on Sinology*, Taipei, August 15–17, 1980 (Taipei: Academia Sinica, 1981).

the evils of the past and the glories of the future in the expectation that everyone will identify with the promised future that is around the corner, and hence can easily endure current pain and problems.

But when the euphoria is shaken, disappointment turns into suspicion, especially about the conduct of the leaders. The aloofness of the leadership that contributed to the aura of optimism may now suggest abandonment and the idea that authority has not played fair. Learning about reality and the hard facts of national life induces first frustration and then anger.

Because Leninist leaders of a people's republic cannot appeal to the past for their legitimacy, promises of the future have inordinate importance; legitimacy therefore rests entirely upon promises of what the future will bring. This state of affairs, of course, only contributes to the need to be vague about the actual state of progress—a vagueness that is often protected by issuing a welter of statistics which give the impression of concreteness and progress but which in fact only muddles what needs to be known.

In spite of a long record of disappointments that goes back well before 1949, it has been remarkably easy for the leaders to sustain the spirit of wishful thinking. Optimism is sustained partly because of the strong and positive nurturance in early childhood, which makes Chinese children feel that they are indeed special. The attitude is reinforced by a cultural resistance to introspection, which blocks out profound self-doubting, and an uncomplicated situationally oriented calculus for action that suggests that new circumstances can always provide the chance for new opportunities. These propensities of Chinese culture help sustain a general bias toward optimism. The bias is so strong that even when the mood is despondent the belief can persist that only a slight change of circumstance, such as the death of a few octogenarians, will be enough to restore hope for progress.

206

Whether Chinese politics at any moment is in a phase of optimism or depression, the cadres' unwavering concern must be to establish, behind the screen of consensus, their personal security through the informal associations that are the factions basic to Chinese politics.

The Bases of Factions

To understand the role of factions in Chinese politics, it is necessary to put out of mind the analogue of interest-group politics or even of bureaucratic politics in industrially developed societies. Factions in the People's Republic rarely represent clearly defined institutional, geographic, or generational interests. This does not mean, however, that institutional, geographic, or generational considerations may not contribute to the formation and maintenance of particular factions.

The prime bases of factions are power constellations or clusters of officials who for some reason or other feel comfortable with each other, who believe that they can share trust and loyalties, and who may recognize common foes. More often than not, the real motivation is career security and enhancement, whether it be at the lowest county or provincial committee level or among those on the Politburo and the State Council jockeying for greater influence. The glue that holds factions together can thus be either mutual career self-interest or the highly particularistic sentiments associated with personal ties in Chinese culture, that is, the spirit of *guanxi*. The concept of *guanxi*, which describes the personal bonds of acquaintanceship and mutual belonging and gives vivid context to the networks of personal associations in Chinese culture, is quite different from patron-client relationships in that it gives considerable scope to the subordinate and can burden the superior with demanding obligations. It operates among near equals, and usually the advantaged position is that of the person who can "pull *guanxi*," that is, extract favors from the more fortunate partner.

Chinese factions lie between the extremes of the intimately knit cliques and the diffuse mass parties that are common in the politics of other countries. Although cadres are capable of being highly aggressive in protecting each other, the networks that shape the factions are seldom strongly motivated to assert generalizable policy interests. Factions are thus more latent than manifest, more capable of bureaucratic obstructionism than of policy initiation or implementation, and generally diffuse and imprecise with respect to policy matters, except when it comes to pragmatic considerations of career and power.

The question of the relationship between policy choices and factional alignments in Chinese politics has been extensively debated.[2] Unquestionably, certain leaders do become identified with particular policies, and therefore their supporters are also inclined to champion certain policies and oppose the policies of competing factions. Indeed, certain policies can become the trademark of particular factions. Similarly, the introduction of new policies can be interpreted as favoring the well-being of cadres in a particular faction and damaging those in other factions. In these respects, factions are related to policy.

Yet it would be dangerous to jump from these observations to the conclusion that factions are usually formed in response to policy preferences. Active political participants in China seldom have the luxury of deciding their policy stands on the basis of an objective weighing of all the pros and cons. Quite the contrary, cadres invariably find themselves constrained

---

[2] The issues have been well laid out in such works as Kenneth Lieberthal and Michel Oksenberg, *Policy Making in China* (Princeton: Princeton University Press, 1988); and David M. Lampton and Kenneth Lieberthal, eds., *Bureaucratic Structure and Policy Process in China* (Berkeley: University of California Press, 1991).

by a host of past commitments, personal relationships, and obligations. Usually their only realistic option is to go along with the position that appears to favor the well-being of their faction. One has only to consider the marginal role that substantive policy issues can play in the decisions of American politicians concerning, for example, which of their party's presidential aspirants to support for nomination, and then to recognize that in Chinese politics personalized relationships are orders of magnitude more intense, to understand why policy cannot be the prime basis for factions in China. Chinese cadres simply have far less room for maneuvering.

Labeling factions according to presumed ideological or policy tendencies can produce grotesque results. It was, for example, absurd for Hua Guofeng to have declared that the Maoist "Gang of Four" were "Ultra-Rightists," and it was equally ridiculous for Western journalists after Tiananmen to call the orthodox, Marxist central planners "conservatives." Chinese politics is not structured according to the Western idea of progress that has produced the natural division between those who value change and those who uphold the past. The rhythm of Chinese politics is usually not the pendulum swings of left and right, of change versus continuity; rather, it is framed within the hierarchical structure of government, and thus follows the up-and-down motions of centralizing and decentralizing, tightening and relaxing, controlling and loosening, *shou* and *fang*.

Leaders can, of course, be seen at different times as having certain policy tendencies, but it would be dangerous to assume binding consistency. Chinese leaders are granted great flexibility and find it easy to shift their positions as circumstances change. Both Mao and Deng were generally comfortable with their policy zigs and zags. American public figures have to go through all kinds of contortions to prove that they have always held the same views, and consequently they are often uneasy that someone will expose their contradictions.

209

In China, followers can accept significant policy changes by their leaders because their bonds are of a more personal nature.

On the rare occasions when factional strife punctures the veil of consensus, the Chinese ruling elite usually appears to be divided into contending groups. Furthermore, Chinese rhetoric about intraparty conflicts invariably describes the struggles as being between "two lines." Yet such clear bipolar divisions in fact have been the exception, occurring only at times of extreme crisis. The more normal condition is a pattern of factional distribution in which groupings of officials are scattered within the hierarchy of Chinese politics. Much of the time the groupings are latent, nurturing themselves by providing the individuals involved with increments of security as frequently as is necessary or possible. Sometimes the networks are lax to the point of apparent nonexistence; at other times they are agitated into action, whereupon coalitions and alignments of networks take on the character of aggressive factions.

Leaders do not necessarily strive consciously to build up networks of followers—in fact there is a taboo in the ethics of the party against precisely such endeavors, a taboo so strong that senior officials are not supposed to engage in explicit talent searches among the younger cadres. Instead, the networks tend to take a hierarchical shape and eventually strive to attach themselves to particular leaders. Consequently, any leader who has had a successful career in the party will inevitably find that he has developed a chain of potential supporters. Unless he acts to satisfy their needs, they will, in time, abandon him for another, more supportive leader. As a result he will be alone, and as his peers discover his vulnerability, competitors will arise to seek his downfall in order to use his position to satisfy their own networks of supporters. At the same time a superior cannot be seen as overly protective, for this would violate the taboo against being an active patron. Deng Xiaoping, in spite of carefully nurturing both Hu Yaobang and Zhao Ziyang as his successors, had to dispassionately wash his hands of them when they each got into trouble.

The fact that factions are generally mobilized out of latent networks of associations, through the introduction of highly symbolic communications, indicates how loosely structured these critical units of Chinese politics are. The boundaries between factions tend to be vague, and there is often uncertainty as to whether certain officials in fact belong to one faction or another. Even at the core of factions, relations can be more tacit than explicit.

Consequently, when a faction comes under attack there may be two diametrically opposite reactions: Those at the periphery often choose to fade away, denying whatever associations they may have had, while those at the core seek to strengthen their bonds, taking on a siege mentality. For example, in 1978 the Chinese press issued dark hints about the enduring power of three factions: the "slip-away faction," composed of people who would drift away from meetings when denunciations of the Gang's followers became vehement; a "swivel faction," which would adjust its posture to any change in the political climate; and a "wind faction," which pleaded that the past for which they were being attacked was "gone with the wind." Similarly when first Hu Yaobang and then Zhao Ziyang fell from power most of those who had been their most loyal followers soon drifted away and made no attempts to maintain the power of their respective groups. It was the students and not his former associates who used the occasion of Hu Yaobang's death for political purpose.

The same structural constraints appear to operate when a faction is on the rise, since there can be considerable uncertainty as to how the benefits should be distributed within the coalition. Those who lose out become disaffected, while those who benefit most must hang together, for they will eventually become the targets of attack by the next emerging faction.

The tacit nature of factions is accentuated by the process of accretion whereby networks of associations are expanded at different times, under different conditions, and for different reasons. Thus, the very things that hold a faction together at one time may become the cause for dissension under changed conditions. Given the tortuous history of the CCP, nearly all power groupings contain people who would disagree now about the merits of past events.

These considerations were shaped by Mao Zedong's profoundly important decision that the CCP would not follow Stalin's practice of applying the death penalty in party purges. Although we now know that thousands of people were "persecuted to death" during the Cultural Revolution, the usual Chinese practice has been to stress rehabilitation through re-education, which has meant that not only can purged victims be restored, but also most organizations contain people who have been hurt and who thus have scores to settle once the opportunity arises. While it is true that dismissed cadres may not be directly punished, the practice of keeping them at home under a form of house arrest can be not only humiliating but also psychologically damaging. Both Hu Yaobang and Zhao Ziyang are reported to have become seriously depressed after they were removed from office and isolated at home. Also the uneven and arbitrary pattern of punishment after the Tiananmen Massacre has demoralized cadres who were not themselves prime targets of punishment.

The Power of Personal Ties

Because of its critical importance in providing the psychological foundations of the factions, it is appropriate to pause briefly to examine in greater detail the Chinese cultural phenomenon of *guanxi*. The key ingredient of factions is this

212

distinctly Chinese concept, which has no exact counterpart in other cultures. It has dimensions and overtones that go beyond such relationships as particularistic bonds or patron-client ties, and therefore it is not easily appreciated by foreigners. Until recently most Western commentators have ignored the importance of *guanxi* and have favored instead such other cultural traits as the Chinese concern about gaining or losing "face" (*lien* or *mienze*). Possibly this has been because such concepts as "face" or "filial piety" presumably have a more positive ethical quality, distinguishing as they do honorable from possibly shameful conduct.[3] In contrast, foreigners and modernized Chinese alike have tended to see *guanxi* as a somewhat sordid form of unenlightened favoritism that should disappear once the "restoration" of Chinese culture occurs. Consequently, there has been little explicit analysis of the concept of *guanxi*.[4] Yet, even though it would be impossible

[3] On the psychodynamics of the Chinese concept of "face," see Hua Hsien-chin, "The Chinese Concept of Face," *American Anthropologist*, 46 (1944), 45–64; Warner Muensterberger, "Orality and Dependence: Characteristics of Southern Chinese," *Psychoanalysis and the Social Sciences*, 3 (1951), 37–69; John H. Weakland, "The Organization of Action in Chinese Culture," *Psychiatry*, 13 (1950), 361–370; and Weston la Barre, "Some Observations on Character Structure in the Orient: II, The Chinese," *Psychiatry*, 9 (1976), 215–237.

[4] Studies that implicitly acknowledge the role of *guanxi* in pre-Communist Chinese political relations include Andrew J. Nathan, *Peking Politics, 1918–1923* (Berkeley: University of California Press, 1976) chap. 2; Lucian W. Pye, *Warlord Politics* (New York: Praeger, 1971); and Hsi-sheng ch'i, *Warlord Politics in China, 1916–1928* (Palo Alto: Stanford University Press, 1976), 36–76.

Analyses of Communist Party politics that recognize the importance of *guanxi* include William W. Whitson, *The Chinese High Command: A History of Communist Military Politics, 1927–1971* (New York: Praeger, 1973); Thomas W. Robinson, "Lin Piao as an Elite Type," in *Elites in the People's Republic of China*, ed. Robert A. Scalapino (Seattle: University of Washington Press, 1972); Frederick C. Teiwes, *Provincial Leadership in China: The Cultural Revolution and Its Aftermath*, Cornell University East Asia Papers, no. 4 (Ithaca: Cornell University Press, 1974); Michel Oksenberg, "The Exit Pattern from Chinese Politics and Its Implications," *China Quarterly*, no. 67 (September 1976); and idem, "Getting Ahead and Along in Communist China: The Ladder of Success on the Eve of the Cultural Revolution," in *Party,*

to test such a hypothesis quantitatively, there is considerable evidence suggesting that instead of declining in importance, *guanxi* may have increased as Chinese have experienced all the unsettling effects of revolution and social change.[5] *Guanxi* involves far more than just the Western notion of social contacts and connections related to influence. In the West, the key to the flow of personal influence in particularistic relations, say, in the "old boy network," is actual acquaintanceship; in the case of *guanxi,* it is enough that the social roles are seen as related, even though the individuals may not have previously known each other.

To a limited degree, however, it is helpful for understanding *guanxi* to think of the analogy of acquaintanceship networks in American society. As a result of increased communication, particularly through the professions, the number of people in the chain of acquaintanceships necessary to link any two Americans has probably declined over the last hundred years. Certainly within any of the major professions, such as any academic discipline, it is usually possible for any reasonably centrally placed member of the discipline to get a "reading" on even the most obscure member with only one or two phone calls, and it is estimated that at the most it requires only six or seven people to connect any two Americans in an acquaintanceship chain. In their latent state, these potential chains

---

Leadership, and Revolutionary Power in China, ed. John W. Lewis (Cambridge: Cambridge University Press, 1970).

[5] An excellent analysis of *guanxi* is J. Bruce Jacobs, "A Preliminary Model of Particularistic Ties in Chinese Political Alliances: Kan-ch'ing and Kuan-hsi in a Rural Taiwanese Township," *China Quarterly,* no. 78 (June 1979), 237–273. His typology of the bases of *guanxi* for studying a contemporary Taiwanese township seems applicable for the personalistic relations of early Republican China, and although he is cautious about generalizing to the PRC, his model seems to be appropriate for handling the place of *guanxi* in contemporary Chinese politics. A good case study of the role of *guanxi* in factional relations in a Chinese community is Barbara K. L. Pillsbury, "Factionalism Observed: Behind the Face of Harmony in a Chinese Community," *China Quarterly,* no. 74 (June 1978).

of acquaintanceship are essentially the same in America and China; the big difference, of course, is the purposes for which they can be used once they have been activated. In the American case, it is true that one can, with some delicacy, go beyond merely asking for an objective "reading" of the abilities of another; in China, there is no question that greater demands can be made. It is not just that the dividing line between acquaintanceship and friendship is different in the two cultures; there is also a difference in what can be legitimately expected of even the most limited connection.[6]

The first thing to note about *guanxi* is that it is thought of as having an almost physical objective existence, and therefore it is not merely a subjective phenomenon, knowable only to participants. Thus it is perfectly reasonable for one person to inquire of another as to whether two other people do or do not "have *guanxi*," and if the answer is yes, then it is assumed that the third party should be able to give a precise reading of the exact "quantity" and not just the "quality" of the *guanxi*.[7]

A more important characteristic of *guanxi* is that its existence or nonexistence affects not only the behavior of those directly involved in the relationship; it can potentially affect all who are to any degree related to either of the principals. Thus, if X inquires of Y whether A and B have *guanxi,* and it is established that they do and that Y has a relationship with B, then it can be assumed that X should be able to establish a claim upon A. This is, of course, the nature of the latent

[6] For an outstanding analysis of how the Chinese concept of *ganging,* or the affect in *guanxi* relations, differs from the Western concept of friendship, see Morton A. Fried, *Fabric of Chinese Society: A Study of a Chinese County Seat* (New York: Praeger, 1953).

[7] Someone who is not acquainted with the Chinese concept of *guanxi* might, on reading Bruce Jacobs' analysis (note 5 above), conclude that his schematic model for measuring the value of *guanxi* was an example of mechanistic social science searching for the illusion of quantification. In fact, however, his model is true to the Chinese spirit of objectifying and quantifying *guanxi* relations.

215

networks among the cadres. The fact that Y has played a key role in making the network possible puts him in the highly esteemed Chinese position of middleman—which means that he can expect benefits from all the parties. Furthermore, the more substantive the outcome of X and A's new relationship, the more Y and B can expect to benefit. Hence there is less reluctance than might be expected for people to mediate actively in order to expand a *guanxi* network, since all the middlemen can conceivably benefit more than either of the principals who are the poles of the network.

Guanxi, however, must not be confused with the concept of patron-client relationships, which has recently become a popular way of describing alliances between the well-to-do and less well-to-do in rural Asia and other Third World regions. (Those who have helped popularize that concept have also, I believe, unfortunately stripped it of much of the richness of cultural variations in their efforts to make all cases fit various abstract models of the relationship.)[8] The patron-

[8] James C. Scott has been a leader in expanding the concept of the dyadic relationship of patron-client (landlord–peasant tenant) into a more general theory of moral economy. The basic assumptions of moral economy are that the traditional patron-client relationship, involving peasants and landlords, concerned norms about justice and fairness that were the bases of the "moral" community of traditional societies, and that the introduction of market forces associated with the rise of capitalism threatened the security of the peasants, making them prone to rebellion. See such studies as James C. Scott, *The Moral Economy of Peasants* (New Haven: Yale University Press 1976); idem, "Patron-Client Politics and Political Change in Southeast Asia," *American Political Science Review*, 66 (March 1972), 92–113; idem, "The Erosion of Patron-Client Bonds and Social Change in Southeast Asia," *Journal of Asian Studies*, 22 (November 1972), 5–37; Carl Lande, "Networks and Groups in Southeast Asia: Some Observations on the Group Theory of Politics," *American Political Science Review*, 67 (March 1973), 103–127; Eric Wolf, *Peasants* (Englewood Cliffs, N.J.: Prentice-Hall, 1966); and idem, *Peasant Wars of the Twentieth Century* (New York: Harper & Row, 1969).

The moral economy theory has been challenged by advocates of a political economy approach, who hold that peasants have responded rationally to market opportunities, that the patron-client ties can be understood in terms

client relationship assumes a more substantial difference in the resources available to parties involved than has to be the case with *guanxi*. In some respects, it is surprising that, given the great emphasis upon hierarchy in Chinese culture, there is not a sharper sense of "patron" and "client" in *guanxi*. Yet the very essence of *guanxi* is that the relationship is in the first instance based upon a shared particularism—a common place of origin, a shared teacher, grandfathers who were friends, and the like—and thus there is a pretense of equality even as there must be the subtle recognition of superior and inferior. Also, in contrast to patron-client relations, in *guanxi* there is much greater acknowledgment that the inferior can victimize the superior, and there is also much greater use of stratagems in creating feelings of responsibility and obligation on the one hand and indebtedness on the other.

In *guanxi* there is a complex blend of affect and calculation. In contrast to Western culture, it is good form in Chinese culture to show explicit interest in the selection of the best stratagem or ploy in expanding or manipulating *guanxi* ties. On the other hand, in Chinese culture it is not necessary to dramatize or inflate the affective considerations; it is assumed that only the shameless will not honor their particularistic obligations.

---

of cost-benefit analysis, and therefore that reactions to change reflect the objective conditions and not just subjective feelings about justice and fairness. See Samuel L. Popkin, *The Rational Peasant* (Berkeley: University of California Press, 1979).

The character of the ties among Chinese officials falls between these two views about patron-client relations. In line with the moral economy theory, we recognize the importance of culture, but our understanding of the cultural factor is not limited to moral norms about justice and fairness; it includes all the learned behavior and practices that are deemed to give security in interpersonal relations. In line with the political economy approach, we recognize that there is considerable rational calculation guiding the behavior of superiors and subordinates, but we also maintain that what is "rational" can be understood only in the light of cultural predispositions and not according to an abstract calculus.

The Suppression of Bureaucratic Interests

In relation to the dynamics of factions under the rule of orthodoxy and consensus, a strange paradox of Chinese politics is that even though almost all the action takes place in the context of a status hierarchy the alignments of the factional networks usually do not reflect bureaucratic interests.

In most political systems it is assumed that departments, ministries, agencies, and other formal organizations have their own institutional interests, and that there will inevitably be clashes among these interests. Sometimes the conflicts involve broad and fundamental issues, such as agriculture versus industry, or light versus heavy industry; at other times, the conflicts are quite narrow and center on the allocation of resources or questions of authority and jurisdiction. Such conflicts lie at the heart of most governmental processes and, described as bureaucratic politics, they are taken as a normal fact of life in most countries.

Not so in China. The very admission of the normality of such conflicts would be to debase the importance of consensus. Indeed, precisely because any faction based upon institutional or organizational considerations would be a challenge to the ideal of consensus, the Chinese go to great lengths to prevent the emergence of such bureaucratic interests. Government institutions are supposed to fit together as cogs, and no leader should assert his special interests over the collective interests.

Mao, of course, did legitimize what he called "nonantagonistic contradictions," but these were of a more general nature, largely between the people and the party, and they did not involve clashes between parts of the government that in theory should work together smoothly. The Marxist-Leninist doctrines of the unity of theory and practice and of the correctness of party line have also contributed to the conviction

218

that institutionally based conflicts are abominations that
threaten the integrity of the regime.

Although Mao's assertion that the history of Chinese communism could be encapsulated in his theory of the struggle
between "two lines" was an admission that intraelite conflicts
were possible, it is significant that all struggles between the
"two lines" have been officially described as manifestations
of personal ideological failings; never has there been a hint
that clashes over the correct line arose out of the logic of
different institutional interests. The "ten great line struggles"
that Mao spoke of and the two additional struggles identified
by the current leadership, involving the purges of Lin Biao
and the Gang of Four, all presumably represented the failings
of individuals. The Chinese refuse to entertain the notion that
their intraparty disagreements, such as the post-Tiananmen
clashes between "hardliners" and "reformers," might in any
way reflect the interests and perspectives of particular institutions.

Significantly, in imperial China, although political life was
structured around a centralized bureaucracy that was divided
into ministries or boards, the factional politics of the mandarins also rarely reflected institutional interests. The Chinese
have historically been extremely sensitive to the dangers of
officials' becoming contentious, especially in efforts to represent their bureaucratic interests. The principal defense employed in traditional China was that of preventing specialization. In the earliest period, the highest officials around the
emperor did not represent functional boards and hence particular interests, but were designated in entirely meaningless
symbolic ways, such as according to the points of the com-
pass. (To a curious extent, some of the members of the current Chinese Politburo are equally free-floating and have no
specialized responsibilities.) Later, as the six ministries or
boards became more formally institutionalized, the Chinese
continued to protect themselves against bureaucratic politics

by ensuring that officials did not develop institutional loyalties that would drive them to excessive zeal in championing the interests of any department. The tradition of "gentlemanly power" among mandarins required that officials never become too interested for too long in the technical problems of any ministry. By conscious design, enthusiastic advocates of any upsetting policies in any particular ministry could expect to be reassigned so as to have to work against the very programs they had initiated. A high official in, say, the Ministry of War could be certain that if he pushed too hard for greater allocations to the military he would shortly be transferred to the Ministry of Finance, where he would be expected to advance with equal enthusiasm all the arguments against his previous pleas for more funds for the Ministry of War. To a startling degree, cadres who reach high positions today also tend to have careers that have forced them periodically to alter their enthusiasms for specialized institutional interests.

In Chinese politics, policy issues have long been relegated to second place behind questions about legitimacy and propriety. Whether it was mandarins seeking to rule an extensive empire or cadres today straining to govern a billion people, the first priority has always been the need to uphold correct conduct in order to preserve the social order. Both mandarin and cadre discovered from experience that their first concern always had to be adherence to their respective norms of propriety, which in the spirit of consensus always included the rule that everyone else should also conform. Historically, Chinese bureaucracies have been wondrous institutions for providing the inertia necessary for governmental durability. By being impervious to the costs of stalling actions and of obstructing policy initiatives until the illusion of consensus has been realized, and by being hypersensitive to the psychic rewards of condescension toward the lesser orders, Chinese bureaucrats, both those of long ago and those of today, have proved that the continuity of regimes resides more in being than in doing.[9] Rather than chase the will-o'-the-wisp of accomplishments, they have valued the universal instinct of deference for the exemplar of a culture's ideals, even if the ideals are only of the moment—the "model" worker, peasant, cadre, or leader, or the quintessential Confucian scholar-mandarin.

The key structural or organizational reason for the muting of bureaucratic interests is that Chinese procedures prohibit communication among subordinates in different ministries or departments. Interministry or interdepartment coordination must generally take place at the very top. Thus, instead of the constant flow of telephone calls and meetings among subordinates that occurs in most bureaucratic systems, subordinates communicate up or down only within their own ministry. The responsibility for coordinating policy and settling organizational conflicts is reserved for those at the center. Junior officials are denied the possibility of seeking allies in other ministries or departments and are not able to impress their superiors with having outnegotiated competitors in other hierarchies. Superiors do not expect their subordinates to test the positions of other ministries or even to explore ahead of time the views of potentially contending power centers.

Evidence about the lack of interdepartmental communication comes from the testimony of numerous foreign businessmen who, much to their amazement, have had Chinese in one ministry ask them about the views and positions of officials in another ministry. The Chinese have explained their need to ask Americans to serve as middlemen on the grounds that it is improper for them to contact directly people in another chain of command.

Thus the flow of policy-oriented demands can move directly

---

[9] For an exceptionally illuminating explanation of why concerns for proper conduct and form had to take precedence over substantive issues in imperial China, see Ray Huang, *1587: A Year of No Significance* (New Haven: Yale University Press, 1981).

upward only within separate encased hierarchies, an organizational arrangement that from time to time contributes to the impression that the Chinese are about to surge ahead on all fronts—with no sense of priorities—as each ministry or organization seeks in its own way to carry out the general policies of the day. Only when all the separate bureaucracies have made their "commitments" or their "demands" and these have been passed up to the State Council or the Politburo are there any dampening effects from the ultimate imperative that resources are scarce and priorities must be set. Instead of the complex game of governmental politics in which almost no one is too humble to seek outside allies or to strive for recognition by winning interagency battles over substantively trivial issues, the Chinese system permits subordinates to push whatever policy initiatives they have only toward the top of their own ministries.

When such initiatives do reach the top, they cannot become the stuff of open, bureaucratically based politics because of a peculiar lack of congruence at the pinnacle: For reasons that have never been explicated but seem to be ingeniously clever—given the Chinese commitment to repress all policy conflicts—the Chinese have more ministries than vice-premiers. Thus individual vice-premiers have to take responsibility for several related ministries, resolving in their own way any potential conflicts.

The Primacy of Power

Our analysis thus leads to the fundamental proposition that in Chinese factional politics power considerations are generally decisive because power is seen as the least ambiguous and most predictive of all factors in social life. Institutions, organizations, generational identities, and geographic affiliations all provide bases for factional alignments in Chinese politics, but although these considerations do at times suggest policy preferences, they are less important than pure power calculations. Leaders can shift their positions according to all the other considerations, but in the end they have to recognize that power is sovereign.

Given the Chinese leaders' preferences for unambiguously defined situations and their comfort with hierarchical relationships, it is understandable that they place a premium on their perception of the distribution of power. Power, they like to believe, is an ultimate reality. It is noteworthy that when the Chinese had a multipolar political system, in the 1920's, the warlords did not always adhere to the classical rules of balance-of-power politics but frequently followed a distinctively Chinese pattern. Instead of a potentially dominant actor causing the lesser actors to coalesce as a balancing force, the weakest warlords usually tried to learn what they could gain by identifying with strength, and only then would they explore the payoffs of forming an alliance of the weak. The more generous the strong, the more readily they became magnets. (Note that this was precisely the way the warlord era ended, when Chiang Kai-shek steadily bought off his opposition.) By allying himself with strength, a lesser warlord could greatly heighten his power status, particularly relative to those who had no alternative but to oppose the emerging threat. Thus, for the Chinese warlords, autonomy was not the ultimate value, as it was in the traditional European balance-of-power calculation; rather, they based their decisions upon associating with power.

In today's China, given the cross-pressures of political life, it is often difficult to determine the realities of power as precisely as the Chinese would like. Institutions are real and do have a solid base, but it is never clear how far a particular institution can extend its influence as compared with another. Generations are readily recognizable and they provide a clear basis for status differences, but they provide almost no guidance as to effective power. In the end, for most cadres the most reliable key to evaluating relative power is their judgment about the scope of influence of particular individuals.

The inordinate importance of such personalized power in Chinese Communist politics derives in part from the absence of a system of rule by law. Cadres cannot count on one another to act predictably according to impersonal rules. To make matters worse, there is no longer the binding role of custom or tradition, which could also limit the importance of personalized power. Thus in Chinese politics the two traditional limitations on power, law and custom, are missing. And the prospect is that power is likely to become even more important because the rather fragile Communist form of restraint, ideology, will probably erode faster than a system of law can be established.

In seeking to fathom the obscurities of Chinese elite power relationships it is best to be guided by three cardinal principles. Unfortunately, they are not consistent, but their very contradictions help illuminate a basic source of the pervasive uncertainty of Chinese politics. The three principles will by no means make Chinese politics completely understandable to the outsider, but this should not be cause for discouragement; as Vietnam's Prime Minister Tran Van Dong once explained to Ambassador Maxwell Taylor, "Don't feel badly about not understanding Vietnamese politics; we don't understand it ourselves."

The first principle of power in China is that the people tend to conceive of power relationships as a single coherent hierarchy, and therefore they try to reduce as much as possible the discrepancies between their formal and informal structures of power. (Americans, on the other hand, tend to take it for granted that congruences are unlikely between formal officeholders and actual power-wielders.) The most telling evidence of this feature of Chinese political behavior is the fact that of all the countries that have experienced Communist rule, the

Chinese have had the greatest difficulty in maintaining the conventional dual hierarchies of state and party. While the Soviet Union and the Eastern European countries have routinely institutionalized the dual formal and informal structures of state and party, the Chinese Communists have been uncomfortable without a single line of authority. Unable to work smoothly with a dual power hierarchy, the Chinese—contrary to both conventional Communist practices and the near-universal fantasy about the supremacy of hidden powers—have given primacy to the more formal powers. (In doing so, they have, however, still acceded to the human propensity to mystify authority by making obscure the workings of formal, public authority.)

The second principle about power, which qualifies but does not contradict the first, is that status tends to imply power and is not treated as being merely symbolic. To be more precise, symbolic matters are treated as manifestations of genuine power, and hence status becomes power. Anyone who visited China in the early post-Mao years will agree that two decades of egalitarian ideology did not blunt the Chinese sensitivity to status differences. Indeed, the elimination of explicit differentiating by such obvious, though crude, measures as wealth has made the Chinese even more alert to the subtleties of status differences.

The uncompromising obligation to defer to those of higher status makes it easy for such persons to use power. Consequently, ceremonial appointments can be readily transformed into actual power roles if the incumbent chooses to assert authority. Old men may be appointed to high offices as tokens of respect, but there is the risk that such appointees will not be passive and will exploit their potential for influence.

The third principle, which can operate to contradict the other two, is that power is readily transmitted through linkages of personal relationships. Indeed, the very basis of the

225

power networks in Chinese politics is the pattern of personal bonds that are strengthened by Chinese concepts of friendship and *guanxi*.

This aspect of personal relationships introduces an extraordinary element of uncertainty into Chinese politics: Could it be that X, who otherwise has no claim to fame, is in an honored position merely because of his old age, or could he be the ally of a very powerful figure? Is the obscure man behind the scenes wishfully pretending to be, as the Chinese call it, a wire-puller, or is he legitimately an associate of one óf the principals in the political game? Indeed, the initial appearance of any figure in the topmost circle, whether he be a venerable worthy or a youthful aspirant, immediately raises the question of who was the sponsor who has just demonstrated an inflation of his power.

Clearly, these three principles collectively work to complicate, and hence obscure, the realities of power for a people who believe that it is imperative to be able to read the delineations of power.

The fact that politically conscious Chinese find it difficult at times to perceive the realities of relative power and therefore are filled with anxieties about misjudging the situation does not, however, generate what might be called a paranoid style of politics. Instead, those who are confused tend to constrict their vision, ignore what they cannot fathom, and concentrate their attention on the most immediate linkages to power available to them. Thus, uncertainty strengthens personal ties, the very phenomenon that introduces the greatest imponderable into the power calculation. The result is a vicious circle.

And, of course, the importance of the third principle is precisely what contributes to the opaqueness of Chinese politics. The supposition that much must be going on that defies perception suggests that private linkages have intruded into public affairs. At every level in the political system, anyone's power may be orders of magnitude greater than first impressions would indicate, but then again the opposite could also be true.

Hence, in spite of all the striving for certainty in the calculations of power associated with the first two principles, the third principle operates to ensure that an element of mystery constantly surrounds the facts of power in Chinese politics.

The Search for Clarity Exaggerates the Difference between Friend and Foe

When we examine the interaction of these three principles more closely, many obscure patterns of Chinese political behavior become intelligible.

The speed with which leaders have risen and fallen in Chinese politics can be explained partly by the inconsistency of the three principles. A surprisingly rapid rise may occur because the routine assignments that make up one's only public record may mask more significant relationships behind the scene. The distinctively Chinese characteristic of such cases of dramatic promotions is that they almost never depend upon quality of performance in publicly observable roles; rather, they depend upon behind-the-scene developments. This is paradoxical, given the Chinese propensity to attach more importance to formal than to informal power hierarchies.

Even more distinctive is the management of the fall from power in China. In view of the deserved renown of the Chinese in dealing with matters of "face," it is surprising that they have generally been brutal in removing people from office and have not engaged in ritual promotions to ceremonial offices. The problem here is that the Chinese have been hoisted by their own cultural petard: Believing in rule by men and not by law, they find it difficult to define a high-status office that cannot be used as a power base, and thus it is impossible to "promote" a man to a high position that has been stripped of power by legalistic regulations.

People in high ceremonial positions can all too easily seek to translate status into power and use personal ties with those who command other, more literal forms of power. Furthermore, the tactic of "kicking someone upstairs" does not seem to work in Chinese politics because those who do the kicking may be envious and may ask. "Why should he get all the rewards and comforts of high station rather than one of us?"

The practice of leaving compromised leaders in official positions for even a brief time fits the Chinese tendency to underplay the importance of ensuring that power and responsibility are combined. The importance of status and of personal ties has meant that people can wield considerable power without being held accountable. Leaders with high status but little administrative responsibility may erratically intervene in the policymaking process and create confusion. Politburo members without appropriate administrative duties may use their high status for random interventions which they may not be able to sustain and which could provoke erratic governmental activities.

All of these causes of uncertainty in power patterns, combined with the belief that nothing is possible without understanding the realities of power, encourage the Chinese to attach extreme importance to perceiving accurately the friends and the enemies of each principal leader. When power relations are confused, the simplest way to find order is to determine precisely who is associated with or opposed to whom. This need promotes a tendency to exaggerate the differences between friends and enemies and to reduce the category of neutral. Friends must be nurtured, they cannot just be taken for granted; enemies have to be defended against, they cannot just be ignored.

The Awesome Powers of Denial and the Limits of Chinese Nationalism

Our discussion of power and factions brings into the open subjects that are deeply repressed in Chinese public discourse. As we have noted, not only is there a profound aversion in Chinese political culture to speaking openly about power, but Chinese leaders will uniformly deny the existence of factions. The interplay of power and factions must therefore take place behind the curtain of orthodoxy. The imperative of conformity and consensus also means that factional power struggles have surprisingly little impact upon the established ideology. Although the popularity of different slogans and code words can signal the fortunes of the different factions, the more fundamental content of ideology does not usually provide an accurate scoreboard as to who is up or down. Ideology is treated as of such great importance in form and ritual that it has to be largely isolated from the realities of power and the consequences of power struggles. The object of the cadres is not to change the substance of the formal ideology but to maximize their security.

The cumulative effects of the Cultural Revolution and the repeated disappointments and frustration over the utopian promises of Communism have, however, eroded the potency of Marxism–Leninism–Mao Zedong Thought and thereby undermined the legitimacy of the party elite. At the same time, however, the awesome powers of denial in the culture have prevented the factions from emerging publicly as advocates of different sets of interests and hence of different visions of what China should become. Unable to perform the task of interest articulation and interest aggregation, the networks of cadres have been unable to move China ahead in political development to a stage of real politics.

Battered though Marxism-Leninism-Maoism has become, it remains the only orthodoxy, performing the critical function of upholding the myth of consensus. Some China specialists argue that soon the ideology may be quietly set aside in favor of Chinese nationalism. This development, however, will not necessarily open up Chinese politics enough to legitimize the competition of factions. Indeed, there are some problems with Chinese nationalism which we can only touch on here but which suggest that it may lack sufficient content to hold the ring for more open partisan competition.

The biggest problem is that much of what is usually thought of as Chinese nationalism are really powerful sentiments of racial and cultural identity and not feelings about the nation as a state. Nationalism is a modern sentiment that appeared only with the emergence of the nation-state in Europe, and it should not be confused in the Chinese case with such historic attitudes as "Han chauvinism" and the "Middle Kingdom complex." The distinction is important because the two perform quite different political functions. Ethnic identity can provide the basis for distinguishing the collective sense of "we-ness" from all the others who are the "they." However, for ethnicity to become a part of a true nationalism something more is needed. Nationalism as a state of feelings about the nation as a state needs to have specific content such as the ideals, symbols, and myths which can inspire a people and help regulate their public lives. Nationalism must speak not only to what is unique about one's own country but also to how, as a state in a world of states, the country meets the international standards of modern statehood.

More importantly for our purposes, nationalism also establishes constraints on the behavior of the elite by setting standards as to what is expected of true national leaders. Thus in their respective partisan politics there are certain things that, say, British, French, or American leaders cannot do because those things would violate their respective nationalistic norms. The problem with Chinese nationalism is that it lacks the content necessary to constrain partisan leaders. The Communist leaders are able to insist that they represent the nation, and anyone who disagrees with them is by definition "unpatriotic." The lack of any distinction between Chinese nationalism on the one hand and the partisan positions of either Communist or Kuomintang leaders means that all dissenting critics run the risk of being labeled subversive enemies of the Chinese people. In a sense the constraints of nationalism should serve as the basis for the "unwritten constitution" that establishes the arena for partisan politics. In the Chinese case, there is not enough content to what might be called Chinese nationalism to distinguish it from the self-interested position of whoever dominates the system at any moment.

For more than a century Chinese spokesmen have been trying to articulate a vision of nationalism that would have more substance. Often this has taken the form of looking back to when China was "ahead" of the world (whatever that might mean) and then calling for China to "catch up" (whatever that may mean). No nation has built a spirit of meaningful nationalism out of mere material accomplishments. The pride and honor of the British has nothing to do with being the homeland of the Industrial Revolution but rather comes from the glory of king and Parliament, and from all that was associated with once bearing the "White Man's Burden." Similarly, the French think in terms not of GNP but of such values as the Enlightenment and the cry of "liberty, equality, fraternity." And of course American nationalism is built upon the Declaration of Independence, the Bill of Rights, and the dream of democracy and human rights. In contrast China lacks the idealistic substance of a modern form of nationalism which can provide either inspiration for popular mobilization or disciplining constraints on elite behavior. Instead an overwhelming sense of ethnic identity operates to obscure the fact that there are very few specific ideals for defining unambiguously the meaning of "Chineseness." Chinese nationalism is not something Chinese society can use to limit the Chinese state. Rather, Chinese nationalism is what the leaders of the day say it is, and this means that it becomes a defense of their formulation of what the consensus should be.

Consequently the dynamics of Chinese politics continues to operate according to the tension between conformity to formal orthodoxy and factional striving for power and security among the cadres. The result is also a gross imbalance between state power and society, to which we turn next.

ERRATIC STATE, FRUSTRATED SOCIETY

Why does China thwart, frustrate, and even embarrass those who try to help? For all who befriend China, the story is the same: high hopes then disappointment. The exhilaration of the Beijing Spring followed by the rage at the Tiananmen Massacre was only the high-theater version of the countless commonplace ways in which China continually brings hope and then despair to its well-wishers. In world politics all governments, whether democratic or Communist, have had their special problems in maintaining smooth relations with Chinese authorities. But it is of course Chinese people themselves who are the most hurt and frustrated.

China seems to evoke in others, particularly Americans, an irresistible desire to serve as China's teachers in the ways of the modern world, and thereby presumably help China improve itself. Yet, from the time of Lord Palmerston's efforts to get the Chinese to accept the conventions of Western diplomacy, to President George Bush's attempts to alter the behavior of Beijing's current rulers, China seems impelled to reject the helping hand and to act in ways that, to those who believe they have the country's interests at heart, seem perversely self-damaging.

Western frustrations with the conduct of Chinese officials began with the first efforts to "open" China. Even after 1842, when the Qing court agreed in the Treaty of Nanking to establish state-to-state relations, the British were driven again to use military muscle, in part to get the Chinese to establish a foreign office and conduct "normal" diplomatic relations. Faced with *force majeure* the Chinese reluctantly gave up their tradition of "managing barbarian affairs" through the offices of the Board of Rites, where specialists in protocol could teach uninformed foreigners the "usages of the empire," including how to get down on all fours when kowtowing to the August One. They did indeed set up a crude facsimile of a foreign office. The British, however, were driven to exasperation, for they were convinced that in staffing the new office, the Tsung-li Yamen, the Chinese must have diabolically scoured the imperial bureaucracy to find the most dim-witted of officials, mandarins who could not keep the train of thought through a conversation, who kept forgetting the point at issue, and who were always losing their papers and correspondence. To add insult to injury the Chinese had placed the foreign office on a back street in a rundown building, where passersby could press their noses to the windows to watch Western diplomats attempt to lecture Chinese mandarins on why foreign affairs should not be treated as a mere nuisance.

It is of course understandable and hardly noteworthy that cultural differences should arise in relations among people with quite different traditions. The disappointment with China, however, is of a more troublesome sort. Indeed, the difficulties are particularly frustrating precisely because outsiders usually seem to have an easy time establishing comfortable, often warm, relations with individual Chinese. The problems almost invariably arise from the actions of the government and the ways in which power and authority operate in China. Chinese authority causes trouble not only for foreigners but for the vast majority of the Chinese people. Just when all appears to be going well, Chinese officials create problems for seemingly unaccountable reasons.

234

It is hard to pinpoint the intentions behind their disruptive acts because, in a world glutted with irrational political systems, China's is possibly the most bizarre. Can it be that one year after Tiananmen more than one billion sullen people are left mute and passive victims awaiting the outcome of power struggles among enfeebled strongmen, the one with top billing holding no posts at all, his presumed principal opponent's only claim to legitimacy being membership in an "advisory commission" of "retired" leaders? The problems are far more than just those associated with conventional Communist oppression. China has a political system in which accountability seems to be absent altogether, in which no one appears to know where the responsibility should lie anyway, and, consequently, in which awful things can happen to the ordinary citizen.

The accumulation of American frustrations with China can lead to feelings of betrayal. Americans may even come to believe that, with the end of the Cold War, China has lost its geopolitical relevance. But, because a quarter of humanity cannot possibly be irrelevant, it is important to try understanding why the Chinese government, in contrast to the Chinese people, has been and remains such a disappointment. Unfortunately, the problems are not ephemeral; their roots extend deep into China's historical experience. True understanding of these problems, therefore, calls for an analysis of the complex and unique ways in which the Chinese state and society have evolved.

The starting point for understanding the problem is to recognize that China is not just another nation-state in the family of nations. China is a civilization pretending to be a state. The story of modern China could be described as the effort by both Chinese and foreigners to squeeze a civilization into the arbitrary and constraining framework of a modern state, an institutional invention that came out of the fragmentation of Western civilization. Viewed from another perspective, the miracle of China has been its astonishing unity. In Western terms, it is as if the Europe of the Roman Empire and of Charlemagne had lasted until this day and was trying to function as a single nation-state.

The fact that the Chinese state was founded on one of the world's great civilizations has given inordinate strength and durability to China's political culture. The overpowering obligation felt by Chinese rulers to preserve the unity of their civilization has permitted no compromises in Chinese cultural attitudes about power and authority. Whereas pragmatic considerations have readily guided the Chinese in other spheres of life, this has not been possible with respect to the most fundamental values which determine the basis of legitimacy of the state and which govern the relationship between state and society.

Chinese civilization produced a distinctive and enduring pattern of relations between state and society. Although affairs of state were always secret and tainted with the suspicon of scandal, the realm of government projected grandeur and thus gave all Chinese a right to pride and dignity. Chinese society, on the other hand, was peculiarly passive toward the government, made no claims on state policies, and concentrated its energies on the private domain. Having always been composed of inward-looking groupings, it was cellular in structure. Civil society in China existed only at the local level; there were no national social institutions such as the church in Europe. Thus the state existed alone at the highest collective level.

One secret of the unity of China has been a conspiracy of make-believe that masks the strengths and limitations of both the state and society. The Chinese state, both imperial and Communist, has always pretended to omnipotency, but in reality its policy-implementing authority has been surprisingly limited. Chinese society for its part has gone along with the pretense of official omnipotence while following its own lead

236

and making almost no demands on the government. Rulers and subjects have thus tended to keep their distance from each other while pretending to be harmoniously close.

This peculiar relationship sets the stage for the great Chinese political game of feigned compliance. Central authorities will issue their "absolute" orders and local authorities proclaim their obedience, even as they quietly proceed to do what they think best. Higher-level authorities are hesitant to check too carefully about implementation of their orders for fear that doing so might reveal their impotence and shatter their pretenses of absolute power. Lower-level authorities are careful not to be too blatant in disregarding the more troublesome orders, while being overzealous in carrying out those that are untroublesome. Once embarrassed, however, central authorities can act with mad fury.

In traditional China, as in present-day China, the clash of politics occurred among the topmost rulers and their bureaucracies. The people as a whole had almost nothing to say or do about public affairs, despite the fiction that all policies were executed in their name. Factional political struggles among the elite operated to neutralize policy initiatives, and thus spared the population undue obtrusiveness. The Confucian mandarins understood that the purpose of bureaucratic government was to uphold the ideal of stability, which is best achieved when bureaucrats bend all their wits and energies toward blunting one another's initiatives.

Although government in the People's Republic involves more concerted policy efforts, it is one of the great illusions of the day that Chinese authorities are as omnipotent as they pretend to be. In a host of fields, from tax collecting to controlling economic activities in Guangdong, Fujian, and other dynamic provinces, central authorities know that feigned compliance still reigns and that it is best not to attempt the impossible by demanding obedience. Sovereignty, after all, calls for theatrical representation.

In the meantime the Chinese people ignore the buffoonery of their aged leaders when the latter shrilly promise the imminent collapse of capitalism. The words of officialdom can hardly be taken seriously by an intelligent, pragmatic people when their leaders simultaneously call for more foreign investments. The regime mounts a campaign warning that the West is plotting for China a "peaceful evolution" from socialism to democracy, a danger the people can only hope will come sooner rather than later. The political language of the elite at times loses contact with reality. It speaks of the "bad old days" of Western domination, when only 2 percent of China's national income was related to foreign trade and investment; it touts a proud new anticapitalist, anti-imperialist era when nearly one-third of China's national income depends upon the world capitalist system. State and society in China have quite different realities indeed.

This distinctively Chinese relationship between the state and society was historically sustained by a shared belief in a moral order, the upholding of which gave government legitimacy, and the existence of which gave the people security and peace. Although most traditional societies had comparable moral orders, elsewhere the process of modernization has involved transitions to political orders based on competing economic and social interests. With successful modernization, the balance of power shifts in favor of society and the emerging interests of the people. The authority of government comes to depend upon the outcome of political processes. Instead of being derived from an orthodox moral order, legitimacy is invigorated by the play of politics as codified in a system of laws.

In the case of China, however, significant competing interests never emerged. Instead of a drive toward pluralism and toward a system of legitimacy anchored to the realities of political processes, there was a frantic search for a new moral order to replace the eroding Confucian one. Marxism-

238

Leninism in its Maoist form became the new moral order that reenergized rulers' pretensions to moral superiority and invincibility. The result is a distinctive system, which can be called Confucian Leninism, in which rulers (especially under Mao) claim to have a monopoly on virtue, society is guided by a moralistic ideology, and the hierarchy of officialdom is supposedly composed of exemplary people skilled in doctrinal matters. This continuing emphasis on a moral order explains the exaggerated importance of ideology in the Maoist years, the current propensity to revert to orthodoxy at every sign of political difficulties, and the generally erratic behavior of the state.

Mao sought to do something the Chinese emperors and mandarins were far too prudent to try. He sought to use the legitimacy of the moral order to mobilize people for material advancement, especially during the Great Leap Forward and the Cultural Revolution. When these efforts failed, the legitimacy of the new moral order eroded, and there was a crisis of faith. For a brief time Deng Xiaoping reestablished a sense of legitimacy by providing immediate material payoffs from his reforms. When economic problems began to emerge after 1985, however, the government had neither a moral order nor the benefits of a political process to provide legitimacy. The only immediate alternative was repression. Tiananmen has become the universally acknowledged code word for repression in the search for legitimacy.

For a time the horrors of the Cultural Revolution seemed great enough to extinguish any lingering legitimacy from Marxism-Leninism-Maoism. When Deng initiated his economic reforms a debate was under way between party theorists advocating the "Two Whatevers"—whatever Mao said and whatever Mao did—and those advocating "seeking truth from fact." The debate confused the issue of what should be the criterion for evaluating policies with the larger question of what should be the basis of legitimacy now that Mao, the

Superthinker, was dead. The pragmatists' argument that "practice is the sole criterion of truth" provided far too risky a basis for state legitimacy. No society has been so foolish as to make successful policies the basis of the legitimacy of its government, since the very essence of legitimacy is that it should sustain the government regardless of how partisan policies are working out. In practical terms, Deng used the debate long enough to eliminate his rival Hua Guofeng and his "Whatever" faction, and then reasserted the authority of the "Four Principles," which gave primacy to the party and to the moral order of Marxist-Leninist-Maoist Thought. The debate helped party leaders to liberate their thinking from the silliness of Maoist rhetoric, but it failed to usher in a new basis of legitimacy for the state.

The inestimable importance of the moral order for political legitimacy has made Chinese leaders, both Confucian and Communist, dogmatic believers that values can be vividly categorized into those that are at the core or essence of the moral order; those that are foreign but useful, such as Western science and technology; and those that are an abomination because they contaminate the purity of the core values. The third are to be vigilantly guarded against and denounced, for example, as they are today, as "spiritual pollution" and "bourgeois liberalism." All Chinese leaders, starting with the reformers at the end of the Qing dynasty, have steadfastly followed this formula in trying to modernize China while preserving its civilization. Serious troubles arise, however, when in practice it proves impossible to ensure that the three categories of values are being kept neatly separated. Panic grows at the thought that the purity of the core values is being contaminated by Chinese who are supposed to be learning only practical matters from alien cultures.

The vivid manner in which Chinese leaders have differentiated Chinese values from foreign knowledge has, surprisingly, created problems for the development of a modern sense of

Chinese nationalism. Modern nationalism calls for integrating the parochial culture of a people with the universal qualities of the modern world culture. It is success in this blending of values, and not the artificial preservation of the parochial, that gives vitality to nationalism and the drive for modernization. The Chinese approach has tried to separate what needs to be combined.

This hypersensitivity to what is precious in the Self and what may be useful in the Other makes the Chinese more extreme than other transitional peoples in having at the same time a superiority complex and an inferiority complex, a contradiction that does not particularly bother them. Enough has been said elsewhere about the "Middle Kingdom complex," but what needs to be noted here is that this complex is accompanied by a keen awareness of the need to learn from others, to send students abroad, to search for what is best, and to replicate it in China—with little regard for patents or copyrights. In this process the Chinese have elevated science and technology to core values and have come to revere science in much the same spirit as the earlier mandarins did Confucianism. Thus, instead of having the liberating effect it did in the West, in China science has become a new orthodoxy for a state-supported technocratic elite. The Chinese political approach to science and technology therefore has an absolutist character; it is assumed that there is always a single, best answer to all technical problems.

The Chinese tradition of orthodoxy suggests that technocrats should have a common solution to any problem, with disagreements fought out within the circle of the elite, in the style of defenders of a moral order. Chinese political leaders have refused to recognize that technical problems usually have multiple solutions, and that choosing among them involves the clash of values and power inherent in competitive politics. In other countries debates over alternative technocratic solutions have generally widened political participation

241

and strengthened pluralistic tendencies. This is not so in China, precisely because "science" has been made a part of the Chinese core values that, ironically, must be protected from contamination from other aspects of Western culture that are not "science."

Expecting that science should provide absolute certainty, like answers to arithmetic problems, Chinese political leaders are easily angered by the fact that technology generally calls for probabilistic thinking. They thus imperiously demand the single "correct" answer to a policy problem. Of course political leaders in other countries also have their frustrations with the contingent nature of applied scientific knowledge. Harry Truman, for example, once complained that he wished he could find a one-armed economist, one who would not always be talking about "on the one hand, and on the other hand." In China, however, the authoritarian traditions of the emperors and of Leninism-Maoism combine to produce hostility toward any suggestion of ambiguities and probabilities. Chinese rulers' reactions thus tend to be of the old imperial stripe: "Don't tolerate; exterminate."

This dogmatic approach to science, along with adherence to "scientific" Marxism-Leninism, has produced a psychological problem for Communist leaders as they try to preserve the dichotomy between essential "Chinese" values and the "dangerous" values of foreign cultures. The core values to be defended are, in fact, foreign imports: science and Marxism-Leninism. In an effort to get around this awkward reality, the leadership talks of "building socialism with Chinese characteristics." This formula does not solve the problem, however, because for forty years the party has been denouncing just about every feature of Chinese culture as a feudal abomination that should be obliterated. In the end it is not easy to articulate what exactly are the Chinese qualities that should now be defended. In practice all that is left of "Chineseness" is the belief that leaders have a claim to moral superiority as the defenders of the moral order, even if this involves acting in erratic and arbitrary ways that set back the nation.

Not Interest Groups, but Protective Associations

The stunted growth of interest groups in China is rooted in part in the nature of traditional Chinese society, which was essentially agrarian, and in which the only established channel for upward mobility was the government bureaucracy. China did not have the diversities that emerged in Europe with the rise of the cities, the development of a merchant class, the growth of the professions and occupations, and all the other social changes that contributed to the pluralism basic to modern Western politics. In the West the rise of interest groups in society was also fueled by religious beliefs that valued the individual and gave legitimacy to individualism and the search for self-realization. In China the society was community oriented; individuals were expected to find their identities as part of a group and to conform to the conventions of the collectivity.

This characteristic of Chinese culture profoundly affected the way Chinese political life developed, and it explains why today the government can be so troublesome. The fact that all Chinese derived their identities from being members of a group, starting most importantly with the family and the clan, gave stability to China's unique structure of state-society relations, making it relatively easy for the government to rule. In the Ming dynasty as few as 100,000 officials managed an empire of 100 million people, and a single magistrate was responsible for a county population of about 50,000. Collectivities governed themselves, and the state could rely upon the principle of collective responsibility. In policing it was not necessary to apprehend the particular person who committed a crime. Chinese justice could be administered by arresting, torturing, and punishing the culprit's father, grandfather, or head of his or her clan. Since fathers had no desire to suffer for the bad acts of their sons, they could be counted on to go to great lengths to bring them up in the right way. Filial piety had its practical as well as spiritual implications.

Society also benefited from this system, in that individuals could derive a strong sense of security from being a part of solidarity groups that provided mutual support. Under the Chinese system of social connections, called *guanxi,* an individual might also have access to reciprocal ties and people beyond his or her primary group. An individual could thus become a part of a complex network of associations extending outward from the family to people from the same town, province, school, or other institutions. People who shared any commonly recognized identity could count on one another.

For both the mandarins of the past and the cadres of today, these networks of personal relationships have, as we have seen, provided the latent structures of factional Chinese politics. *Guanxi* ties, however, have not always provided security. John K. Fairbank recounts that the Hongwu emperor of the Ming dynasty became so furious with his prime minister that he had him beheaded, along with all the members of his extended family. His fury still unappeased, the emperor then went after everyone who was known to have been in any way associated with any of them, to the extent that this early Stalinist-style purge exterminated over 40,000 people. Fairbank observes, "*Guanxi* has its dangers."[1]

Since Tiananmen, state terror has been reimposed with ease partly because the students and dissidents who need to use *guanxi* can never be certain that their networks have not been penetrated by informers. An environment has evolved in which people feel safe in trusting each other only if they have damaging information in reserve to be used if necessary

---

[1] John K. Fairbank, *China: A New History* (Cambridge, Mass.: Harvard University Press, forthcoming).

244

against the other. The problem of distrust has splintered opposition to the regime even among those outside the country.

The group-oriented character of Chinese society also makes governing easier because the collectivities are expected to look after their own members, while not making demands on the government. China has always had protective associations, but not pressure or interest groups. In traditional China these associations were the family and clan; today they are the work unit and the "iron rice bowl." Just as individuals are not supposed to assert their personal interests above those of the group that provides their identities, likewise all subordinate interests in China's hierarchical society are expected to defer to higher interests.

The taboo on the articulation of interests no doubt contributed to the unity of China, but it also set sharp limits on political development, even to the point of dictating the scope of discourse and determining who was a spokesman on public affairs. As a result China never developed a real political economy in the sense of openly acknowledging that political power might be harnessed to advance economic interests. Those with interests that might be affected by governmental policies could not publicly call for allies or seek to mobilize opinion in favor of their interests. They could instead only try to operate quietly by seeking special favors in the implementation of policies, and thus risk being seen as a source of corruption. Consequently, although China has great regional differences, ranging from the rice economy of the south to the millet and wheat economies of the north and from its cosmopolitan coast to its provincial interior, these differences have never been openly recognized. Everyone has simply gone along with the pretense that whatever the central authorities advocate is in the interest of all Chinese.

The prohibition against asserting material interests has made selfishness China's ultimate sin. Since advancing personal interests is seen as dishonorable, severe limits have been placed on even the vocabulary of Chinese politics. The language of Chinese politics has always been limited largely to supporting the values of the moral order. Political discourse thus becomes moralizing rather than analyzing problems. No matter what scoundrels they may be as individuals, as self-conscious members of a supposed virtuocracy Chinese officials are trained to praise all acts of the government as morally unassailable. Other Chinese are limited to two acceptable levels of discussion: the ad hominem level of remonstrating against specific officials for their selfish wrongdoings, or the lofty plane of boasting of their own selfless patriotism. Thus Chinese political discourse is either thick with charges of corruption against selfish officials or, as people seek to demonstrate their selflessness, highly idealistic and patriotic.

The imperative of always appearing selfless also limits who participates in political discussions. Most people remain mute for fear of being reviewed as selfish and concerned only with their own material interests. Intellectuals and students thus receive a near monopoly on speaking out, for they are thought to have no special interests beyond their prime responsibility of defending the moral order. This responsibility has made them prisoners of the status quo, unable to advocate genuinely alternative approaches. China never had the clash of church and state, of religion and science, that in the West established the intellectual as a legitimate outside critic of authority. As a result the Chinese governmental process has rarely had the benefit of intellectual criticism. It is true that many noteworthy Confucian scholars bravely remonstrated against officials of the imperial government, or even against the emperor, but they almost always did so in orthodox terms.

The story of intellectual dissent in the People's Republic has been much the same. Intellectuals have criticized the personal failings of officials, and some at great risk even questioned the correctness of Mao's and Deng's policies. The tyranny of patriotism, however, has imposed a form of self-censorship.

246

The Chinese tendency to blur the distinctions between party, government, and country has made it dangerous to challenge fundamental policies or the basic character of the political system for fear of appearing to be unpatriotic and subversive. Liu Binyan, China's famed investigative reporter, even after twenty-two years of exile in the countryside, until Tiananmen never questioned the values of the party and sought only to expose individual wrongdoing. In his essay "A Second Kind of Loyalty," which electrified the Chinese reading public, Liu suggested that, in addition to the good soldier Lei Feng's simpleminded obedience to the party, there was a second kind of loyalty, typified by two people who had chastised officials for their failings.[2] As late as Tiananmen few intellectuals questioned whether Liu was still too bonded to the party to recognize that there might be an even higher kind of loyalty, that of criticizing socialism out of love for China. What makes Fang Lizhi, China's Sakharov, stand out among Chinese intellectuals is his outspoken acknowledgment that China has been cursed with what he calls "the problem of patriotism," which stops all reasoning because once you "criticize someone for being unpatriotic it will shut him right up."[3]

A further problem in a society in which self-interest must be masked and people must pretend to selflessness is that people never feel they know where others really stand. Everybody knows of course that people have hidden interests. There exists, therefore, considerable suspicion about hidden agendas and real motives. From ordinary social relations to international politics, inordinate attention has to be given to determining the real position of others. Are they potentially

---

[2] Liu Binyan analyzes the reactions to his article and his own responses in *A Higher Kind of Loyalty* (New York: Pantheon Books, 1990), 192–201.

[3] Fang Lizhi elaborates the problems Chinese dissidents have had with the issue of patriotism in *Bringing Down the Great Wall: Writings on Science, Culture, and Democracies in China* (New York: Alfred A. Knopf, 1991), p. 244.

friends or foes? Stratagems abound, but they have to be followed with the greatest care because of the danger of causing the other party to "lose face," which is the grievous pain people experience when their masks are stripped away.

The social imperative not to offend, especially in face-to-face relations, produces an astonishing double paradox in contrasting Chinese and American political behavior. American politicians, operating in a democratic political culture, paradoxically discount what other politicians say publicly ("He had to say that for his constituents"; "It was only said for election purposes"), while believing that the hard currency of political communication is found in the privacy of meetings held behind closed doors, where they can talk "man to man."

Chinese leaders, operating in an authoritarian political culture, follow the opposite rule. They believe face-to-face meetings are where hypocrisy prevails. That is where it is obligatory to tell others what they want to hear, where ceremonial rituals must be carefully observed so that relations go smoothly; no one loses "face" and there is no hint of confrontation. In Chinese political culture one discerns where the other person stands only by reading between the lines of public statements and attaching importance to the code words employed.

This paradoxical difference between the Chinese and American evaluations of private communications makes even more puzzling the secret visit to Beijing after Tiananmen by President Bush's national security adviser, Brent Scowcroft. According to American logic, the trip's purpose might have been to reassure Beijing that the U.S. president was not as angry about Tiananmen as his public statements may have suggested and, further, that Bush's subsequent public statements about trying to keep China "open" should be discounted as conventional American hypocrisy employed to pacify his political constituents. Seen from a Chinese point of view, however, the trip was merely a ceremonial visit consisting of flattering

6/19/99 5:15 PM

www.COLLEGEBOOKSTORE.ORG
Visa/Mastercard   20.18
ACCOUNT NUMBER 4521385235251 0S02
APPROVAL 595925

TOTAL   20.18
P 5% SALES TAX   1.23
SUBTOTAL   18.95
PYE INC/SPIRIT OF   MDS 1   18.95
5B0674832404 TRADE

03 CASH 1   5949 0905 201

CARLETON COLLEGE BOOKSTORE

toasts, to be dismissed according to the conventional Chinese hypocrisy of face-to-face meetings.

The need in Chinese social and political life to probe where others stand as they uphold the ideal of selflessness makes the identification of friend and foe a constant concern. This produces layers of ritual about friendship that only further obscure whether or not the reality exists in any particular relationship. In Chinese culture people can become instant "old friends," but the obligations of friendship are vague; there is only the general notion that the more fortunate party ought to be helpful. Even a slight sign of coolness, however, can raise the suspicion that the relationship has become adversarial. This is not the place to analyze the complex sentiments associated with friendship in Chinese culture, but suffice it to say that friendship is a highly valued ideal that is nonetheless hard to realize in practice. It is also an inappropriate ideal in institution-to-institution relations, for, ironically, just as cooperation seems attainable, trouble becomes more likely.

China still actively plays on the theme of friendship in the old tradition of treating well those who have come from afar to partake of its wonders. True, there is currently some embarrassment over the old Maoist slogans "We have friends everywhere" and, in sports, "Friendship first, competition second." Yet it is striking how few allies China actually does have and how easily its relations with others tend to sour. Usually trouble arises just when relations seem to be improving: as with the Soviet Union in the late 1950's, India in the early 1960's, Vietnam in the late 1970's, and Japan and the United States in the late 1980's. In the post-Mao era of "opening" to the world, China has of course been seeking "normal" international relations. Over the last few years, however, when Chinese officials have been systematically questioned as to the countries with which they have the closest and easiest relations, they have generally been hard put to specify any country other than their formal ally, North Korea. Few knowledgeable people believe that China and North Korea are really close friends.

The overriding duty to defend a great civilization by upholding a moral order seems to cause Chinese leaders to discount the risks of irritating other governments. At the same time they are themselves hypersensitive to perceived slights. Thus Chinese officials generally strive to claim the moral high ground in any diplomatic negotiations. Just as Chinese rulers traditionally believed that they could shame their subjects into correct behavior, and much as Chinese parents use shaming to socialize their children, so Chinese leaders today seem to believe that it is to their advantage to tell other governments that their relations with China are either "bad" or not as "good" as they should be. They will speak of "a cloud over the relationship" and claim that relations can be improved only if "he who tied the knot unties it." There is no hint of offering a quid pro quo, however, no concrete indication as to what it might be worth for the other party to improve its relationship with the Chinese. Other governments should simply do what is "right" and be thankful to China for providing moral instruciton and guidance. The Chinese tactic of blaming others for any setback in relations is remarkably effective in dealings with the United States. America's puritan instinct dictates that if something has gone wrong it is proper first to suspect that the fault is probably one's own; and even if it turns out to be the other's, one should remain as close-mouthed as possible for fear of making things worse. This tendency in turn only compounds the problem, because Chinese culture takes for granted that an accused party who offers no defense must be guilty.

There is an additional twist to the differences in American and Chinese thinking about the role of morality in international affairs. As George Kennan, Hans Morgenthau, and others have pointed out, the United States tends toward a moralistic approach to foreign policy that inhibits the advancement of American interests and allows others undue advantage. Chinese leaders, as the practiced guardians of a moral order, turn the issue of morality the other way around. They use arguments of "right" and "wrong" as a way to inhibit the actions of other countries, thereby advancing China's own practical interests—interests that of course they pretend are of secondary concern. Chinese leaders' commitment to the advantages of being morally superior is so great that even after the horrors of Tiananmen they still thought they could benefit by blaming the United States and others for what happened.

Change Is Easy, but Development Is Difficult

The erratic behavior of the Chinese state in both domestic and international affairs is exacerbated by the Chinese belief that benevolent government requires rule by men and not by law. (The Chinese tradition of rule by law was one of arbitrary and harsh authoritarianism.) The Confucian ideal of rule by superior men acquired new vigor when China adopted Leninist elitism, and the Confucian-Leninist hybrid has produced a system that gives successive top rulers extraordinary freedom. Consequently, and paradoxically, ultimate power in a society that is otherwise group oriented rests largely in the hands of individual personalities.

The peculiarly personal quality of sovereign authority has made leaders acutely sensitive to the need to take advantage of their every opportunity and to cling to power for as long as possible. Without a system of laws they cannot be sure that their policies will survive their hold on power. New rulers bring new policies. As a result questions of succession dominate Chinese politics. When things are going well, people wish "long life" to the paramount ruler; when they are going badly, people look forward to the arrival of the Grim Reaper. Since

251

a leader's influence ends at the grave, it is natural to try to hold on to power as long as possible. Gerontocracy is the result. The "Eight Ancients" today rule over the entire political system, and generational change is excruciatingly slow. Indeed, aspiring Chinese leaders seem to get old faster than those ahead of them die.

Further exaggerating the zigs and zags of Chinese policies made possible by the rule of men rather than law is the Chinese spirit of pragmatism, which holds that changes in circumstances should prompt changes in action. In contrast to American politicians, who go into contortions to prove that they have been consistent in their views through thick and thin, Chinese leaders find it painless to change their positions as circumstances change. For them it is a sign of wisdom to adapt to the logic of a situation, and it is an indication of power to be able to order policy changes. Since proving that one has both wisdom and power is a combination hard to beat in any culture, it is not surprising that Chinese leaders will confidently alter their policies. Americans are puzzled that Deng Xiaoping, who brought about the liberalizing reforms, could also be the butcher of Tiananmen. They forget that he is the same man (although then his name was then spelled Teng Hsiao-p'ing) who in 1957 proposed the Anti-Rightist Campaign and in doing so sold Mao on the idea of sending intellectuals down to the countryside to rusticate. Most Chinese leaders have likewise had several political incarnations.

The tradition of government by superior people, acting as the guardians of a moral order, has inhibited the institutionalization of government in China to the point that there is widespread speculation about how much of the Communist system, built up over half a century of struggle, will outlast the octogenarians who are now the supreme rulers. Yet, paradoxically, in spite of the apparent fragility of a noninstitutionalized system of government, communism, which is in crisis nearly everywhere else, endures in China in its Confucian-Leninist form.

Optimists take heart from actuarial considerations and from the doctrine that "nothing succeeds like a successor." Pessimists observe that the Chinese gerontocracy hangs on while American administrations come and go: an infirm Mao outlived Richard Nixon's presidency, and now an elderly but vigorous President Yang Shangkun is a good bet to outlast the current U.S. administration. Beijingologists scanning the ranks of the leadership to spot a possible future reformer place their hopes on a Li Ruihuan, the former carpenter and now party propaganda czar, or on a Zhu Rongji, the mayor and cheerful booster of Shanghai. It is wishful thinking, however, to believe that the Chinese political system is a well-integrated machine ready to respond to one man pushing a button labeled "reform", and thereby restore the happy visions of the early 1980's. Prediction is made difficult precisely because the Chinese political system is susceptible to sudden zigs and zags according to the whims of a few men, while simultaneously carrying the burden of being true to a great and only slowly changing civilization. In a rhythmic way China's strengths turn into its weaknesses, and its weaknesses become its strengths.

It is prudent to have guarded expectations about the immediate actions of the leaders and the outcomes of their factional power struggles. It is, however, possible to be more certain about the evolution of modern China. It will probably continue to be the story of a society composed of people with remarkable talents for adapting to the modern world but cursed with a political culture that constantly dashes hopes for smooth progress. The distinctive state-society relationship that has worked so successfully in preserving the unity of China also works to make progress erratic.

The failure of significant interests to emerge politically suggests that there is little prospect in the foreseeable future that the balance will shift from the state in favor of society, as has occurred in Eastern Europe and is occurring in Taiwan, South Korea, and the other countries that are leading the worldwide transition away from authoritarianism. Dissidents trying to think through the future of China are mired in utopian debates that would at best call for heroic efforts to reestablish a moral order. Some talk about a "third way" between capitalism and socialism; others dream of returning to the heady days of the early 1980's, before the reforms ran into increasingly daunting problems and it became apparent that without solid political support there is no easy exit from a centrally planned economy. The prospects of such support are made dimmer by the Chinese tradition of believing that all successful leaders must be supermen, for today there are no charismatic figures among the dissidents.

Still others take hope from Chinese history. Out of the chaos of a disintegrating dynasty there have repeatedly emerged energetic founders of new dynasties. Such a reliance on historical analogy is questionable, however, because in the past the Confucian moral order remained in place, ready to be reinvigorated by the new dynasty. It is harder today to identify the norms that could give vitality to a new political order, and therefore the drift of inertia becomes a guiding force. The strongest consideration uniting the opposition is a passion for revenge, for "settling scores," but there is no agreement even about which scores need settling first. Today there is widespread hope that "democracy" could become China's new moral order, but it is hard to imagine that a democracy could exist without a politics of competing interests.

China's distinctive state-society relationship has contributed to the peculiar rhythm of its politics. The factional struggles within the elite have produced not the Western pendulum swings between left and right, liberal and conservative, but

254

an up-and-down motion of centralizing and decentralizing, of tightening and loosening the state's penetration of society. The vast majority of people live as peasants in some five million hamlets and villages with their own largely self-contained social and political systems. They see the workings of government as much like the weather, to be thanked when favorable and cursed when bad. The urban population is not organized into interests, but rather is made up of strata or segments, such as the intellectuals and technocrats, industrial workers, managers, service people, entertainers, journalists, and owners of small enterprises. Their response to the politics of the state is largely one of mood: when things are favorable for them they are capable of enthusiasm; when things go wrong, of alienation. Most of the strata joyfully welcomed the early Deng reforms, but by 1985, and especially since 1988, they have one by one become disenchanted. Swings in mood between enthusiasm and alienation are humanly significant, but they are not a substitute for real politics.

Although it is hard to find a silver lining in the clouds, Chinese society, in spite of current repression, continues to have surprising dynamism. The coastal provinces have fought back the forces of political repression and economic recession; consequently, economic progress at the local level continues. The modernizing elements in the society seek to expand their international contacts as best they can. Just as Soviet society made significant progress in urbanization, education, and professionalization during the political stagnation of the Brezhnev era, so it is likely that Chinese society will advance regardless of its anachronistic government.

China's peculiar state-society relationship allows its leaders to rejoice in their presumed omnipotence, and its bureaucrats to engage in their factional struggles, while the Chinese people are left to seek comfort and security in personal groupings that can protect them from more extreme political storms. Acts of make-believe smooth over the obvious contradictions and ensure that Chinese civilization will change slowly regardless of the zigzags of an erratic state. The unshakable idea that China remains a great civilization fuels a comfortable superiority complex and makes the vast majority of Chinese optimists, for they must believe that it is only an anomaly that things are as bad as they presently are, and that greatness will inevitably return.

In coping with this civilization masquerading as a state, the rest of the world has every reason to follow its own optimistic instincts and try to build ties with elements of China's distinctive society. At the same time, it should give careful heed to the historically erratic ways of China's political system. The fundamental goal in dealing with China should be to strengthen elements within Chinese society that can in time serve as more effective checks against the troublesomeness of the state. Thus, even though official U.S.-China relations have been "bad" since Tiananmen, trade has expanded and American contacts have continued to give support to a wide variety of elements in Chinese society. Ultimately the place China will come to occupy in the world community will be determined more by the evolution of an increasingly assertive and pluralistic Chinese society and less by the pretensions of its political leaders. For, as the society changes so will the foundations of the political culture, and the result will be a new spirit of Chinese politics.

INDEX

Bureaucratic politics
  lack of specialization, 219–221
  suppression of, 218–222
Burmese people, 64, 80
  father-son relationships of, 98–99
  inner world of, 150
Bush, George, 233, 248

California Institute of Technology, 46n
Canton, study of, 24
Cathay, 52
Chan, W. T., 47n
Chang Tchang, 94n
Chao Jung-chi, 138n
Charismatic leaders, 27
Ch'en, Jerome, 120n
Ch'en Yi, 136
Ch'i, concept of, 151–155
Chiang Kai-shek, 31, 39, 128, 184, 223
Chiang Yee, 94n
Chien Chiao, 204, 205
Ch'in, concept of, 151–155
Chin, Ai-li, 90n, 109n
China
  bureaucracy of, 14, 178
  civilization of, 4
  as a developing society, 2–4
  modernization of, 2, 4
  political systems of, 36
  specialists of, 1
  traditional, 12, 16, 25, 29, 31, 180
  as a transitional society, 2
Chinese Communist Party. *See* Communist China, party organization of
Chinese diplomatic corps, 44–45
Chinese medicine, 150–155
Chinese military, 3
Chinese nationalism, 10, 70–71, 127, 229–233
Chinese poetry, 103
Chinese political class, 14, 47–49
  clash with educated class, 49
  domination of all subsystems, 24–28
  lack of interest groups in, 18–24
  parochial identity as Chinese, 49

performance of, 2
political system and, 29
power holders, 26, 49, 94
Chinese political culture, 10, 12–16, 34–35, 67
  aggression in, 28–35
  ancestor worship in, 92
  anti-intellectualism in, 40–47
  avoidance of responsibility in, 157–159
  brutality of, 43
  central place of political order in, 24–28
  commitment and opportunism in, 176–179
  compulsive behavior in, 135–137
  controlled sentiments in, 186–188
  destruction of parental authority in, 116–117
  elites in, 11
  emotions in, 49, 70–75, 81–84
  energy in, 143–148
  family system in, 87–89
  friend and foe, 78–81
  frustrations of participation in, 43, 188–193
  hostility and hate in, 44, 49, 67–68, 70, 81–82
  humiliation in, 62, 68, 71–73, 77, 95
  inertia in, 135–137
  importance of private morality in, 15–16, 82–83
  increasing bureaucratization in, 83
  inequality in, 77–78
  links with society, 16–22
  loyalty concept in, 180–184
  moral masochism in, 74
  moral rectitude in, 69
  model of discipline in, 194–196
  modern, 30, 35, 130
  mystique of Chinese greatness in, 53, 80
  need for ideology in, 13–16
  Oedipal period in, 99
  paradox of, 55
  power in, 76
  "racial arrogance" in, 51

Violation of Chinese air space by
  U.S., 72
Vogel, Ezra, 24

Warlords, 3, 9, 48, 49, 181
  politics of, 62
Watson, B., 74n
Weakland, John H., 93n, 95n, 100,
  213n
Weiner, Myron, 39
Wen Su, 153–154
Western impact, 51–52, 213
  Chinese response to, 61–65, 180
Whatever faction, 239–240
Willpower, concept in Chinese cul-
  ture, 125–126, 137–148

different from energy, 143–148
relationship to efficacy and mo-
  rality, 141–143
Wolfenstein, Martha, 95n
Wong, Jede Snow, 94n
Wright, Arthur F., 14
Wu, K. L., 106n

Yang, C. K., 90n, 11n
Yang Shangku, 253
Yellow River basin, 12
Yen Ching-yueh, 87n
Yuan Shih-k'ai, 8
Zhao Ziyang, 211
Zhu Rongji, 253